Fictional Games

Also available from Bloomsbury

Every Game is an Island: Endings and Extremities in Video Games,
Riccardo Fassone
Material Game Studies: A Philosophy of Analogue Play, ed. Chloé Germaine
and Paul Wake
Video Games, Violence, and the Ethics of Fantasy: Killing Time,
Christopher Bartel
Intermedia Games – Games Inter Media: Video Games and Intermediality,
ed. Michael Fuchs and Jeff Thoss

Fictional Games

A Philosophy of Worldbuilding and Imaginary Play

Stefano Gualeni and Riccardo Fassone

BLOOMSBURY ACADEMIC
LONDON · NEW YORK · OXFORD · NEW DELHI · SYDNEY

BLOOMSBURY ACADEMIC
Bloomsbury Publishing Plc
50 Bedford Square, London, WC1B 3DP, UK
1385 Broadway, New York, NY 10018, USA
29 Earlsfort Terrace, Dublin 2, Ireland

BLOOMSBURY, BLOOMSBURY ACADEMIC and the Diana logo are trademarks of Bloomsbury Publishing Plc

First published in Great Britain 2023
This paperback edition published 2024

Copyright © Stefano Gualeni and Riccardo Fassone, 2023

Stefano Gualeni and Riccardo Fassone have asserted their right under the Copyright, Designs and Patents Act, 1988, to be identified as Authors of this work.

For legal purposes the Acknowledgements on p. xv constitute an extension of this copyright page.

Series design by Charlotte Daniels
Artwork © Rebecca Portelli (character design and illustration), Franz-Peter Manias (3D graphics and layout) and Stefano Gualeni (concept design)

All rights reserved. No part of this publication may be reproduced or transmitted in any form or by any means, electronic or mechanical, including photocopying, recording, or any information storage or retrieval system, without prior permission in writing from the publishers.

Bloomsbury Publishing Plc does not have any control over, or responsibility for, any third-party websites referred to or in this book. All internet addresses given in this book were correct at the time of going to press. The author and publisher regret any inconvenience caused if addresses have changed or sites have ceased to exist, but can accept no responsibility for any such changes.

A catalogue record for this book is available from the British Library.

A catalog record for this book is available from the Library of Congress.

ISBN: HB: 978-1-3502-7708-3
PB: 978-1-3502-7712-0
ePDF: 978-1-3502-7709-0
eBook: 978-1-3502-7710-6

Typeset by RefineCatch Limited, Bungay, Suffolk

To find out more about our authors and books visit www.bloomsbury.com and sign up for our newsletters.

Contents

List of Figures		vii
Foreword		ix
Acknowledgements		xv
Introduction		1
	Four uses of fictional games	8
	Chapter outlines	10
	Glossary	13
	References	16
1	On Fictional Games	19
	1.1 Playing fictional games?	24
	1.2 The unplayability of fictional games	31
	1.3 Ground and figure: The gestalt of fictional games	46
	References	52
2	Fictional Games and Ideology	59
	2.1 The representation of virtues and vices in fictional games	68
	2.2 Play without labour in *Quintet*	73
	2.3 Conclusions	79
	References	81
3	Fictional Games as Utopian Devices	87
	3.1 The game of Azad and indeterminacy	95
	3.2 Thinking outside the game in *The Running Man*	102
	3.3 Conclusions	110
	References	112
4	Fictional Games as Deceptions and Hallucinations	117
	4.1 *Roy: A Life Well Lived* (within the Machine)	125
	4.2 Being played by *The Game*	133
	4.3 Conclusions	141
	References	142

5	Fictional Games and Transcendence	145
	5.1 Transcendence and technological fatalism in *Diamond Dogs*	152
	5.2 Transcendence of the self in *eXistenZ*	158
	5.3 Conclusions	165
	References	167
6	Concluding Thoughts	171
	6.1 Meta-referential fictional games and satire	174
	6.2 Directions for future research	178
	References	180

Appendix: A Compendium of Fictional Games Cited in the Book	183
Index	195

Figures

0.1 A screenshot from the fictional video game *Global Thermonuclear War* as played in the 1983 film *WarGames*, directed by John Badham.   3
1.1 A screenshot of the 2012 video game *Mass Effect 3* (BioWare) showing a game of Kepesh-Yakshi. Analogous to popular board games in the actual world, Kepesh-Yakshi requires its fictional players to optimize their resource management and strive for territorial domination.   26
1.2 A game of Muggle Quidditch, a playable version of the fictional sport Quidditch in the *Harry Potter* series of novels. The term 'muggle' is used in the novels to designate someone who lacks magical abilities.   30
1.3 A playable version of Cyvasse, complete with a board and a set of official (as well as alternative) rules. The game was adapted and integrated by the Bristol Design Forge on the basis of how the game is described and played in the fantasy novel series *A Song of Ice and Fire*.   31
1.4 Calvin and Hobbes playing a game of Calvinball.   37
1.5 The rules of Whack-Bat as explained in Wes Anderson's 2009 film *Fantastic Mr. Fox*. The protagonist of the film, Mr. Fox, is a skilled player of this humorous adaptation of the game of cricket.   38
1.6 A frame of the 1977 film *Star Wars: Episode IV – A New Hope*, directed by George Lucas, showing an ongoing game of the holographic board game Dejarik.   47
1.7 The fictional game *Domination* is played by James Bond (Sean Connery) and Maximillian Largo (Klaus Maria Brandauer) in this frame of the 1983 film *Never Say Never Again*, directed by Irvin Kershner.   51
2.1 A game of Rollerball: a ruthless sport combining skating, motorcycling, and American football, played in the 1975 film with the same name, directed by Norman Jewison.   65
2.2 A screenshot of the 2014 video game *Dragon Age: Inquisition* (BioWare) in which some of the characters are playing a game of Wicked Grace.   71

2.3 A frame of Robert Altman's 1979 film *Quintet*. The characters of the film play a game of Quintet on its five-sided wooden board using custom-made tokens. 76

3.1 In the 2009 digital game *Every Day the Same Dream*, the player experiences various episodes within the monotonous life of a white-collar worker in a short, playable reflection on existence, alienation and the refusal of labour. 92

3.2 The final confrontation between Ben Richards (Arnold Schwarzenegger) and the show host Damon Killian (Richard Dawson) in the 1987 film *The Running Man*, directed by Paul Michael Glaser. 107

4.1 The entrancing game found in *Star Trek: The Next Generation*'s episode 'The Game'. The characters' addiction to the game is so profound that they eventually put their own survival (and that of their ship) at risk. 121

4.2 A frame taken from the episode 'Mortynight Run' of the animated series *Rick and Morty* capturing Rick Sanchez playing *Roy: A Life Well Lived*. The social context of the pan-galactic arcade hall and its orientation towards entertainment and performativity is evident in this figure, with the spectator-friendly screen showing the game progress while the active player lies unconscious in their seat. 131

4.3 In this frame, Nicholas Van Orton (Michael Douglas) signs the contract that initiates the game that will lead him to the brink of insanity in David Fincher's 1997 film *The Game*. 137

5.1 At a Chinese restaurant, Ted Pikul (Jude Law) – the protagonist of the 1999 film *eXistenZ* – is compelled by the game to shoot a waiter with a gun made on the spot using the bones of a mutant fish. Directed by David Cronenberg. 162

6.1 In the fictional video game *My Dinner with Andre*, the player appears to be guiding the conversation among the characters. This scene both reflects sarcastically on the tone of the film that inspired the fictional game and serves as a moment of indirect characterization for Martin Prince Jr. *The Simpsons*. 175

Foreword

Playing fiction-games with fictional games

Daniel Vella

In Olga Tokarczuk's 1996 novel, *Primeval and Other Times*, Squire Popielski, a wealthy landowner in the village of Primeval, which is 'the place at the centre of the universe' (2010: 9), falls into a profound depression. It is 1932, and he is thirty-eight years old. He has lost his religious faith, grown disillusioned with the political promise of the newly independent Polish nation and been abandoned by his artist lover. In his despondency, he is visited by a rabbi, to whom he poses three questions: 'Where did I come from?', 'What can a person actually know?' and 'What should a person achieve, how should he live, what should he do, and what not?' (ibid.: 75–6). By way of an answer to these questions – and a fourth that the rabbi adds to the list: 'Where are we heading? What is the goal of time?' – he receives an old wooden box. Inside are the components of a mysterious game – a complex circular labyrinth printed on cloth; a set of brass pieces representing people, animals and objects; an eight-sided die and a book of instructions labelled '*Ignis fatuus*, or an instructive game for one player.'

The game takes over the Squire's life. He loses interest in his family and business concerns and notices the German soldiers who come to occupy his village during the Second World War only as an unwelcome distraction. As the novel proceeds and we learn of the events that befall Primeval and its inhabitants over the course of the upheavals and tragedies of the twentieth century, the game – and the Squire's playing of it – remain a vital element, interwoven with the novel's many other strands and reflecting the personal and national histories to which we bear witness. In this way, *Primeval and Other Times* can be spoken of in relation to numerous other works of fiction – novels, stories, films, TV shows and even digital games – in which fictional games occupy a significant narrative or thematic role, so much so that, in many cases – as in Hermann Hesse's *The Glass Bead Game*, in Suzanne Collins' *The Hunger Games* or in A. S. Byatt's 1967 novel or David Fincher's 1997 film, both simply called *The Game* – these fictional games occupy a pivotal position reflected in the work's title.

Given this preponderance of examples, it is somewhat surprising that, as Stefano Gualeni and Riccardo Fassone observe in this book, there has been very little sustained critical engagement with fictional games. It is precisely this lack that *Fictional Games* sets out to tackle, and it does so with aplomb. Gualeni and Fassone's achievement, I would argue, is twofold. First – a necessary, foundational contribution in a field so underexplored – they offer a wide-ranging survey of fictional games across literature, cinema, TV and digital games. Although the book does not aim for encyclopaedic exhaustiveness, the Appendix, which lists the ninety-two fictional games covered in the book, might well represent the first available transmedial *corpus* of fictional games, providing the reader with a rich whistle-stop tour of fictional games in all their variety, and the scholar with an invaluable resource for any future studies on fictional games.

As significant a contribution as this is, the charting of this corpus, of course, is only the first step for Gualeni and Fassone's project. Their main aim in this book is to delve into the question of the significance of these fictional games. Again, for a work that tackles a relatively unexplored domain, this is another necessary move: a work like this needs to answer the question, *why is it worth paying attention to fictional games?* This question is addressed insightfully and incisively in *Fictional Games*, making a case for the polyvalence of the games we encounter in works of fiction. Different chapters explore the significance of fictional games as embodiments, and representations, of the ideological structures of the societies in which they are played, as spaces of utopian possibility that afford resistance to, and transgression of, those same ideological structures, as deceptions or hallucinations that blur the distinction between reality and representation (and between multiple levels of representation), and as contexts for transcendental possibility.

As the field of study requires, Gualeni and Fassone's approach is inherently multidisciplinary, being informed by game studies, literary theory, media studies, cultural studies and philosophy, among others. Given the focus on games, not to mention the authors' previous work, it is hardly surprising that the book's theoretical foundations delve most deeply into game studies. Here, though, a crucial question arises. One of the most enduring tenets in the field of game studies has been the idea that the game scholar needs to be an engaged player-researcher (Aarseth 2003), and that the perspective which is most fundamental to understanding the significance of a game is that of 'the game as played, as referring to the object of study for game studies from the player's perspective' (Leino 2009: 6). This has been challenged from a number of directions, notably through examinations of zero-player or idle games (Fizek 2018) and the development of posthumanist, relational understandings of gameplay (Janik 2018), both of which decentre the player from the experience and meaning of the game. Nonetheless, the difficulty remains: how does one develop a critical and analytical perspective on games that are – by definition, as Gualeni and Fassone point out – unplayable?

Their response is to thematize the unplayability of fictional games, making their incompleteness and unavailability to player experience an intrinsic aspect of their expressivity, rather than a limitation to be overcome. This is an approach which aligns well with the second main theoretical foundation of the book – for the intersection of games, play and fiction – particularly literary fiction – is not entirely untrodden academic ground. Patricia Waugh notes that the idea that the creative activity of art is inherently playful – that, say, a work of fiction is the outcome of an imaginative game played by its creator – is an established one (1984: 34). Similarly, in philosophy, Hans-Georg Gadamer claims that the work of art is the 'transformation into structure' of the free movement of play (2013: 114). To take one example of this conventional idea of the process of imaginative artistic creation as a game, Christopher Nash's appositely titled literary-theoretical work *World-Games* (1987) describes the fiction-games (as opposed to fictional games) involved in the creation of 'anti-realist' works of fiction, whether in the neocosmic vein (fiction-games that lead to the formation of fictional worlds that are coherent but diverge from representing the world we perceive as actual) or in the anticosmic one (fiction-games that reveal the artifice of, and destabilize, fictional worlds).

The foregrounding of fictional games within works of fiction, then, can be understood as a *mise en abyme* of the process of imaginative creation, a text-within-a-text or a world-within-a-world, a recursion into a second nested layer of fictionality or representation that constitutes a 'laying bare of the rules of the game' (Waugh 1984: 41). Gualeni and Fassone are attuned to this, paying special attention to the meta-reflexive qualities of fictional games – the way they can lead us back to thinking about games, play, representation and fictionality, by foregrounding their complex interweaving within the texts and the fictional worlds they are contained in. However, as we have already mentioned, fictional games are, by necessity, incompletely specified and unattainable. Like the verbal descriptions of the films of Hector Mann in Paul Auster's *The Book of Illusions* (2002), or the 'Navidson Record' videotape in Mark Z. Danielewski's *House of Leaves* (2000), what we have is the symbol of an unreachable original, the sign of an absence that haunts the text.

This is very evidently the case in *Primeval and Other Times*. As readers of Tokarczuk's novel, we learn something of the game throughout the course of the novel – but not enough for us to be able to recreate and play it for ourselves. We learn the labyrinth consists of eight concentric circles, with each circle having double the number of exits out to the next circle as the one before it had; thus, the first circle has 1 exit to the second circle, the second circle has 2 exits to the third, and so on, until the player arrives at the eighth circle, which has 128 exits out of the labyrinth. We know that each circle represents a new attempt at creation by an increasingly exhausted and dispirited God and that, as such, the game represents the cosmology of a tired universe in which the tragedies piled up by Walter Benjamin's Angel of History (2003: 392) are the signs of an inevitable decline, as God withdraws further and further from His creation. We know that the boundaries between the game and the outside world are blurred, or perhaps that the game expands to incorporate the entirety of the world so that, in one instance, Squire Popielski cannot proceed until he has a dream of being a dog, and, in another instance, the arrival of officials from the newly installed post-war district administration to discuss the nationalization of his properties appears to satisfy the conditions for him to move on to the next circle.

The game, then, is as vast as the world, containing an entire cosmology in miniature; at the same time, it is as small as the contents of one person's consciousness. It constitutes an example of what Waugh termed the 'black boxes' so prevalent in postmodernist fiction (1984: 39) – an apparent solution to the recursion of meaning and signification that, however, is swallowed up by the absent centre of the novel's fiction-game: as readers, we can never be privy to the metaphysical revelation Squire Popielski receives from the game. In fact, the inaccessibility of the game's answer to all the novel's questions is evident: even within the novel's fictional world, the game constitutes a private obsession for a single character in a highly multivocal novel. After Squire Popielski's death, his family members find the components of the game in a drawer and react with sheer incomprehension at the idea that this sparse collection of junk represents their elderly relative's decades-long obsession. The game, then, becomes a physical token of an unreachable, solipsistic interiority – as private and inscrutable as the roughly made crucifix clasped in Sebastião Rodrigues' hand as he is cremated at the end of the Martin Scorsese film *Silence* (2016), representing the faith he kept secret for decades, or, more to the point, Cassandra's papers locked in a trunk at the end of Byatt's aforementioned *The Game*. In this way, the game in *Primeval and Other Times* reflects, in its multifaceted, ambivalent significance, and in its very inaccessibility, the range of meanings that fictional games accrue as meta-reflexive textual constructs. Accordingly, over the course of *Fictional Games*, we encounter, among many others:

> games whose rule-structures codify the ideological structures of the society that produced them, making visible those higher-level structures in all their artificiality and – often – their cruel arbitrariness;
> games that present themselves as hermetic systems embodying an occult metaphysical understanding of reality, thereby threatening the stability of the dominant reality systems of science, religion, history and politics, resulting in an overdetermination of meaning in which no reality system can appear definitive or comprehensive;
> games that expand and blur the boundary between themselves and the world, incorporating more and more elements into their own system until the map becomes the territory, or the territory becomes the map, and the world is revealed as a great game – in all its ludic arbitrariness, but, at the same time, in the rigidity of its predetermined order;
> and games that speak to the unattainable centre of meaning of the individual human consciousness, that embody private worlds of imagination and obsession, that are the trace of the separation between interior and exterior worlds.

All of this conceptual and thematic breadth is what Gualeni and Fassone take up as their remit with *Fictional Games*. I consider it a mark of their success that this book, in shining a light on a hitherto underexamined field, invites – even calls out for – further studies that can use the ideas and insights developed herein as a springboard for deeper dives into individual fictional games, for even more wide-ranging surveys, or for unpacking even more tropes and meanings in fictional games. However, even if such future work fails to materialize, we are still left with this remarkable study as an invaluable resource for tracing the elusive meanings, and unpacking the actual significances, of fictional games. Why is it worth paying attention to fictional games? Read on and find out.

References

Aarseth, E. J. (2003), 'Playing Research: Methodological Approaches to Game Analysis', in the Proceedings of the Digital Arts and Culture Conference, Melbourne, May 19–23.

Auster, P. (2002), *The Book of Illusions*, London: Faber.

Benjamin, W. (2003), *Selected Writings 1938–40*, H. Eiland and M. W. Jennings (eds), Cambridge, MA: Harvard University Press.

Byatt, A. S. (1992), *The Game*, New York: Vintage.

Danielewski, M. Z. (2000), *House of Leaves*, New York: Pantheon.

Fizek, S. (2018), 'Interpassivity and the Joy of Delegated Play in Idle Games', *ToDiGRA: Transactions of the Digital Games Research Association*, 3 (3): 137–63.

Gadamer, H.-G. (2013), *Truth and Method*, J. Wertheimer and D. G. Marshall (trans.), London: Bloomsbury.

Janik, J. (2018), 'Game/r-Play/er-Bio-object: Exploring Posthuman Values in Video Game Research', in the Proceedings of the 2018 Philosophy of Computer Games Conference, Copenhagen, 13–15 August.

Leino, O. T. (2009), 'Understanding Games as Played: Sketch for a First-Person Perspective for Computer Game Analysis', in the Proceedings of the 2009 Philosophy of Computer Games Conference, Oslo, 13–15 August.

Nash, C. (1987), *World-Games: The Tradition of Anti-Realist Revolt*, London: Methuen.

Scorsese, M. (2016), [film] *Silence*, Paramount Pictures.

Tokarczuk, O. (2010), *Primeval and Other Times*, A. L. Jones (trans.), Prague: Twisted Spoon Press.

Waugh, P. (1984), *Metafiction: The Theory and Practice of Self-Conscious Fiction*, London and New York: Routledge.

Acknowledgements

This volume would not be complete without the possibility for us to express gratitude for the help of some very special people. These people assisted us in a number of ways that often went beyond academic criticism, text editing and logistical support. We are thankful to Esther MacCallum-Stewart, Cristina Di Maio, Johnathan Harrington, Dan Hassler-Forest, Giaime Alonge and Daniel Vella for their invaluable criticism and suggestions. This book would also be less complete and pleasurable had it not been for the hard and inspired work of Jennifer B. Barrett, Rebecca Portelli and Franz-Peter Manias. We also extend a heartfelt 'thank you' to Liza Thompson and Lucy Russell from Bloomsbury Academic and to Federico Campagna for helping to make this book possible.

Finally, we are grateful to our families, who had to endure innumerable trials and tribulations during the long months leading to the completion of this volume. This book is dedicated to you, Francesca, Alice and Nele.

Introduction

Games are important things. At least since the Neolithic age, they have contributed to the construction and establishment of shared customs and beliefs in human communities. Games can be used to train and educate, and they can signal and influence cultural shifts, as well as contributing to defining a social group's tastes and aspirations.

Playing games is a cognitively complex and socially multilayered activity that most people perform at various stages of their lives, and it is unsurprising that the intricacies, paradoxes and deep-seated, personal meanings of play have perplexed philosophers, sociologists, psychologists and game (and play) scholars for centuries.[1] In their attempts to answer questions about the cultural relevance of play and the definition of 'game', these scholars have proposed an assortment of frameworks and definitions to orient their work. In most cases, these forays have focused on ludic practices and games that exist in our world and that have been – or still are – actually played. Very little attention has been devoted to games and playful activities that are solely encountered in works of fiction, where they often play an important narrative role. In a fictional context, games can be used, for example, as a synecdoche for some of the moral or political assumptions underpinning a certain social group, or they can be described in

---

[1] Presenting a genealogy of studies on games and play is beyond the scope of this work, but a more granular account of that historical process can be found in Brian Sutton-Smith's (1997) effective and provocative summary of reflections on these topics.

passing, serving as background elements that contribute to making a fictional world feel vibrant and interconnected.

This book is about games that can be grouped under the umbrella term 'fictional games'. We utilize this term to indicate playful activities and ludic artefacts conceptualized as part of fictional worlds. Fictional games are meant to trigger the imagination of the appreciator of a work of fiction and cannot actually be – or at least were not originally meant to be – played (see Gualeni 2021). Games in fictional worlds are not typically presented in formally complete ways; rather, authors often simply hint at these games' rules, affordances, boundaries, exceptions and criteria for success, defining them just clearly enough to achieve their intended functions within the work of fiction. As will become clear in the next chapter, we will not treat the incompleteness and unplayability of fictional games as a lack or a fault in the set-up or representation of fictional games. Instead, we recognize these aspects as crucial to the functioning of fictional games as thematic, expressive devices and as central to these games' expressive value and aesthetic appeal. Inspired by Christopher Thi Nguyen (2020), we could characterize our aesthetic relationship with fictional games as 'an aesthetics of imagined agency'.

As we will clarify later, in discussing and analysing fictional games, we do not take a hard stance on what constitutes a game. Additionally, we are not particularly concerned with how short-lived, vague or incomplete the representation of a fictional game may be within a work of fiction, nor are we especially bothered by the fact that fictional games, by definition, cannot be accessed and manipulated by players. In this book, when an artefact or structured activity is literally (i.e. non-metaphorically) presented in a work of fiction as a game, we simply consider it to be one. This decision not only made our work simpler as authors but also accounted for the fact that several fictional games that captured our interest – especially fictional games played under hegemonies in works of dystopian fiction – could not technically be considered games, at least according to classical game studies. As noted by Boschi (2017), almost all dystopian fictional games transgress some of the necessary conditions for something to be considered a game proposed by the forefathers of game studies such as Huizinga and Caillois. Such dystopian fictional games, Boschi claims, are not voluntary and free activities, nor are they without repercussions on one's actual life (ibid.). The fact that the hegemonies that control dystopian fictional games often intervene during gameplay by changing the rules or setting new victory conditions is also irreconcilable with the notion that a game is ultimately a fair and egalitarian social contract of sorts, instead further emphasizing the

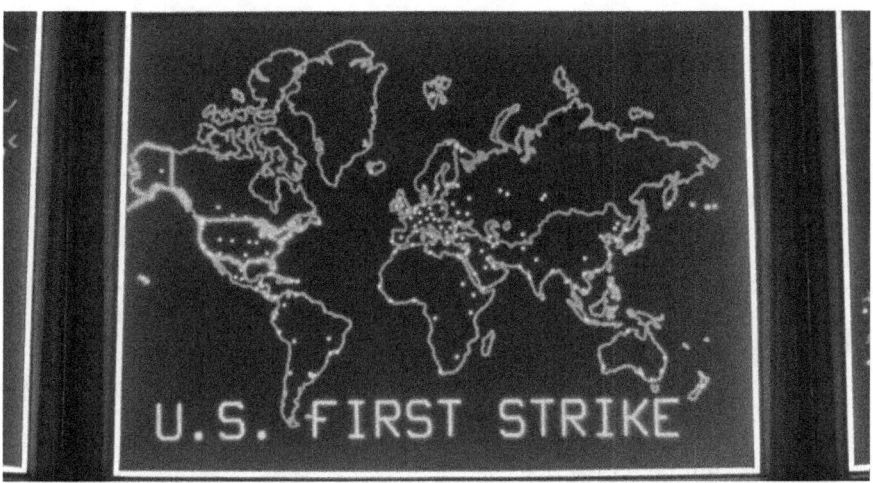

Figure 0.1 A screenshot from the fictional video game *Global Thermonuclear War* as played in the 1983 film *WarGames*, directed by John Badham © United Artists 1983. All rights reserved.

unfair and absolutist systems of power that dominate the fictional world in question (ibid.).

In this book, we analyse and discuss a subset of the types of games that appear in works of fiction. We do not consider, for example, works of fiction that describe or reference the game of chess, as chess does not fit our definition of a fictional game. Likewise, we do not analyse novels such as Dostoevsky's *The Gambler* (2017), Kawabata's *The Master of Go* (2006) or Bolaño's *The Third Reich* (2011), as these works describe games that also exist outside the realm of fiction (i.e. roulette, Go and Avalon Hill's 1974 tabletop wargame Rise and Decline of the Third Reich). The games represented in such novels were part of our cultural heritage long before their appearance in a fictional work, and they are still played in the physical world. In this book, we focus instead on fictional games that are *only* fictional games and that do not (or did not originally) exist as actually playable artefacts. Put more simply, a fictional game like *Global Thermonuclear War* – whose simplified wireframe graphics and ominous apocalyptic undertones (see Figure 0.1) are part of the fictional world of the film *WarGames* (Badham 1983) – is the kind of cultural phenomenon we discuss in this book, whereas the filmic representation of the actual game of basketball in Spike Lee's *He Got Game* (1998) is not.

At this point, we imagine the reader may be wondering why one should write – or read, for that matter – a whole book about games that do not actually exist and cannot be played. Our answer to this question involves a combination of the three following observations:

1. The work has merit because it concentrates on an area of cultural production that, to date, has been almost completely unexplored.
2. As we hope to show and explain in this book, fictional games are interesting and relevant in their functions as philosophical and literary devices.
3. This book integrates and extends the disciplinary boundaries of academic fields including game studies, the philosophy of fiction, science-fiction studies, the philosophy of games and narratology by offering a methodological and conceptual toolkit for the critical analysis of fictional games as cultural productions.

Our rather selective definition of fictional games is informed by a broader discussion on the nature and characteristics of games in general. Are there recurrent features, functional elements or modes of utilization that determine when something is considered a game? The question of what constitutes a game as a social object is famously problematic, and the great variety of artefacts that are referred to as 'games' – or that were historically referred to as such – is perhaps the most glaring manifestation of the ambiguity that characterizes our relationship with games. This ambiguity underpins the oft-invoked claim that a complete answer to the question of what constitutes a game can never be achieved (see Arjoranta 2014; Aarseth and Calleja 2015; Laas 2017); games can be defined in a multitude of reasonable and valid ways, but none of these definitions can encompass the full spectrum of what games are or can be. To be clear on this point, we are not suggesting that the word 'game' cannot be defined: it is self-evident that a number of definitions can be proposed and suitably used in a variety of contexts. Instead, we want to emphasize that each definition can only capture a glimpse of the vast horizon of what games are and what they could be. Thus, definitions of 'game' have been devised and used for restricted purposes such as filing a patent for a new product, writing a book about games, analysing a new video game release for a popular magazine or determining legislation concerning games.

Recognizing that the conceptual boundaries of what constitutes a game are flexible, porous and resistant to complete analytical categorization is arguably not at the forefront of players' everyday relationships with games. We contend that players who are sufficiently familiar with the conventions of the particular media form can effortlessly understand (and adapt to) how a certain game combines operational interdictions, aspects of make-believe and social conventions. Beyond merely understanding and aligning with a game's rule set, its affordances, spatiality and narratives, we argue that sufficiently game-literate players intuitively and habitually treat these elements as preconditions for playing with (and within) a game. Having made this point, we also want to emphasize that we do not consider semantic or conceptual ambiguities trivial matters when adopting perspectives such as that of the scholar or the legislator. As authors of academic works in the field of game research, we must often explicitly subscribe to one of the many possible game definitions to present a clear and satisfactory argument. However, we also enjoy the absence of precise classificatory criteria as one of the most interesting traits of playful artefacts and playful activities, and we must acknowledge that this book about fictional games would not exist without our fascination with the theme of uncertainty in general and, more specifically, with uncertainty in how games are understood, played and discussed.

In light of these observations, we decided to adopt a double definition of what constitutes a game as our operational method. As stated above, we embrace a nominal and rather loose definition of what a game is. However, we also consider a fictional game to be a game by virtue of its being literally understood as a game or a sport by the characters inhabiting a fictional world – and thus being potentially available for them to play. As an example to illustrate our approach, although we may understand tarot reading as a game in a broad and unspecific sense, if this practice is presented in a work of fiction without being explicitly understood as a game by (at least some of) the characters in that work, it does not qualify here for analysis as a fictional game.[2]

Aside from being a space where we can present a definition of what we mean by 'fictional games' and introduce our operational stance towards the definitions of 'game', this introduction gives us the opportunity to clarify why we decided to focus on this particular relationship with games. In this book, we attempt to use the speculative and often prophetic lens of fiction to explore what games could potentially be, as well as the sociocultural effects that could be pursued through them. In this pursuit, fictional games will often be compared with – and used as – philosophical thought experiments (see the definition of 'thought experiment'

---

[2] Similarly, the fatal game that is central to the narrative of the film *Saw* (Wan 2004; see Chapter 1) could be considered a fictional game because some characters refer to it as a game in a non-metaphorical way. Conversely, the chase orchestrated by the killer in the film *Seven* (Fincher 1995) is defined by elements of rituality and playfulness, but it is never literally addressed as a game and thus would not be considered a fictional game.

in the Glossary). In fact, some fictional games are not simply meant to be imagined but are also explicitly devised to assist us in thinking through hypothetical situations that reveal limitations and contradictions in our thought and action.[3] Such fictional games, in particular, challenge fiction appreciators with logical and ethical conundrums that often feature extraordinary elements such as magic spells, sentient artificial agents, outlandish body augmentations and encounters with alien species and civilizations. We are not suggesting that the expressive and philosophical potential of fictional games is limited to their being aids to the imagination or serving as critical devices. In this book, we explore a variety of other possible uses of fictional games, including their functioning as tools for meta-reflexivity. We use this exploration to demonstrate the capability of fictional games for inviting deliberate reflections on games and play, and to make an argument regarding how games are currently designed, played, sold, manipulated, experienced and understood as cultural productions (see Gualeni 2016). Our insight into the flexible and permeable boundaries that define games will be particularly central in Chapters 4 and 5, which focus on fictional games as, respectively, means of deception and tools for transcendence.

Beyond fictional games' already-mentioned thematic, critical, deceptive and meta-reflexive potential, in this book, we discuss other expressive uses of these games – for comedic effect, as utopian devices and to elicit a sense of estrangement among their appreciators. Notably, these speculative, transformational, political, meta-reflexive, misleading, comic, utopian and estranging qualities are not unique to fictional games. In fact, these experiential effects have often been recognized as emerging from fictional elements within fictions (such as fictional novels within actual films or novels). Moreover, the aspirations of contributing to the development of self-awareness, orienting an individual's moral compass, offering critical perspectives on socio-political circumstances, mounting meta-referential claims, and entertaining and estranging audiences can certainly also be recognized as an aspiration of actual games and video games. Existing games customarily grouped under categories such as 'games for change', 'serious games' and 'critical games' are playable artefacts that explicitly pursue – through gameplay – the formation of citizens who are better informed, more aware and

---

[3] Elgin (2007) raised a similar point in relation to literary fiction in her essay, 'The Laboratory of the Mind'. Like a thought experiment, Elgin writes, 'a work of fiction selects and isolates, manipulating circumstances so that particular properties, patterns, connections, disparities and irregularities are brought to the fore. It may localize and isolate factors that underlie or are interwoven into everyday life, but that are apt to pass unnoticed because they are typically overshadowed by other, more prominent concerns' (Elgin 2007: 47).

more congenial. Although this capability is particularly evident in games that openly and deliberately pursue positive social effects, every game experience is potentially transformative (and also potentially dangerous). Our experiences of play inevitably disclose values and ideologies in a variety of modes, such as through aesthetic representations, the spatial and interactive boundaries that a game imposes, as well as its prescribed criteria for success and failure. To further clarify this point, it might be important to emphasize that it is not infrequent for philosophers to include playing games among the practices that enable people to test, exercise and exhibit values that have significance at both the individual and the societal scale (see MacIntyre 2007; Nguyen 2020; Gualeni and Vella 2020). Similarly, the work of academics and designers operating at the intersections of game studies, game design and social activism hinges on the recognition of the existential significance and rhetorical (as well as transformative) potential of our relationships with games. Such scholars investigate the sociocultural impact of games from the perspectives of both game creators and players (see Bogost 2007, 2011; Flanagan 2009; 2018; Grace 2012; Flanagan and Nissenbaum 2014; Gualeni 2015, 2016; Rusch and Phelps 2020).

To explain the salience of this book, it is important to highlight, again, that – within the current discourse surrounding games – their sociocultural and existential significance has been examined exclusively in relation to actual games.[4] For our purposes, it is crucial to point out that not all the possibilities and themes presented and explored in the form of fictional games are also expressed (or can be expressed) through the interactive experience of actual games. Reflections on this asymmetry are among the most original philosophical contributions offered in our book.

As a final methodological note, when referencing existing, actual games in this book, we follow the guidelines that we ourselves proposed in a 2019 paper (Gualeni, Fassone and Linderoth). This decision is motivated by the fact that, unlike established citation styles, our recommendations are mindful of the characteristic hybridity and instability of the medium, and address various bibliographic tensions and deficiencies that characterize the ways in which games are currently referenced in books and in academic literature.

---

[4] That is, games that we could actually engage with as players. In the academic field of game studies, only a few authors have approached games in a way that is not strictly dependent on their existence as playable artefacts. Perhaps the most relevant among the perspectives of these authors is that of 'hypothetical games', as discussed by Björk and Juul (2012) in their paper, 'Zero-Player Games – Or: What We Talk about When We Talk about Players'. The idea of hypothetical games, however, is only briefly outlined in their paper, which does not fully examine the expressive and transformative potential of hypothetical games.

Four uses of fictional games

To facilitate the navigation of the various perspectives and arguments concerning fictional games that are woven together in this volume, we group them into four broad (and often overlapping) thematic categories. We understand fictional games as parts of a fictional world that reflect (and can influence) the values, beliefs and political orientations of its inhabitants; provide them with access to forms of spiritual and corporeal transcendence; and infiltrate their reality, becoming deceptively indistinguishable from it. This book separates these functions into four chapters. After establishing the theoretical framework for the book in Chapter 1, we introduce the thematic chapters with a discussion of the ideological bearing of fictional games in Chapter 2, where we examine fictional games whose primary expressive function is that of emphasizing – as well as adding detail to – contextual features of the fictional worlds of which they are a part, mirroring in ludic form the dominant values and beliefs of a fictional society. Serving as a counterpoint to Chapter 2 on the repetition and normalization of ideologies in fictional games, Chapter 3 is about the use of fictional games as tools to subvert the sociopolitical status quo. In this chapter, we focus on fictional games that function as utopian devices within their respective fictional worlds, leading to changes in the political thinking of the fictional characters while also stimulating the political imagination of the reader. Next, Chapter 4 concentrates on how fictional games can be deceptive and how they can blur and transgress the boundaries between the contingency of play and the seriousness of actual life. Finally, before the concluding chapter, the last thematic chapter, Chapter 5, explores how fictional games can be conducive to the transcendence of particular ways of existing as human beings, catalyzing and guiding the overcoming of human finitude and subjectivity.

The four functions that we identified and discussed in this book should not be considered exhaustive in terms of the potential of fictional games, nor should they be understood as an all-encompassing summary of how fictional games are used in literature, cinema or other media forms. As an example of a notable function that was excluded from our editorial structure, fictional games can possess comedic qualities for fiction appreciators, as is the case for the drinking game True American, a fictional game played in the television series *New Girl* (Merriwether 2011–18), whose severe under-specification often gives rise to a variety of exhilarating and paradoxical situations. Other potential uses and functions of fictional games that are discussed only in passing in this book and that do not receive the extensive attention devoted to the themes mentioned above involve satire and parody – the utilization of fictional games that have already been discussed by Bakhtin (1968) in the context of the bizarre games found in the work of French humanist François Rabelais. Another valuable cultural role for fictional games which is still related to satirical and critical aspirations consists in their already mentioned meta-referential use, which will be explored in the conclusion, Chapter 6.

Each of the thematic chapters of this book takes an interdisciplinary approach to the challenge of mapping the uncharted territories that are specific to its expressive goals. In general, our efforts draw from disciplines such as existential philosophy, the philosophy of fiction, literary criticism, game studies, film studies and media studies. Beyond referencing and outlining games that appear in existing works of fiction in examples and corollaries of our arguments, each chapter also offers the in-depth analysis and criticism of two fictional games that we consider particularly relevant or telling in relation to the themes being presented. These two exemplary fictional games are chosen from a variety of forms and genres of fiction and serve the purpose of grounding specific theoretical perspectives in the practice of analysing fictional content.

Before introducing the thematic chapters and case studies, it is necessary to present a cautionary note. We want to acknowledge that most of the detailed case studies discussed in these chapters are drawn from the work of English-speaking authors. Although we present some examples that were originally produced in languages other than English (i.e. Italian, Spanish, Japanese and French), our engagement with the texts was mostly through the mediation of the English language. We consciously made the decision to take this approach, deciding to take on only those works of fiction where we felt we could leverage a reasonable degree of familiarity with the narrative and broader cultural conventions employed by these artefacts in the analysis. This meant choosing case studies written in familiar languages (or with available translated versions), as well as presenting notions of games and play that we felt culturally equipped to discuss and criticize. We have tried to compensate for this shortcoming by drawing examples from a variety of media, portraying different political and social sensibilities and giving voice to different identities within the production of fiction that could be labelled as 'Western'. We hope that this research may inspire others to discuss fictional games found in different contexts and belonging to other canons.

Chapter outlines[5]

To maximize the accessibility of our content, this section offers a short description of the chapters of *Fictional Games*, adding to the very brief description above and indicating the types of fictional games discussed as detailed case studies in each thematic chapter.

Chapter 1: On Fictional Games

Following the basic methodological observations offered above, Chapter 1 lays the theoretical foundations for our foray into fictional games. With its preparatory and connecting role, this chapter begins by offering a definition of fictional games that sets them apart from similar cultural objects (such as minigames, referential games, nested games and in-game side quests). It provides an initial analysis of salient examples of fictional games and homes in on one of their more interesting expressive traits – their deliberate incompleteness. This first chapter also discusses a few fictional games that, after their appearance in a work of fiction, were formally completed and partially redesigned so that they could be played in the physical world. It concludes with proposing a gestalt psychology-inspired distinction between fictional games that function as background elements in a work of fiction, and fictional games that hold, instead, a more focal narrative role.

Chapter 2: Fictional Games and Ideology

This chapter focuses on how fictional games are presented within a fictional world to mirror (and to succinctly communicate to the audience) the dominant ideologies and values within a fictional society. Here, games act as a synecdoche for the larger social and political organization presented in the work of fiction. To demonstrate the specific relevance of games in the construction and

---

[5] This book is the result of the authors' collaborative effort. Nevertheless, due to the idiosyncrasies of the Italian research evaluation system, we are required to provide a breakdown of the authors' contributions. As mentioned, despite this formality, we encourage the reader to consider this book as the outcome of the authors' teamwork.
  Stefano Gualeni is the main author of sections 1.1, 1.2.1, 1.2.3, 1.3 and 2.1, the introduction to Chapter 3, sections 3.1 and 4.1, the introduction to Chapter 5, section 5.1, the introduction to Chapter 6 and section 6.1.
  Riccardo Fassone is the main author of the introduction to Chapter 1, sections 1.2.2 and 1.2.4, the introduction to Chapter 2, sections 2.2 and 3.2, the introduction to Chapter 4 and sections 4.2, 5.2, 6.2.

normalization of ideologies, we draw our examples in this chapter from a variety of authors working in different media. In the concluding section of this chapter, we argue that certain specificities of games and play make them particularly efficient in encapsulating sociopolitical orientations and values. Robert Altman's film *Quintet*, the first case study, is used to illustrate how a fictional game can act as the centrepiece of the description of a dystopian society. The second fictional game analysed in detail in this chapter is the game of Virtues and Vices, a fictional game played by the Utopians in Thomas More's 1516 book *Utopia* (2003).

Chapter 3: Fictional Games as Utopian Devices

Drawing on game studies, utopian studies and science-fiction studies, our third chapter examines fictional games as utopian devices. At the centre of this approach is the recognition of the utopian potential latent in characteristic traits of the activity of play, such as uncertainty and contingency. In the pursuit of the utopian relevance of fictional games, our first case study is the game of Azad, described in Iain M. Banks' 1988 science-fiction novel, *The Player of Games*. By presenting relationships of power through a game (and, finally, as a game), fictional games like Azad serve as a reminder that all sociopolitical circumstances – even the most dystopian ones – are ultimately indeterminate and that they always retain the possibility of change. The second exemplary game presented in this chapter is pivotal in the dystopian world of the novel *The Running Man* (King [1982] 2012) and its film adaptation of the same name (Glaser 1987). This fictional game is an example of a 'gladiatorial game' in a hegemonic society that becomes the catalyst (and the occasion) for a utopian act.

Chapter 4: Fictional Games as Deceptions and Hallucinations

This chapter offers a reflection on instances when games are utilized as deceptive constructs. In popular narratives such as David Fincher's (1997) film *The Game*, playfulness can be impossible to be distinguished from the seriousness of one's 'real life'. Games that are camouflaged as non-games can pose a series of epistemic issues both for the characters in the work of fiction and for the fiction appreciator. As a starting point, this chapter begins with the assumption that games are not entirely separate from 'real life' and that this ambiguity is constitutive of the very understanding of the activity of play. The case studies discussed here provide examples of how this fundamental ambiguity has been used to articulate labyrinthine narratives in which games blur the boundaries between the factual and the fictional. The mind-game film *The Game* and Roy: A Life Well Lived, a fictional game in the science-fiction animated series *Rick and Morty* (Roiland and Harmon 2013–present), are discussed as relevant examples of this strategy.

Chapter 5: Fictional Games and Transcendence

Could fictional games be a context for pursuing various forms of transcendence, from the dissolution of the boundaries of knowledge disciplines to the fall of human individuality? Could these games be opportunities to abandon our organic bodies and live a fuller, less constrained existence? There are works of fiction in a variety of media forms in which games have precisely this transformative – and even evolutionary – role. Although we also discuss examples of fictional games that do not pursue transcendence through the use of advanced augmentation technologies (e.g. Hermann Hesse's 1943 novel *The Glass Bead Game*), most of this chapter is deeply involved with notions and orientations emerging from the philosophy of technology. Alastair Reynolds' (2003) novella *Diamond Dogs* and David Cronenberg's (1999) film *eXistenZ* are discussed as cases where games are leveraged as thought experiments concerning our posthuman future and the new roles and possibilities for play within it.

Chapter 6: Concluding Thoughts

The final chapter summarizes the relevance and uses of fictional games and the insight gleaned about them throughout *Fictional Games*. It homes in on an expressive function of fictional games that is transversally present in all the philosophical reflections and close readings offered in the thematic chapters of the book – their capability to function as meta-referential devices. Approaching fictional games in terms of their potential for meta-referentiality, this concluding chapter discusses their aptitude for suggesting critical and/or satirical perspectives on how actual games are designed, played, sold, manipulated, experienced, understood and utilized as part of our culture. Furthermore, this coda addresses the book's limitations and potential developments, opening avenues for further research at the intersections of the philosophy of fiction, science-fiction studies and game studies.

Glossary

actuality We employ the adjective 'actual' to indicate things or events that are currently the case in the world we natively belong to as biological creatures. The indexical specification 'actual' (as in the case of one's 'actual body') serves to clarify that we are not referring to a body that can be found or inhabited within a fictional world (see **fictional world**) but to one's own biological anatomy and the related possibilities for perceiving, thinking, feeling and acting.

agency As noted by Nguyen (2020) and Jennings (2021), the notion of 'agency' is inherently ambiguous and problematic, and this concept is especially foggy in the field of game studies. As an operational definition for this book, we propose understanding agency in a broad sense that aspires to account for the plurality of fictional agencies (human and non-human, digitally mediated and non-digitally mediated) represented in fictional games. We therefore apply the term 'agency' in relation to games to indicate the possibility for players to take deliberate, intelligible action, and to experience the results of their choices (see Murray 1997: 126). This way of approaching agency therefore 'implies that the player [...] explores and manipulates the game environment and seeks to influence it' (Schott 2006: 134).

author In this book, we often refer to a singular author as the figure responsible for the vision and content that characterize a work of fiction. Although acknowledging that creative works including collaborative works of fiction such as movies or digital games are often better understood as the product of distributed authorship (see Jennings 2016; Gualeni, Fassone and Linderoth 2019), we decided to follow Currie in considering it unproblematic to posit one implied creator even in such cases. In his 1990 book *The Nature of Fiction*, Currie clarified that he refers to authors and their actions as though every work were the product of a single author, even though that is not always the case:

> Although it is not true, no great harm will be done by assuming that it is. For I take it that an act of joint authorship is exactly that: an act engaged in by more than one person rather than several distinct acts undertaken individually and patched together. This does not mean that every word must be the joint product of all the authors, merely that it should be understood between them that they are engaged in a

common project and that each has, in engaging in it, the kind of intention I have called a fictive intention.

1990: 11–12

fatal challenge/ fatal game/ deadly game These terms, which can be considered interchangeable for the purposes of this book, describe fictional games where the welfare of some involved beings is at stake. This is a relatively common narrative trope that is generally employed to emphasize a growing tension around challenges that the characters must face. It is also employed to engender moral dilemmas for the protagonists of a narrative to solve. Deadly games do not need to be considered or understood as games by all the participants, who often have very little agency or information about the activities that are taking place. In works of fiction, deadly games are often regarded as games only by their designers or masterminds. Notably, such games have historically existed. Well-known examples of actual fatal challenges are the gladiatorial games of ancient Rome and deadly trials such as Russian roulette or chicken run (a fatal challenge that involves two or more drivers simultaneously performing deadly stunts with cars – usually stolen – where the winner is the last driver to abandon their vehicle).

fiction Philosophers of fiction understand 'fictionality' as a quality of mediated content. Fictional content, they claim, is supposed to be imagined – and not believed – by their audience (readers, players, movie-goers or radio-drama listeners and so on). From this perspective, an expressive artefact can be labelled 'a work of fiction' when it encourages – and supports – acts of make-believe.

In other words, engaging in fiction consists of accepting the authors' invitation to imagine the characters and events presented in their work (Currie 1990: 30).

fictional world In the philosophical tradition of phenomenology, the term 'world' indicates a set composed of entities understood together with all their properties and mutual relationships. More specifically, a 'world' describes that set as it is experienced by one of the beings participating in the set itself. According to this tradition, to be identified as a world, properties and mutual relationships need to be experienced by the being in question in a way that is persistently perceivable and behaviourally consistent (Gualeni 2015: 6). In this book, we apply terms like 'fictional world' rather informally, in a way that builds on the phenomenological tradition, yet slightly deviates from it. With 'fictional world', we indicate that the environments and events described in a work of fiction (or encountered during gameplay) are meant to be imagined as being experienced – or having the potential for being experienced – as worlds by the fictional characters who inhabit them (see Ryan 2013).

ideology An ideology is understood, in the context of this book, as a set of socially shared beliefs that contribute to constituting an individual's goals and determining their actions. Ideologies tend to be initially embraced and enacted by the dominant class of a society and are then shared among the rest of a social group in ways that are typically implicit. This implicit quality – the adoption of ideologies in unspoken, pre-reflexive ways – is what sets them apart from values, which are, instead, explicitly presented and accepted as guiding principles for a certain society (e.g. in codes of law, religious commandments and precepts and proverbs).

rule A rule is an explicitly stated prescription for action. Rules guide and formalize agents' behaviours in various contexts, ranging from the traffic code, to how one is supposed to eat soup at a dinner party, to how sports and games are played. These prescriptions are typically meant to be mentally and behaviourally upheld by agents who intend to follow a certain code of conduct. This is also clearly the case when one engages in card games, table-top games, sports, puzzles, quizzes and analogue kinds of games more generally. Not all the prescriptions that bind and structure in-game agencies (see **agency**), however, are explicitly stated or enforced by the players themselves; some are implicitly imposed by elements or properties of the gameworlds. In the game of tennis, for example, agents such as air, gravity and friction cannot be understood as rules of the game. They are, instead, game affordances: properties or elements of the game environment that invite, inhibit or negate specific actions. Digital games typically present playful worlds that are defined by digital affordances rather than rules. One does not typically have the freedom to deviate from the kinds of behaviours and possibilities disclosed by a game, even if self-applied restrictions to one's behaviour can still occur in games, as is seen in deliberate acts of digital sportsmanship. An example of something that is a rule in a game but is instead an affordance in a digital game is the banning of touching the ball with one's hands in football. Whereas one must refrain from this behaviour in an actual football game (and punishment will follow an accidental or voluntary breaking of this rule), the possibility of grabbing or touching the ball with one's

thought experiment avatar's hands is simply not offered in interactive, digital renditions of football.

thought experiment A thought experiment is an imaginative act that consists of engaging with a hypothetical situation (or scenario). The scenario presented in a thought experiment is often one that would be unlikely to be encountered in the actual world, or that is categorically impossible in a particular socio-technical context. Thought experiments are not meant as blueprints for future activities; like fictional games, their function is to stimulate the imagination and subjective reasoning of recipients. With that objective, thought experiments employ a variety of cognitive tools, from moral imagination to lateral thinking. Their philosophical value consists of assisting recipients in reflecting on their mental habits and on the moral principles that guide their beliefs and behaviours. Among the most discussed examples of thought experiments are the trolley problem (Foot 1967), the experience machine (Nozick 1974; see Chapter 4) and Swampman (Davidson 1987).

worldbuilding Originally applied in relation to works of literary fiction, the term 'worldbuilding' indicates the efforts on the part of the authors to present a detailed and plausible fictional world. It is used when analysing and discussing works in literary genres such as science-fiction and fantasy. The utilization of the term 'worldbuilding' to indicate the process of setting up a fictional world has recently transcended its literary origins to encompass a wider variety of media forms, including film, games and video games.

References

Aarseth, E. J. (2007), 'I Fought the Law: Transgressive Play and the Implied Player', *Proceedings of the 2007 DiGRA International Conference*, Tokyo, September 24–28.

Aarseth, E. J. and G. Calleja (2015), 'The Word Game: The Ontology of an Undefinable Object', *Proceedings of the 10th International Conference on the Foundations of Digital Games (FDG 2015)*, Pacific Grove, CA, 22–25 June.

Arjoranta, J. (2014), 'Game Definitions: A Wittgensteinian Approach', *Game Studies: The International Journal of Computer Game Research*, 14 (1).

Avalon Hill (1974), [Board game] Rise and Decline of the Third Reich, designed by John Prados and published by Avalon Hill.

Badham, J. (1983), [Film] *WarGames*, United Artists, Sherwood Productions.

Bakhtin, M. (1968), 'The Role of Games in Rabelais', *Yale French Studies*, 41: 124–32.

Banks, I. M. ([1988] 2012), *The Player of Games*, New York: Orbit.

Björk, S. and J. Juul (2012), 'Zero-Player Games – Or: What We Talk about When We Talk about Players', *Proceedings of the 2012 Philosophy of Computer Games Conference*, Madrid, 29–31 January 2012.

Bogost, I. (2007), *Persuasive Games: The Expressive Power of Videogames*, Cambridge, MA: The MIT Press.

Bogost, I. (2011), *How to Do Things with Videogames*, Minneapolis, MN: University of Minnesota Press.

Bolaño, R. (2011), *The Third Reich*, New York: Farrar, Straus and Giroux.

Boschi, A. (2017), 'Let the Games Begin! – *La Figura del Gioco Distopico nel Cinema e Nella Letteratura Fantascientifica*', *Cinergie – Il Cinema e le altre Arti*, 12: 269–80.

Currie, G. (1990), *The Nature of Fiction*, Cambridge: Cambridge University Press.

Davidson, D. (1987), 'Knowing One's Own Mind', *Proceedings and Addresses of the American Philosophical Association*, 60 (3): 441–58.

Dostoevsky, F. (2017), *The Gambler*, London: Alma Books.

Elgin, C. 2007, 'The Laboratory of the Mind', in W. Huemer, J. Gibson and L. Pocci (eds), *A Sense of the World: Essays on Fiction, Narrative, and Knowledge*, New York: Routledge, 43–54.

Fincher, D. (1995) [Film] *Seven*, Cecchi Gori Pictures & Juno Pix, New Line Cinema.

Fincher, D. (1997) [Film] *The Game*, Propaganda Films. Scriptwriters: John Brancato & Michael Ferris.

Flanagan, M. (2009), *Critical Play: Radical Game Design*, Cambridge, MA: The MIT Press.

Flanagan, M. and H. Nissenbaum (2014), *Values at Play in Digital Games*, Cambridge, MA: The MIT Press.

Foot, P. (1967), 'The Problem of Abortion and the Doctrine of Double Effect', *Oxford Review*, 5: 5–15.

Grace, L. D. (2012), 'Critical Gameplay: Designing Games to Critique Convention', *Proceedings of the 20th ACM International Conference on Multimedia*: 1185–8.

Gualeni, S. (2015), *Virtual Worlds as Philosophical Tools*, Basingstoke: Palgrave Macmillan.

Gualeni, S. (2016), 'Self-Reflexive Videogames: Observations and Corollaries on Virtual Worlds as Philosophical Artifacts', *G A M E – The Italian Journal of Game Studies*, 5 (1): 11–20.

Gualeni, S. (2021), 'Fictional Games and Utopia: The Case of Azad', *Science Fiction Film & Television*, 14 (2): 187–207.

Gualeni, S. and D. Vella (2020), *Virtual Existentialism: Meaning and Subjectivity in Virtual Worlds*, Basingstoke: Palgrave Pivot.

Gualeni, S., R. Fassone and J. Linderoth (2019), 'How to Reference a Digital Game', *Proceedings of the 2019 DiGRA International Conference*, Kyoto (Japan), 6–10 August.

Hesse, H. ([1943] 2000), *The Glass Bead Game*, London: Vintage.

Jennings, S. C. (2021), 'A Meta-Synthesis of Agency in Game Studies: Trends, Troubles, Trajectories', *G A M E – The Italian Journal of Game Studies*, 8 (1): 85–106.

Kawabata, Y. ([1951] 2006), *The Master of Go*, London: Yellow Jersey.

King, S. ([1982, as R. Bachman] 2012), *The Running Man*, in *The Bachman Books*, London: Hodder & Stoughton: 707–978.
Laas, O. (2017), 'On Game Definitions', *Journal of the Philosophy of Sport*, 44 (1): 81–94.
Lee, S. (1998), [Film] *He Got Game*, 40 Acres & a Mule Filmworks, Touchstone Pictures.
Liesberger, S. (1982), [Film] *Tron*, Walt Disney Productions.
MacIntyre, A. (2007), *After Virtue: A Study in Moral Theory*, 3rd edn, Notre Dame, IN: University of Notre Dame Press.
Merriwether, E. (2011–18), [TV series] *New Girl*, 20th Century Fox Television.
More, T. ([1516] 2003), *Utopia*, ed. George M. Logan and Robert M. Adams, Cambridge: Cambridge University Press.
Murray, J. H. (1997), *Hamlet on the Holodeck: The Future of Narrative in Cyberspace*, New York: The Free Press.
Nguyen, C. T. (2020), *Games: Agency as Art*, Oxford: Oxford University Press.
Nozick, R. (1974), *Anarchy, State, and Utopia*, New York: Basic Books.
Raynolds, A. ([2003] 2006), *Diamond Dogs, Turquoise Days*, New York: ACE Books.
Roiland, J. and D. Harmon (2013–present) [Animated series] *Rick and Morty*, USA: Warner Bros. Television Distribution.
Rusch, D. C. and A. M. Phelps (2020), 'Existential Transformational Game Design: Harnessing the "Psychomagic" of Symbolic Enactment', *Frontiers in Psychology*, 11.
Ryan, M. L. (2013), 'Fictional Worlds in the Digital Age', in R. Siemens and S. Schreibman (eds), *A Companion to Digital Literary Studies*, Hoboken, NJ: John Wiley & Sons, 250–66.
Schott, G. (2006), 'Agency in and around Play', in D. Carr, D. Buckingham, A. Burn and G. Schott (eds), *Computer Games: Text, Narrative and Play*, Malden, MA: Polity Press, 133–48.
Sutton-Smith, B. (1997), *The Ambiguity of Play*, Cambridge, MA: Harvard University Press.

1

On Fictional Games

Games and sports frequently appear in works of fiction. In this book, we focus on the expressive possibilities and philosophical relevance that games and sports – playful activities in which prescriptions for action and criteria for success are formally defined – have when they are presented within such works. Our specific interest lies in the use of these games as thought experiments and meta-reflexive devices. Throughout this book, we will build a case for the meta-reflexive potential of fictional games, elaborating on their capability for inviting deliberate reflections on games and play and making claims regarding how games are currently designed, played, sold, manipulated, experienced and understood as social objects (see Gualeni 2016).

Representations and mentions of games have been common elements of fiction since ancient Greece. Aeschylus' 467 BCE play *Seven Against Thebes*, for example, repeatedly references dice games and the lottery to emphasize the low probability of a certain occurrence in the fictional world he is describing (i.e. that Eteocles and Polyneices will meet at the same gate of Thebes during the Argives attack on the city). Perhaps because of the stigma of frivolity and moral disreputability that was – and to some extent still is – associated with them, games only started to play a more central role in works of fiction several centuries after Aeschylus' work. Texts such as *The Book of One Thousand Nights* (c. 850) and Giovanni Boccaccio's ([1353] 2003) *The Decameron* are examples of works of literature in which games play a role that is more substantial than being a passing reference or part of the narrative background. As discussed by Fassone and Huber (2017), early modern Italian literature abounds with examples of games having a focal relevance in texts that straddle the line between fiction and theory. Pietro Aretino's ([1543] 1992) *Le Carte Parlanti*, written in 1543, and Torquato Tasso's ([1581] 1858) dialogue *Il Gonzaga Secondo*, written in 1581, are striking examples of this phenomenon.[1] Subsequently, games and sports have frequently been used as narrative devices, and their use in fiction is now common.

Notwithstanding their recurrence in the history of the production of fiction and the fact that they are frequently mentioned, featured and fictionally played in contemporary works, little academic interest has thus far been dedicated to the meaning and the expressive potential of the representation of games within works of fiction. Greater scholarly efforts have been dedicated, instead, to both the role of fiction within games (see Aarseth 2007; Van de Mosselaer 2020) and the possibility for literary fiction to be playful or game-like for readers (see Hutchinson 1983; Suits 1985; Edwards 2013).

The first academic treatment of games and playfulness as components of literary fiction is found in Robert Detweiler's 1976 essay, 'Games and Play in Modern American Fiction'. In this essay, he nominally defines games as 'contests of some sort that have a traditional formal structure or an easily identifiable game configuration' (49). According to Detweiler, the representation of games within a work of fiction is only one of the three possible ways in which (modern, American) fiction can be considered 'ludic'. Several years later, Bernard Suits published an essay entitled, 'The Detective Story: A Case Study of Games in Literature', where, in a way that is similar to Detweiler's 1976 book, he proposes a small taxonomy of ways in which a literary work can 'correctly' (i.e. non-metaphorically) be considered a game (1985: 200). Among these ways, Suits includes the possibility for literary fiction to be game-like in cases when games are not merely described but are fictionally played within the narrative, thus turning the reader into a spectator of sorts. In contradiction to his opening statement, however, Suits specifies later in the same text that these games are not really *games*, but are – in Aristotle's sense of the word – *imitations* of games (ibid.: 210). In simpler terms, Suits explains that the reader encountering a game within a work of fiction 'is viewing a "game" in the same sense that he is viewing jealousy when he goes to see *Othello*' (ibid.).

---

[1] For more examples and perspectives on the roles and representation of games and play in medieval literature, we recommend the collection of essays *Games and Gaming in Medieval Literature* (Patterson 2015).

Central to Suits' article is the attempt to frame the detective story (a subset of literary fiction) as a sort of intellectual game that the author plays with the reader. The idea that a work of fiction, and its author through it, can institute a playful challenge to the reader has a long intellectual history that can be traced back at least to Van Dine's (1928: 27) claim that 'the detective story is a game. It is more – it is a sporting event', which attests to the existence of a common understanding of the genre as game-like, including among fiction writers. Within the same tradition, Peter Hutchinson focuses his scholarly efforts on the topic of literary play, encompassing both playful writing and the possibility of a ludic relationship between author and reader. Like Suits, Hutchinson does not make the representation of games in fiction a central point of his work. Clues concerning the expressive potential and the literary use of games in fiction do surface, however, in his 1983 book, *Games Authors Play*, where games often feature as examples of literary devices. Of particular interest considering the scope of our work is Hutchinson's discussion of the use of 'parallels' and 'enigmas' in literature, theatre and film. Given their relevance to our book and the frequent recurrence of these terms, we consider it important to briefly introduce these two categories:

1. **Parallels**

    In *Games Authors Play*, Hutchinson (1983: 23) defines parallels as occurring when a work of fiction is represented within another work of fiction in cases where the former mirrors the wider narrative development of the latter. This kind of correspondence can be established with any kind of fiction nested within any other kind of fiction. Instances of this expressive strategy can occur in the form of a book within a book, a film within a film, a book within a film, a game within a theatrical play, a theatrical play within a video game and so on. Several of the examples of parallels discussed in Hutchinson's book are games, including the famous scene of dramatic irony in which Livia and the Mother play chess (Act Two, Scene Two) in Thomas Middleton's 1657 tragedy, *Women Beware Women*, and the game of backgammon played by Keegan and Nora in George Bernard Shaw's 1904 comedy, *John Bull's Other Island* (ibid.: 27–8). Within works of fiction, a game functioning as a parallel presents a barebones version of specific events that are developing in the fictional world as the game is being played. Chess games in Vladimir Nabokov's 1930 novel, *The Defense*, are another obvious example of a game functioning as a parallel in literary fiction. On the basis of evident analogies between games represented in a work of fiction and the wider narrative of this work, Hutchinson analyses a number of possible expressive uses of parallels, including, notably, adumbration (the foreshadowing of events that are still to take place within the narrative), allusion (the referencing of actual historical events or people or to elements and characters that belong to other works of fictions) and parody (a specific form of allusion with evident satirical intent).

2. Enigmas

Games Authors Play presents enigmas as mysteries existing in a fictional world that are typically leveraged to introduce uncertainty and suspense. This category can include several narrative elements that, in their mysterious ambiguity, encourage the reader to assess and question what they know about the fictional world (ibid.). In line with the objectives of the rest of his book, Hutchinson presents enigmas as a particular way in which the authors of literary fictions challenge their readers. He does not discuss them in ways that are specific to – or that make them identifiable with – games, but we can recognize several cases of fictions in which enigmas as discussed by Hutchinson are explicitly presented as games. For instance, in films such as *Jumanji* (Johnston 1995) and *Cube* (Natali 1997) or in the manga series *GANTZ* (Oku 2000–13) and *Alice in Borderland* (Aso 2010–16), the surprising circumstances in which the characters find themselves coincide with the boundaries and prescriptions of puzzling (and potentially deadly) games.

Parallels and enigmas are not exhaustive of the expressive uses of games in fiction, as we are about to show in relation to the representation of sports within works of fiction, and especially so among American scholars and critics. Christian K. Messenger's (1981) pioneering book *Sport and the Spirit of Play in American Fiction: Hawthorne to Faulkner*, for example, explores the relationships between sports and the cultural history of North America, identifying sports as a relatable allegorical context for readers. Messenger argues that a particular (and particularly American) kind of ethos is normalized and celebrated through the figure of the 'sport hero'. Neil David Berman's (1981) book *Playful Fiction and Fictional Players: Game, Sport and Survival in Contemporary American Fiction*, published in the same year, similarly recognizes games and sports as central to the formation and establishment of American identities and values. In one of the five examples analysed by Berman, he also discusses the liberatory potential of games and their roles in highlighting (or even subverting) power relationships within American society. The early scholarly work of Mike Oriard (1982; 1991) and Seán Crosson's 2013 book, *Sport and Film*, can also be cited here as remarkable works concentrating their attention on the representation of sports in fiction as the background for the narrative arc of the sport hero.

Clearly, the occurrence and uses of games in works of fiction have been addressed by some academic literature, mostly in the scholarly fields of literary criticism and film studies. When conducting research for this book, we were surprised to discover that, to date, the representation of games in fiction has received no dedicated interest from disciplines such as the philosophy of fiction or game studies, which one would expect to be prime candidates for significant contributions on the matter. In this book, we aspire to begin addressing this gap in the research by examining and analysing a specific subcategory of games within fiction – fictional games.

What are fictional games, and how do they differ from the representation of actual games within works of fiction? In the Glossary section in the Introduction, we clarified that we qualify media contents as 'fictional' when their existence is meant to be imagined – and not believed – by their recipients (e.g. readers, players, movie-goers and the audience of a radio drama). In other words, engaging in fiction consists of accepting the author's invitation to imagine the characters and events presented in their work (Currie 1990: 30). In accordance with this understanding of fiction, we understand fictional games as playful activities and ludic artefacts that appeal to the imagination of the appreciator of a work of fiction and that cannot be – or at least were not originally meant to be – actually played (see Gualeni 2021).

In this book, we explore fictional games, with a focus on their expressive and philosophical significance. Particularly noteworthy in relation to this pursuit are the scholarly works of Will Slocombe (especially his 2013 paper, 'Games Playing Roles in Banks' Fiction') and Esther MacCallum-Stewart (particularly her 2018 book chapter, 'The Gaming of Players: Jamming Azad'), whose contributions to understanding the relationships between games and fictionality inspired the writing of this book (more on this in Chapter 3). Two other works that are particularly relevant to the aspirations of our book are Chris Bateman's 2011 book, *Imaginary Games*, and Björk and Juul's 2012 paper, 'Zero-Player Games – Or: What We Talk about When We Talk about Players'. These two texts do not explicitly discuss the representation of games and fictional games as part of works of fiction, but both, in different ways, influenced our framing of the relationships between games and imagination.

Imaginary Games

Bateman's book investigates the role of imagination in how we understand and engage in the activity of play. Drawing its premises from Kendall Walton's (1990) theory of make-believe, Bateman's book can be understood as pursuing a project that is the specular opposite of our own. Whereas our book focuses on games that are imagined as belonging in a certain fictional world but that cannot be played outside of it, Bateman's work reflects on how existing, actual games – in both the analogue and the digital domains –function as imaginary props that facilitate and enrich play. In other words, although imagination is a focal notion in both our book and Bateman's, the earlier work discusses imagination and its relevance for games, while our focus is on (fictional) games and their effects on our imagination.

'Zero-Player Games'

Björk and Juul's speculative and highly provocative paper centres its arguments on the questions of what a player is and what a player does. They try to answer these questions by examining playful experiences that are commonly understood to be 'player-less' through the lens of four analytical categories. One of these categories, hypothetical games, directly resonates with the approach we propose in this book, as outlined in the Introduction chapter. 'Zero-Player Games' introduces 'hypothetical games' – games that are meant to be imagined but not implemented; these may be games that are described to examine a certain question (essentially playable thought experiments) or games that actually exist but that, for practical reasons, are unplayable. Albeit only in passing, Björk and Juul argue that sometimes playing games is not as important as imagining them, as their inaccessibility for actual play can function as an incentive for us to examine games and play from other, often unfamiliar perspectives.

The inaccessibility of fictional games in terms of being experienced playfully and interactively (i.e. their unplayability) is clearly a feature that is central both to our definition of fictional games and to Björk and Juul's understanding of hypothetical games. Reflecting the pivotal importance of unplayability in our framing of fictional games, a full section of this chapter is dedicated to it (1.2). Before homing in on the theme of unplayability, in the upcoming section we examine cases that might appear to be ambiguous and/or problematic in our proposed understanding of fictional games.

1.1 Playing fictional games?

As mentioned above, this section is instrumental to further define what can or cannot be considered a fictional game in the context of this book. In it, we explain why neither playable games within digital gameworlds nor actual games that were originally conceptualized as part of a work of fiction fall within our scope. We refer specifically to threshold cases in which games within works of fiction might be playable or could be made playable.

The first threshold case that we want to consider are games that are encountered within interactive works of fiction. Here, we are talking particularly about games that exist within digital gameworlds. Before explaining why these 'games within (digital) games' might constitute exceptional cases, it is important to emphasize that we treat the worlds of digital games – at least in part – as fictional worlds. To be more precise, in our perspective, digital games can be recognized as disclosing playful world-like experiences for their users–experiences that are always characterized by various aspects and degrees of fictionality. In other words, we understand digital games as having been created with the intention of making players imagine both the artificial worlds presented in them and the roles the players take within them. This approach follows scholarly analyses that discuss most digital games as interactive fictions (see Robson and Meskin 2012; Schulzke 2014; Van de Mosselaer 2020). The qualifier 'most' is necessary here because digital games such as *Tetris* (Pajitnov 1984) are not commonly discussed as interactive fictions. We do not elaborate on this issue here, as all the examples of digital gameworlds chosen for this book are taken from games that are rather uncontroversially considered to be works of fiction.

In contrast to most other forms of authored fiction, digital games give their appreciators (i.e. the players) the possibility to interactively engage with fictional content. Depending on the game genre, digital games disclose a variety of agential opportunities that follow from virtually embodying a fictional character and from including the possibility of virtually manipulating elements of a fictional world. As a consequence of these affordances and expressive possibilities, when games are encountered within a digital gameworld, these sub-games are often interactive objects designed so that the player can ludically engage with them. We will discuss these games later in this section, but, first, it is important to emphasize that effectively playable sub-games constitute the majority of cases where a game is encountered within the fictional world of another game. In our perspective, the rare instances where games within games are not interactive playthings but maintain, instead, a degree of under-specification are the only ones that can be considered fictional games. Notable examples of fictional games within digital games include Kepesh-Yakshi, a non-playable chess-like, fictional game within the digital gameworld of *Mass Effect 3*

Figure 1.1 A screenshot of the 2012 video game *Mass Effect 3* (BioWare) showing a game of Kepesh-Yakshi. Analogous to popular board games in the actual world, Kepesh-Yakshi requires its fictional players to optimize their resource management and strive for territorial domination. © Electronic Arts 2012. All rights reserved.

(see Figure 1.1; BioWare 2012), Wicked Grace, a poker-like fictional game in the video game *Dragon Age: Inquisition* (more on this game in Chapter 2; BioWare 2014) and various fictional board games – Wirrâl, The Viticulturist, Archipelagos of Insulinde, Raubritter and Suzerainty – that belong to the gameworld of *Disco Elysium* (ZA/UM 2019). Suzerainty is a fictional board game that contributes to thematically emphasizing the hopelessness and the distinct anti-utopian tone of the larger game. It is described as a civilization-building board game where the player gets to choose a nation and then sets off to colonize and exploit other cultures (ibid.).

Games that are actually playable within a digital game can certainly be called 'games within a fictional world', but we argue that they are better categorized and understood as actual games than as fictional games. Our reason for this claim rests on the fact that such playable sub-games are characterized by aspects such as formal completeness and playability. These playable sub-games can take the form of minigames or nested games. We briefly present these here to offer conceptual and lexical clarity:

Minigames

Minigames are activities within the fictional world of a digital game that are introduced as uninfluential with regard to the main narrative line of the game. In this sense, minigames are typically presented as safely replayable pastimes or sub-games that belong to the wider gameworld but that tend to happen in dedicated areas. Through these activities, the player can hone (and show off) skills that are typically also useful in the wider gameworld. Archery challenges in the *Legend of Zelda* (Nintendo 1986–present) series, the shooting-range skill tests in *Deus Ex: Mankind Divided* (Eidos Montreal 2016) and fishing minigames in a wide variety of game franchises are obvious examples of these kinds of ludic activities. Canonically, players obtain useful rewards for achieving a certain standard of proficiency in these activities. Trophies, achievement markers and pieces of gear are the almost universally expected rewards for succeeding in minigames, and can be shown to other players as a testament to one's commitment to a particular activity or standard of in-game performance.[2]

Nested games

As discussed above, minigames are playable sub-games that are integrated within the wider gameworld of digital games. Their integration is evident in the fact that the skills required to be successful in both typically overlap and that they generally share the same control scheme and fictional space (although minigames tend to be played in dedicated areas of the wider gameworld). Nested games, like minigames, are playable sub-games that are encountered within digital games. Unlike minigames, however, nested games are a 'playable enclave': they are ludically isolated from the wider gameworld that contains them. This isolation does not always extend to the prizes when the player manages to beat a nested game; these prizes are often items and goods that are usable in the main game. The separation between the main game and nested games is often emphasized in the game fiction by the latter being accessible to the player character – and to the player – through devices such as an in-game arcade cabinet, fictional game consoles or specific tables dedicated to that activity. Geometry Wars, a multidirectional action shooter video game that can be accessed and played by turning on a game cabinet in

---

[2] Although very similar to minigames, we decided not to include in-game 'side quests' in this list for reasons we articulate below. Side quests are comparable to minigames in their lack of influence with regard to the main narrative line of a game. In contrast to minigames, however, side quests are not presented or understood as games in their fictional world, and usually involve the use of already acquired in-game skills, instead of new affordances and possibilities. Additionally, side quests typically take place in the broader fictional world as opposed to being somewhat separate from it, and – given their fuller integration with the rest of the game narrative – they often become inaccessible for the duration of the game if they are failed (which is not typically the case for minigames and nested games).

the garage of *Project Gotham Racing 2* (Bizarre Creations 2003) is a clear example of a nested game, as is GamePig, a portable console encountered in *System Shock 2* (Irrational Games & Looking Glass Studios 1992), on which several nested games (reminiscent of Nintendo Game Boy titles) can be played. Other notable examples of nested games are the game of Sinking Ships in *The Legend of Zelda: The Wind Waker* (Nintendo 2002) and the collectible card game of Triple Triad in *Final Fantasy VIII* (Square 1999). With the objective of emphasizing their separateness from the larger gameworlds, it is very rare for nested games to be played in ways that are similar to how the player operates in the broader gameworld.[3] One exception is *Rapunzel*, a fictional arcade video game that can be played on an arcade cabinet in the gameworld of *Catherine* (Atlus 2011).

The argument as to why minigames and nested games cannot be considered fictional games also extends to the case of games that were originally unplayable components of a work of fiction but were later developed into playable artefacts. We argue that, once fully resolved into playable artefacts, what were once fictional games take a different media form. In their new, gameful form, their fictionality is no longer the dominant mode in which their contents are experienced. In this transition, games that were originally imaginative props acquire expressive features and possibilities that characterize their new and interactive media form. For example, procedural forms of rhetoric become part of the expressive arsenal of the author (see Bogost 2007), who can offer the player interactive possibilities for exploring game elements and interpreting game functions in minute detail and in a variety of situations and contexts. At the same time, the expressive possibilities that characterize old media forms become less effective and accessible, or are completely excised from the experience because of their incompatibility with their transparently and instrumentally rational form of games as playable artefacts.

Here, we argue that many of the philosophical and meaning-making possibilities of fictional games emerge from their 'fictional incompleteness' (see the following section on the unplayability of fictional games) – that is, from the particular kind of under-specification that makes them possible to be imagined and speculated about in a great variety of different ways. When fictional games are formally resolved into actually playable artefacts and the functions and meanings of their elements are codified in affordances, rules and exceptions

---

[3] These cases are infrequent because, generally speaking, nested games are often inspired by the arcade video game tradition and tend to be structurally simpler than the larger gameworld of which they are a part.

(achieving something we later discuss as 'teleological crispness'), they become effectively different artefacts with substantially different properties. In other words, in their transition from fictional to actual, games lose their ontological fluidity and with it their possibility to become more than they are.

Examples of this kind of transition abound. Gwent, for instance, was originally a fictional, turn-based collectible card game within the fantasy gameworld of *The Witcher* (CD Projekt RED 2007; the game is also mentioned under a different name in the book series). In the third instalment of the same game franchise, Gwent was formally completed as a playable, nested game (CD Projekt RED 2015). Through this process, Gwent, as a new, playable artefact, was no longer an imaginative prop and inevitably lost some of its potential as a narrative device compared with the original fictional game. Other similar cases can be observed in Fizzbin (a poker-inspired bluff-based card game that made its fictional appearance in the original *Star Trek* and then became a commercially available game in 1976) and Triad (*Battlestar Galactica*'s science-fictional variation of poker, adapted into an actually playable card game in 2012).

A particularly remarkable example of this transition can be seen in the case of Quidditch, a favourite pastime of the students at Hogwarts School of Witchcraft and Wizardry in the fictional world of *Harry Potter* (Rowling 1997–2007). The composition of the teams, the equipment needed to play and the rules of the game are described in detail in the novels of the series, and this has been expanded upon in the films derived from these novels and refined through multiple paratexts (see Whisp 2017) describing the game's minutiae and history. Quidditch is, hence, one of the few fictional games that were originally formally complete but remained unplayable because of supernatural features (see section 1.2.1). In its original form, it can broadly be described as a magical version of hockey played on flying brooms. Points are scored by shooting a ball through a series of rings located at the two ends of the playing field. Each player is equipped with a broom, which is used as a mount to fly across the field. The real-life adaptation of Quidditch leverages the fictional game's formal completeness and is often referred to as Muggle Quidditch (see Figure 1.2) to distinguish it from the fictional game from which it originated (where 'Muggle' is the term found in the *Harry Potter* series of novels to describe people who do not possess or have yet to discover their magic powers). Muggle Quidditch can be described as a variant of Quidditch in which, to use London's (2019: 19) terse and accurate description, 'there is no flying'. Since 2005, the year of its creation, Muggle Quidditch has been an actual sport, and it now boasts several national-level federations and tournaments worldwide.

Figure 1.2 A game of Muggle Quidditch, a playable version of the fictional sport Quidditch in the *Harry Potter* series of novels. The term 'muggle' is used in the novels to designate someone who lacks magical abilities. © Ben Holland (CC BY-SA 4.0). All rights reserved.

Other famous examples of fictional games that were redesigned to become actual, playable board games are Swords and Strongholds (originally a chess-inspired fictional game invented by David Petersen for his *Mouse Guard* graphic novel series), Pai Sho (a Go-like strategic board game within the fictional world of *Avatar: The Last Airbender*), Cyvasse (a chess-like fictional game that originally appeared in George R. R. Martin's fantasy novel series *A Song of Ice and Fire*, see Figure 1.3)[4] and two real-life adaptations of fictional games that originally appeared in Terry Pratchett's *Discworld* series (1983–2015): Thud and Cripple Mr. Onion.

Having addressed cases that could appear to be ambiguous and/or problematic in the context of our understanding of fictional games, in the next section, we articulate the various ways in which fictional games are presented as unplayable in works of fiction.

---

[4] Cyvasse is a turn-based, chess-like fictional game that requires two competing players. The game is said to have originated in the city of Volantis (on the continent of Essos) and features ten types of pieces: rabble, spearmen, crossbowmen, light horse, heavy horse, trebuchet, catapult, dragon, elephant and the king. In the series, Cyvasse is presented as being played on a board that changes from game to game. In the beginning phases of each game, the players set up the tiles on the board with a screen between them, so that neither can see how the other arranges their half of the board (Martin 1996–present).

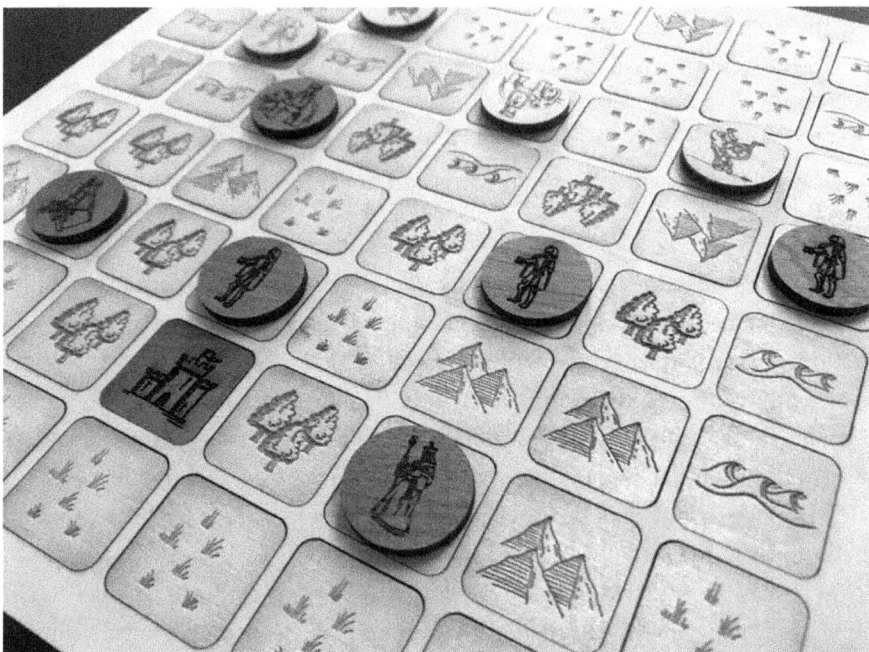

Figure 1.3 A playable version of Cyvasse, complete with a board and a set of official (as well as alternative) rules. The game was adapted and integrated by the Bristol Design Forge on the basis of how the game is described and played in the fantasy novel series *A Song of Ice and Fire*. © Bristol Design Forge. All rights reserved.

1.2 The unplayability of fictional games

Throughout this chapter, we have presented fictional games as playful activities and ludic artefacts devised as components of a larger work of fiction. Thus, fictional games have been discussed as elements of a narrative whose functioning and playfulness are aspects that are meant to be imagined rather than experienced directly by the fiction appreciators. The impossibility of accessing (and potentially enjoying) these games as players is, therefore, a central feature of how we understand fictional games. To emphasize the relevance of this concept, this section is specifically dedicated to the unplayability of fictional games. Here, we propose and elaborate upon four possible sources of this unplayability that can characterize fictional games – four non-exclusive ways in which fictional games are presented as imaginative props and narrative devices that are not supposed to be engaged with in ways that are directly ludic. These four causes of unplayability in fictional games are as follows:

1. Their fictional incompleteness.
2. The current impossibility of their magical or advanced technological features.
3. Their not being meant to be accessed or interacted with by human players.
4. Their clashing with ethical standards and norms that are common in the actual world.

As we elaborate in the following sub-sections, the first two types of unplayability (incompleteness and impossibility) emerge as direct consequences of how a fictional game is represented within a work of fiction. In this sense, a fictional game might be impossible for us (the audience) to play because the author simply did not provide enough detail and information for it to be playable without substantial integrations (see sub-section 1.2.1) and/or because it is clearly not (or not yet) possible to reproduce some of its components and behaviours in the actual world (see sub-section 1.2.2).

Whereas the first two types of unplayability depend on objective qualities of how a fictional game is represented, the second two (being meant for nonhuman players and being unsuitable for the actual world on ethical and legal grounds) emerge from subjective and contextual factors. What we mean is that some fictional games remain unplayable by humans in the actual world not because of impossibilities that characterize the games themselves (or the socio-technical context in which they are played) but rather because of the physical, cognitive and perceptual limitations that (currently) define human players (see sub-section 1.2.3) and/or the interdictions that currently define our moral communities (see sub-section 1.2.4).

1.2.1 The unplayable incompleteness of fictional games

Being in the world as human beings is messy: personal motivations, social conventions and meanings attributed to things and information are often so intricate, dynamic and ambiguous that they are impossible to understand completely and conclusively, let alone reliably predict and act upon. In contrast to our messy engagement with the actual world, the ways in which the meaning of objects and situations are presented in games are generally obvious and unambiguous. Nguyen (2020: 68) calls this quality of our relationship with games and game elements 'teleological crispness'. In his view, games are realms of agency in which the functions of objects and the meaning of actions are entirely obvious (ibid.). The clarity and consistency of rules and affordances are defining traits of the specific and formal manifestations of play that we refer to as games.[5] This crispness is particularly obvious in the explicit ways digital games provide guidance to their players through aesthetic clues and feedback systems (i.e. how players are informed, rewarded and punished within the gameworld). These aspects in the design of the virtual worlds of games as well as training simulations are specifically intended to foster feelings of existential meaning and significant progress among users (Gualeni 2015: 128). Games in general, we argue, can be understood as experiential sub-worlds whose clearly regimented promise of clarity and growth can soothe us and offer an alluring alternative to the complexity, ambiguities, difficulties and inherent absurdity of the actual world (see Gualeni and Vella 2020).

Unlike actual games, fictional games are neither formally complete nor teleologically crisp for the fiction appreciator. Instead, they are typically presented in ways that are deliberately vague and incomplete, and they can undergo surprising changes and transformations. Taking a step back, as we previously mentioned, the rules, boundaries, exceptions and criteria for success in fictional games tend to be simply hinted at in the work of fiction of which they are a part, outlined just clearly enough to fulfil their intended narrative and worldbuilding functions. Why is that the case? Would fictional games not be better components of works of fiction if they were described with full formal and technical details? The author's desire to accommodate the audience's limited capabilities for concentrating, imagining and memorizing only partially answers these questions. Another reason why fictional games are not presented in ways that are completely fleshed out can be identified in the considerable toll that this operation would take on the author in terms of creative effort. Additionally, a fully designed game might – if not correctly paced and regulated in terms of accessibility – threaten the narrative flow and detract from the focus of the rest of the work.

An even more general answer to questions about the incompleteness and vagueness in the representation of fictional games comes from the recognition that all works of fiction are inherently incomplete. The various events that take place in a fictional world, as well as the qualities and backgrounds of its characters and its lore, are inevitably underspecified, unresolved and left open to the imagination and the interpretation of the fiction appreciator (Wildman and

---

[5] In his book, *Homo Ludens: A Study of the Play-Element in Culture*, Johan Huizinga similarly observes that '[i]nside the playground an absolute and peculiar order reigns [...]. [Play] creates order, *is* order. Into an imperfect world and into the confusion of life it brings a temporary, a limited perfection' (1939: 10).

Woodward 2018: 114).⁶ Thus, the presence of gaps and omissions in the imaginings prescribed by a work of fiction (i.e. its fictional incompleteness) is not a trait that is exclusive to the games we label as 'fictional'. Rather, this trait characterizes every aspect and component of a fictional world, including actual games that are represented and discussed as part of it. The rules and strategic possibilities of the actual game of Go, for example, are for the most part sketchily outlined in Yasunari Kawabata's (1954) novel *The Master of Go*, only coming into focus for the reader when they serve very specific narrative purposes. The same point on fictional incompleteness applies to the use of the game of chess in works such as Nabokov's already cited novel *The Defense* and Walter Tevis' (1983) *The Queen's Gambit* (as well as the 2020 period drama Netflix miniseries with the same name).

To further illustrate this point, consider the case of Monarch's Dispute, a strategic, turn-based, two-player fictional board game played in Iain M. Banks' 1998 science-fiction novel, *Inversions* (2012c). *Inversions* is set on a fictional planet resembling late Middle Ages Europe, where a vast empire fell apart about a decade before the events presented in the novel, and the ongoing disputes and conflicts between the factions of what was previously the same empire constitute the plot's sociopolitical background. Monarch's Dispute is mentioned in *Inversions* on a few occasions, when the fictional game is played by two of the main characters, with their in-game behaviour matching the structure and sometimes the very themes of their long conversations. In Banks' book, to use Hutchinson's classification, these Monarch's Dispute games function as parallels (both alluding to and foreshadowing events in the fiction itself). In the second chapter of *Inversions*, the game is described in some degree of detail, and it is introduced as being played in turns on a board that represents two bordering kingdoms. The invitation to imagine a variation of chess is obvious. The points of similarity further increase when the readers learn that, during gameplay, players of Monarch's Dispute move a variety of pieces that include multiple generals, one emperor and one protector (i.e. the emperor's bodyguard). The goal of the game is to protect one's emperor from the assaults of the opponent's army. Not many more details are offered in *Inversions* concerning the game, and it is obvious that, without a description of the board or how it restricts the movement of the pieces and without information such as an indication of the set-up

---

⁶ Literary theorist Maurice Blanchot ([1949] 1995: 75) has described the paucity of information and detail that the audience comes into contact with when engaging with a fictional world in very similar terms. For Blanchot, this 'poverty' is the very essence of fiction (ibid.).

procedures, how turns work, which pieces exist and what the pieces can do on the board, the reader is simply invited to imagine it being played – not to imagine playing it. The narrative relevance of this kind of imagining lies in the fact that the game mirrors, in broad strokes, the socio-technical context in which the game is played. In the specific case of Monarch's Dispute, for example, we are invited to imagine it belonging in a fictional society that values strategic thinking, bluffing, intrigue and the employment of decoys.

There are several examples of fictional games that, unlike Monarch's Dispute, are rendered in rich functional detail. This is the case for the competitive strategic two-player turn-based fictional board game Oråki described in the fourth chapter of Nike A. Sulway's (2013) novel *Rupetta*. The movement rules for the three pawns controlled by each of the two opposing players on the board are provided in detail, as are the rules about losing pieces and the winning conditions. Despite the wealth of formal detail, the lack of functional indications about the Oråki board (and the related absence of set-up procedures) is an unambiguous indication that the game is meant to be clearly understood and imagined but not physically produced or actually played. Sulway presents the board on which Oråki was originally played in the fiction with a focus on its aesthetics rather than its topological or functional aspects:

> The board was a circle of polished and lacquered ebon, five metres in diameter at its outside edge: a dark, gleaming planispheric astrolabe. At its centre a milky orb – the moon – surrounded by the night sky. The stars [the parts of the board that the pawns can occupy] were formed of silver inlay, with pearls at their centre. Facing each other across the board were the chairs for the two players.
>
> Ibid.: 141–2

Having highlighted some of the reasons behind the deliberate vagueness and ambiguity of fictional games, we now emphasize that their fictional incompleteness is not merely an authorial strategy that makes imagining these games a lighter, easier task for both the audience and the author. The under-specification of fictional games can also serve various expressive purposes – first and foremost, surprising the audience with unexpected in-game situations, devious strategies and the revelation of latent in-game possibilities. In general, the fictional incompleteness of fictional games can introduce unexpected events and possibilities in a work of fiction that, if the fictional game were presented in complete detail, could be played out and foreseen by the audience.

Another expressive possibility that leverages the incompleteness of fictional games is bewildering the audience. The sense of unfamiliarity and confusion that can emerge from the deliberate under-specification of fictional games can have a variety of applications: it can be used, for example, to emphasize the inscrutability (and, perhaps, even the hostility) of a universe in which human beings are powerless pawns. In most cases, however, bewildering fictional games are typically employed for comedic purposes (see Saarikoski et al. 2022). Here, we are referring to games that appear to the audience in ways that can be (non-exclusively) in a constant state of becoming and expanding, or so labyrinthine as to make fully understanding them impossible. Instances of these kinds of fictional games include the following:

1. Cups: A fictional card game played in the television series *Friends* (S6E06 – 'The One on the Last Night'; Schwimmer 1999). Chandler (Matthew Perry), one of the protagonists of the series, invents the game and related lexicon on the fly with the intention of losing money to his friend Joey (Matt LeBlanc). The game, as a result, is vague, clumsy and riddled with hilarious exceptions.
2. *Bamboozled*: A bedazzling, fictional quiz show that appears in the television series *Friends* (S8E20 – 'The One with the Baby Shower'; Bright 2002). The rules and various events that constitute *Bamboozled* appear to be as numerous as they are intricate and unpredictable.
3. Calvinball: A game invented by Calvin and Hobbes in the eponymous comic strip. This fictional game has only a couple of fixed rules, one of which is that players cannot play Calvinball in the same way twice. To that end, players can add new rules as each game progresses, making it spontaneous, bizarre and open-ended (Watterson [1990] 2005: 268–73; see Figure 1.4).
4. Mornington Crescent: A conversation-based fictional game featured on the BBC Radio 4 comedy panel show *I'm Sorry I Haven't a Clue*. The game consists of the panellists taking turns announcing a landmark or street, most often a London Underground station. The rules are entirely obscure to the audience and constitute one of the recurrent, hilarious topics of contention on the show. The goal of the game is to be the first player to announce 'Mornington Crescent', a station on the Northern Line.
5. Cones of Dunshire: A fictional board game that is played in the television series *Parks and Recreation* (S8E8 – 'The Cones of Dunshire'). The game, created by one of the protagonists of the series, Ben Wyatt (Adam Scott), is structured by an elaborate series of rules dictating how in-game resources are generated and distributed, defining possibilities for action and movement of the various in-game characters and regulating a number of other bizarre game functions (Robinson 2013).

Figure 1.4 Calvin and Hobbes playing a game of Calvinball. *Calvin and Hobbes* © Watterson 1990. Reprinted with permission of Andrews McMeel Syndication. All rights reserved.

6. Three-Cornered Pitney: Exhilaratingly intricate, this fictional game was invented by Jack Davis and appeared as a five-page story in issue 241 of *Mad Magazine* (EC 1983).
7. Whack-Bat: A fictional team sport that appears in the stop motion animated comedy film *Fantastic Mr. Fox* (Anderson 2009) and can be described as a more outlandish version of the actual team sport cricket. Whack-Bat requires at least thirteen players: three grabbers, three taggers, five twig-runners, one centre tagger and the player at whack-bat. Like other fictional games in this list, the comedic effects ensuing from the encounter with Whack-Bat emerge from the abstruseness and complexity of its rules and scoring system (Figure 1.5).

Another expressive possibility related to the fundamental ambiguity and incompleteness of fictional games is their hinting at the instability and contingency that ultimately define any situation. This particular use of fictional games is the focus of the third chapter of this book, where fictional games are discussed and analysed in terms of their potential as utopian devices – that is, their capability for stimulating imaginings of social and political arrangements that are alternative to the ones that currently characterize our existence.

1.2.2 Unattainable magical or technological features

Fictional games are typically incomplete and underspecified, but some are also unplayable because the fictional world they exist in is radically different from the one we inhabit. Fictional games found in works belonging to the genres of science-fiction, fantasy and horror often imply the use of magic or depend on

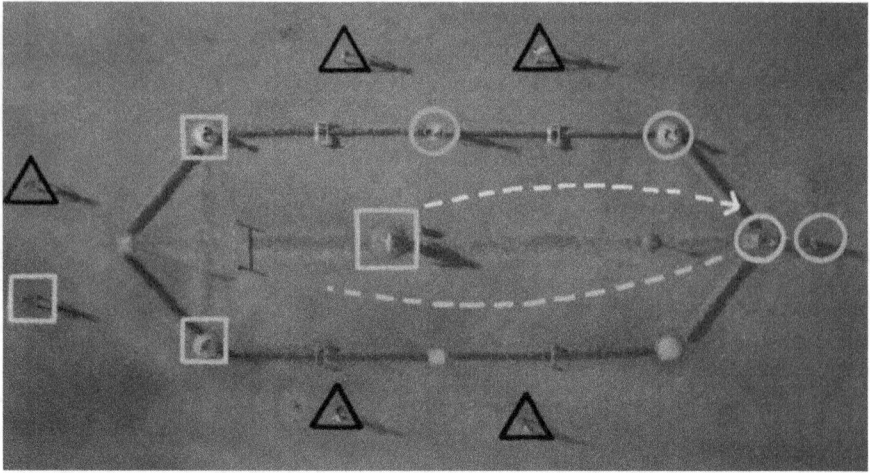

Figure 1.5 The rules of Whack-Bat as explained in Wes Anderson's 2009 film *Fantastic Mr. Fox*. The protagonist of the film, Mr. Fox, is a skilled player of this humorous adaptation of the game of cricket. © 20th Century Fox 2009. All rights reserved.

other supernatural features that are currently inaccessible in our reality. Supernatural, magical, otherworldly or otherwise physically impossible events are a tenet of several genres of fiction. Although supernatural themes have been central to the literary imagination in certain periods, such as European Romanticism (Clery 1995), magic-related themes and paranormal elements are common historical recurrences in most narrative traditions across the globe. Furthermore, according to Natale (2016), a large portion of the contemporary Western media landscape is imbued with – and stems from – a fascination with the supernatural that is rooted in the Victorian period. It comes as no surprise, then, that several of the fictional games analysed in this book also operate according to magical forces or aberrant physical laws that are imagined to be part of a certain fictional world.

Games like Quidditch rely on magic for their functioning (Rowling 1997–2007). Given the global fame of the *Harry Potter* novels, Quidditch can arguably be considered the most popular fictional sport of the last two decades, but both literature and film are rife with examples of sports and other playful activities that are unplayable in the actual world because they require magical or, more generally, supernatural powers. From Howard Waldrop's (1983) Zen-Sumo, a form of sumo involving telekinesis and mind-reading played in the short story 'Man-Mountain Gentian', to the wizard's duel performed by Merlin and Madam

Mim in the animated film *The Sword in the Stone* (Reitherman 1963), all the way to the fictional spirit-casting card game Duel Monsters in the *Yu-Gi-Oh!* media franchise (Takahashi 1996–2004), fictional games are often presented as taking place in a fictional world in which magic and/or supernatural forces are considered common, or at least available, to the protagonists of the narrative.

In an essay entitled 'Hazards of Prophecy: The Failure of Imagination', science-fiction author Arthur C. Clarke (1973) offers three adages about the practice of futurology that are commonly known as Clarke's three laws. The third law states that: 'Any sufficiently advanced technology is indistinguishable from magic' (49). This observation is particularly fitting for fictional games that employ futuristic or currently unattainable technologies. According to this perspective, advanced technologies often serve the same purpose as magic in terms of making certain fictional games particularly intriguing, expressive, surprising or – more to the point of the current discussion – functionally impossible to be played in the actual world. Technologically augmented blood sports such as Motorball, described in the manga series *Battle Angel Alita* (Kishiro 1990–5), or the first-person shooter game Slayers in the movie *Gamer* (Neveldine and Taylor 2009), where – via technologically advanced brain implants – players control the actions of actual death-row inmates who fight for survival in specially created arenas, or deadly light-motorcycle competitions in the fictional world of *Tron: Legacy* (Kosinski 2010) and the futuristic version of boxing imagined by Richard Matheson (2011) in the short story 'Steel' generally portray technological features that are explicitly outside the realm of current achievability.

In fictional games, magical and outlandishly advanced technological features signal the significant alterity of a fictional world when compared with the world we natively share as biological creatures. Nevertheless, fictional games can serve as props and aids to help us imagine potential technologically enhanced futures for play. Although we cannot currently access games that require magical powers or futuristic technologies, we cannot exclude the possibility that some of the features that characterize these games could eventually become part of our world. This claim, of course, belongs to the realm of speculation, but it helps us to frame unplayability as a temporary and contextual feature of some fictional games rather than as an objective quality of these games. Similar to the case of games that we consider unethical and immoral to play in the present situation (but that people may not consider such in the future, or might not have done so in the past), fictional games that involve supernatural forces or advanced technologies might be best understood as only unplayable because of limitations inherent in the socio-technical context that we currently share.

1.2.3 The unplayability of nonhuman fictional games

In the previous paragraphs, we concentrated our exploration of the impossibility of playing fictional games on forms of unplayability that emerge from specific features and elements of fictional worlds that are incongruous with the actual world. We did this by considering games that are impossible to play in the actual world because of the current impossibility of some of their technological or supernatural features. Working in parallel to this previous sub-section, we now turn to forms of unplayability that *do not* depend on unattainable technological or magical features but are rather a function of our perceptual and cognitive limitations as human players. In other words, we now move the discussion to fictional games that cannot be played in the actual world not because they involve warp drives or the option of shapeshifting but because they are incompatible with the qualities and possibilities of our subjective experience.

Before venturing into the expressive use of fictional games that are not meant to be played or understood by human beings, it is important to clarify how the radical form of otherness that we are focusing on here differs from the more familiar category of the 'posthuman'. In an extremely reductive characterization, one can understand the figure of the posthuman as epitomizing the aspiration to challenge the centrality of the human being within our civilization. To that end, scholarly efforts identifying as posthumanist strive to extend moral and political reasoning beyond the generalized and static vision of what constitutes a human subject. This perspective digs its roots in cybernetic discourse and in the idea that the conceptual boundaries of what can be defined as 'human' are flexible, contextual, fraught with issues of power and deeply ideological. Accordingly, posthumanism understands humans as beings that are artificial by nature: since the crafting of the first stone tools, we have been hybrid beings that are constituted, defined and guided both by our attributes as biological organisms and by the possibilities and interdictions that characterize our socio-technological situation (see, e.g., Haraway 1991; Hayles 2008; Wolfe 2010; Braidotti 2013). A relevant manifestation of this orientation can also be observed in relation to its framing of who and what can be considered a stakeholder in a certain process (or, for our purposes, a player in a game); a posthuman understanding of play does not determine one's status as a player on the basis of one's biological, artificial or hybrid constitution.[7]

---

[7] Despite their considerable differences, scholarly inquiries concerning the posthuman have methodological commonalities. One that is particularly significant for the scope of this book is the centrality in both approaches (i.e. the posthuman and the nonhuman) of the theme of agency, and particularly of how agency is conceptualized as interconnected and dispersed, beheld by human animals, nonhuman animals and artefacts alike.

In contrast to posthumanist perspectives, when discussing the nonhuman, we refer to forms of being and experiencing that are inaccessible to humans and that cannot be bridged by means of technological or medical enhancements. In another sweeping simplification, we propose to operatively understand the nonhuman as a form of otherness that is more radical than the posthuman and one that typifies ways of being and acting that we, as human beings, cannot intuitively grasp or (fully) experience without undergoing a drastic alteration of our perceptual and cognitive apparatuses.[8] Based on these premises, a nonhuman understanding of play can be characterized by not specifically catering to the needs or capabilities of human players. From such a perspective, play is an activity that a human being can, at best, partake in and intuit in ways that are partial and insufficient.

Focusing on nonhuman fictional games and how they are beyond our possibility of ever fully perceiving or understanding, we briefly discuss two expressive uses that can be recognized as motivating the incorporation of these radically alien forms of play in works of fiction:

1. Their emphasizing the profound otherness of nonhuman minds and the irreconcilability of their thoughts and world views with those of human beings.
2. Their conveying that there is a vaster background to existence and reality beyond the narrow spectrum that we can currently access with our perceptual and cognitive tools.

These two uses are analogous in many ways. However, they also aspire to elicit diverging attitudes. Whereas the first reveals the nonhuman as ineffable and incomprehensibly distant from our ways of being (and playing), thus denying any hope of ever transcending our physical, perceptual and cognitive make-up, the second expressive use gives hope for further developments in our quest for knowledge and self-understanding. Although this second does not typically suggest or promise a radical overcoming of human subjectivity, it also does not embrace the opposite extreme – resignation.

It is especially in the pursuit of this second expressive objective that fictional games can constitute a playful experimental context in which various forms of

---

[8] For a more elaborate discussion of extending ourselves and our intuitions towards nonhuman ways of being, see, 'What is it Like to Be a Bat?' (Nagel 1974), 'What is it Like to Be a (Digital) Bat?' (Gualeni 2011), *Alien Phenomenology, or, What it's Like to be a Thing* (Bogost 2012) and 'Exploring Speculative Methods: Building Artifacts to Investigate Interspecies Intersubjective Subjectivity' (Hook 2019).

(non-radical) transcendence can be anticipated, communicated in agential form and even actively pursued by the players. In the fifth chapter of this book, 'Fictional Games and Transcendence', we explore the uses and meanings of fictional games in the pursuit of a deliberate and agency-focused form of transcendence. Some examples of fictional games that take this hopeful attitude towards transcendence can be identified in Hesse's (1943) Glass Bead Game; the Blood Spire, a fatal challenge in Reynolds' 2002 science-fiction novella, *Diamond Dogs*; and the computer game *eXistenZ* within David Cronenberg's 1999 science-fiction body horror film with the same title.

Fictional games that, instead, exemplify the first and less hopeful kind of expressive goal are, relatively speaking, quite rare. The fiction work of Banks is particularly rich in terms of expressions of the ineffability of the nonhuman through the narrative use of games. Games played by alien or artificial minds are rather common in his science-fiction novels. One of the most memorable of these is the 'Infinite Fun Space', the ironic name that superhuman artificial intelligences (the Minds) utilize to refer to their most absorbing pastime in the Culture series (a sequence of ten loosely related science-fiction books written by Banks from 1987 to 2012). In the 1996 novel *Excession* in particular, the cognitive and computational capabilities of the Minds are described as being vast enough to run entire universe simulations, allowing them to actively explore metamathical (a fictional branch of metamathematics) scenarios within their imaginations (Banks 2012b). In a way that resonates with the pathological relationship with games that humans can have in the actual world, the Minds experimenting with simulated metamathical universes often find them so interesting and alluring that they completely withdraw from physical reality to explore these simulations and speculate on them for millennia at a time. Because of the computational power of their primitive brains and the consequent limits to their imaginations, humanoids and other flesh sentients in the Culture series know about 'Infinite Fun Space' only vicariously, from discussions with the Minds; these beings cannot directly experience those profoundly nonhuman virtual playgrounds.

As mentioned above, this understanding of nonhumanity, characterized by a hopeless alterity, is rarely expressed in works of fiction in the form of games or playful activities. Such expressions more often take the form of incomprehensible extra-terrestrial languages (for example, in China Miéville's 2011 science-fiction novel *Embassytown*) or of glimpses of world views that are markedly beyond human comprehension (such as those that populate Lovecraftian lore, those of the Tralfamadorians in various novels by Kurt Vonnegut and those in the representation of the composite consciousness characterizing the alien species called 'the Pattern Jugglers' in several science-fiction works by Alastair Reynolds).

1.2.4 Fictional games as moral dilemmas

The moral implications of play and the ethical ramifications of playing certain games are a frequent subject in game studies (Mortensen and Linderoth 2015) and in the philosophy of sports, with scholars discussing the relation between sports and ethical values in cases such as bullfighting (Andrade 2021) and mixed martial arts (Dixon 2015). Furthermore, Mary Midgeley's (1974: 237) blunt – but undeniable – observation that 'Russian roulette is a game, and death is an essential part of it' should be sufficient for prompting a reflection on the complex ethical implications of games. Play is not necessarily a joyful and liberating activity, and games cannot be considered objects whose design is impermeable to ethical concerns.

Brian Schrank and Brian Gabor Jr's Bust A Cup, an experimental game conceived as an exploration and a critique of the notion of danger in playful contexts, addresses what the designers consider to be a misunderstanding of 'the power of play, especially with regard to disruption and risk' (Schrank 2016: 53). In the game, which may be described as a grotesque physical competition, two players are engaged in a duel fought with wooden contraptions to which a ceramic cup and a number of heavy objects such as hammers and chains are attached. Players must smash each other's cup to win the match, but this often results in more or less accidentally hitting one's opponent, with potentially dangerous consequences for their physical well-being. In de-sanitizing play and revealing how harm can potentially emerge from it, the game, together with its paraludic material, encourages a meta-reflexive attitude towards our understanding of what play is and what play is allowed to be within our society. Despite being an exercise in critical game design rather than a fictional game, Bust A Cup raises several questions constructed around moral dilemmas and ethical concerns that are often also posed by fictional games. In works of fiction, games and sports that pose considerable physical risks or demand bodily sacrifices (including the sacrifice of one's life itself) also serve the purpose of giving the appreciator of a work of fiction a glimpse into the disturbing and questionable morality of the fictional society in which these sports and games are played. Depending on contextual, cultural and historical factors, play can thus be framed as a life-affirming, joyful activity or as an ethically problematic and potentially harmful endeavour. This tension is described by Mortensen and Jørgensen (2020) as the paradox of transgression in games: the tendency of certain playful activities to provide experiences and generate dynamics that can be considered transgressive of ethical, moral and legal boundaries in specific contexts (see also Majkowski 2015).

The often bombastic transgression of the ethical norms that are currently shared in our actual social contexts is a characteristic feature of a number of fictional games, and it frequently plays a significant narrative role. In this subsection, we focus on fictional games that would very likely be deemed unplayable in the actual world because of their ethically impermissible features. Below, we offer an operational grouping of how these immoral or ethically questionable games are used in fiction. Although the resulting taxonomy does not aspire to be all-encompassing, it offers a tool for differentiating among the various ethical boundaries that these fictional games can be recognized as transgressing and for identifying the role that these games typically play within the fictional worlds of which they are a part.

The first category of ethically transgressive fictional games that we propose is that of extreme blood sports. Blood sports, which are versions of existing sports where the risky and gory traits are intensified, usually function as a moral commentary on the ethical status of certain sports that actually exist. Scott Sigler's (2009) novel *The Rookie*, for example, imagines a future version of American football in which the players – both humans and aliens – are allowed, and even encouraged, to kill or mutilate their opponents. While the novel does not provide a systematic ethical assessment of the actual sport of American football, it leverages its perceived violence and brutality to provide readers with a familiar reference point whose most controversial aspects are then reworked into an ethically untenable fictional game. Fictional blood sports such as *The Rookie*'s futuristic football can thus be framed as narrative devices that allow us to think about the moral boundaries of actual competitive sports in ways that echo the ethical analysis of boxing offered by Simon (2001), among others.

The second category utilizes transgressive fictional games as a synecdoche for a morally deranged society. A fictional game can offer implicit political or social commentary through how its rules and criteria for success are structured and presented. While the relevance and function of this synecdochic strategy will be discussed in depth in later chapters, it is important to emphasize now that fictional games are often used as a proxy to describe a given social and historical context, relying on the appreciator's assumption that a game is an artefact that reflects some of the values and dynamics of the society that produced it. The film *Rollerball* (1975), an adaptation of William Harrison's (1973) short story 'Roller Ball Murder', describes a ruthless and inhumane society by focusing on its only sport, rollerball, an extremely violent amalgam of roller-skating, American football and motorcycling. The character Johnathan E. (James Caan), the film's most skilful and revered rollerball player, serves as an ethical surrogate for the viewer and – tellingly – ends up choosing to risk his life in the rollerball arena rather than becoming a subservient member of a dystopian order. As we argue in Chapter 2, the fictional game of Rollerball is instrumental not only in encapsulating the main moral tenets of an oppressive society, but also in highlighting a contrast between the fictional world's suffocating social architecture and Johnathan E.'s adherence to the ethically superior, and paradoxically life-affirming, norms of rollerball sportsmanship.

Finally, some fictional games are described or represented as morally or ethically untenable to serve as thought experiments for the appreciator of the work of fiction. In other words, some fictional games act as narrativized instances of what philosophers generally refer to as moral dilemmas. These are hypothetical situations in which 'the decision-maker must consider two or more moral values or duties but can only honour one of them; thus, the individual will violate at least one important moral concern, regardless of the decision' (Kvalnes 2015: 12). Films such as *Saw* (Wan 2004) present viewers with exactly this situation. The film is based on a macabre set of riddles and puzzles, devised by an evil mastermind, that the protagonists must overcome to (possibly) save their lives. The game designed by The Jigsaw Killer for the other characters is certainly unethical by any account. Nevertheless, it is based on a series of moral dilemmas that are presented to the protagonists (and, vicariously, to the viewer) to engage with emotionally and intellectually and to make decisions about. In one instance, Gordon (Cary Elwes) is instructed to kill a man he just met so that his wife and child will be spared. In other cases throughout the franchise (composed of ten films at the time of writing), the characters are instructed to perform acts of mutilation to escape certain situations and save their lives, at least temporarily. Fictional games involving deadly challenges (see the Glossary of Terms), unfettered violence or moral dilemmas may also help to elucidate a general characteristic of play, both fictional and non-fictional. As theorized by Trammell (2020) in his work on torture and play, unethical or oppressive games ask us to focus our attention on the relationships of power in play and demand that we identify who is a player and who is, instead, played.

1.3 Ground and figure: The Gestalt of fictional games

As evident in its title, this chapter was designed to be foundational, providing a space for unpacking and further articulating our understanding of fictional games. In this chapter, we outline the theoretical framework for the rest of the book. Parts of the chapter have also introduced notions and conceptual tools that will be used extensively in our argumentation in the rest of the book, which was hopefully evident in our presentation of four different kinds of unplayability in the previous section.

Before discussing and analysing specific expressive uses of fictional games, each of which will be the focus of a dedicated chapter, we would like to introduce one last 'lens' through which we can scrutinize our object of interest. In this section, we propose a simple dichotomy to define the relevance a fictional game has in the fictional world of which it is a part. In very simple terms, and inspired by the work of Marshall McLuhan, we want to introduce a distinction between the following two roles (or functions) within a work of fiction:

1. Fictional games that serve as background elements that contribute to the fictional world building (i.e. as components of the 'ground' over which more relevant acts of communication and events that are more significant to the plot take place).
2. Fictional games that have a more focal, central role in the fiction as narrative devices (i.e. being of primary importance in how the fictional world is presented and/or has a pivotal function in the plot).

Drawing on Gestalt psychology, McLuhan describes these two functions (specifically referring to any acts of communication) as 'ground' and 'figure'. He explains that 'figure' refers to something that is at the forefront of a certain experience and that requires our active attention, whereas 'ground' indicates all the elements used to give context to certain content or a particular situation. Elements of communicative 'ground' are typically experienced in a state of inattention (McLuhan [1964] 1994; Stalder 1998).

As should be clear after a quick review of fictional games such as those mentioned in this book and collected in the appendix, these games largely play ancillary roles within fictional worlds; most fictional games simply contribute to the fiction as background thematic elements. Typically, they make fleeting appearances in works of fiction, are not crucial to the plot development and serve the purpose of making the fictional world in question feel vibrant and interconnected. Examples of this common variety of fictional games include

Figure 1.6 A frame of the 1977 film *Star Wars: Episode IV – A New Hope*, directed by George Lucas, showing an ongoing game of the holographic board game Dejarik. © Lucasfilm Limited 1977. All rights reserved.

Dejarik (also known as Holochess) in the film *Star Wars: Episode IV – A New Hope* (see Figure 1.6; Lucas 1977); the fatal game of Damage[9] in the novel *Consider Phlebas* (Banks [1987] 2012a); the game Stars and Comets, which features in several novels by Andre Norton; and tri-dimensional chess and the already mentioned Fizzbin in the original *Star Trek* television series.

All the examples of background fictional games listed above are variants of classic games such as chess or poker, which are often enhanced with formal twists or futuristic technological components. The reliance of these fictional games on well-established, actually existing games is better understood as a deliberate decision not to encumber the work of fiction with cognitively demanding details than as a lack of originality on the author's part. Additionally, by referencing experiences that are part of the audience's shared lived background, authors are able to use these fictional games to swiftly and intuitively clarify that the context of a certain situation within the fiction is unserious and likely related to leisure. Furthermore, the similarity of these fictional games to classic games

---

[9] Damage is a fatal fictional card game that is structurally similar to poker. In Damage, players use credits as well as 'Lives' to bet on their card hands. Each time a player loses a showdown, one of their Lives is killed. These Lives are actual individuals brought to the table by each player (including the life of the player him/herself). An important feature of Damage is that all players are linked into a futuristic machine that allows each of them to project their emotions of choice onto other players. Through these emotional links, players can induce their opponents to underestimate (or overestimate) their chances of winning, stimulate reckless in-game decisions and even convince them to commit suicide.

may also be understood as an expressive strategy meant to emphasize the fact that the fictional society in which the games are played attributes importance to ideas and aspirations that resonate with those underpinning actual societies.

Bertolt Brecht's notion of 'the apparatus' might help to elucidate this point. On several occasions, Brecht argued that all forms of expression implicitly reproduce the assumptions underlying the socio-technical context (the apparatus) in which they are produced. He specifically used the notion of the apparatus to explain how all artistic production that takes place under capitalism is inescapably tied to capitalism's modes of production (Brecht 1964: 34–5; see Burling in Bould and Miéville 2009: 50). Likewise, we can understand games as expressive forms that reflect (and are reflected upon in) their ideological and socio-technical apparatus (see Friedman 1999, 2005; Bogost 2007; Pedercini 2014; Möring and Leino 2016). This phenomenon also partly explains why it is difficult for us to imagine games (regardless of their fictional or actual constitution) that are not characterized by activities related to an attitude of instrumental rationality such as the accumulation of resources or the optimization of certain outputs of the game system.

When a piece of fiction presents a society playing games that resemble those played in one's own society, appreciators are implicitly encouraged to assume that the fictional society is underpinned by values, aspirations and socioeconomic relationships analogous to those seen in their own societies. This association – and more generally the role of fictional games in providing clues about the broader sociocultural context of fictional worlds – is further elaborated in the next chapter, 'Fictional Games and Ideology', where, going beyond the use of fictional games as a synecdoche, we also investigate their narrative function of normalizing specific values and reinforcing the sociopolitical status quo, often with the use of coercion.

To contextualize the idea that fictional games can function as clues about trends and values characterizing a fictional society or civilization (*ex ungue leonem*, so to speak), we want to offer a relatable example. One can interpret the rules and criteria for success in chess as a testament to our actual society's orientation towards individualism and the competitive, instrumental utilization of resources and rational faculties. Accordingly, one is invited to imagine fictional societies that play fictional variations of chess to also be undergirded by a feudal-capitalist socioeconomic system or, at the very least, as attaching importance to individual success and the strategic use of one's cognitive faculties. Based on these premises, it is reasonable to expect such a fictional society to be hierarchically stratified, be prone to conflict and hold notions such as instrumentality and efficiency in high regard. Any assumption pertaining to games and playful activities as stand-ins for larger cultural tropes, however, also needs to be understood as contextual. On understanding chess as the epitome of rational instrumentality, for example, H. J. R. Murray (1913) noted that, before it came to exemplify the intellectual game, chess meant different things in different contexts and was used allegorically for a variety of rhetorical purposes. Similarly, in his paper, 'How to Play Utopia', Michael Holquist argued that chess is a kind of *langue*, in the sense that its model of battle is so abstract that it can be injected with any kinds of values, themes and meanings without affecting the structure of the game itself (1968: 117; see also the concluding section of Chapter 3 in this volume).[10]

Going back to the broader discussion on fictional games serving as background elements for works of fiction, it is relevant to emphasize that, for philosopher and literary critic Darko Suvin, as well as for those who were influenced by him such as Frederic Jameson and Raymond Williams, the utopian potential of a work of science-fiction relies simultaneously on both the correspondences and the differences between the world presented in the fiction and the actual world (see Suvin 2016: 88; Williams 1980: 198; also see Farca 2018: 120). It is in this sense that the first category of fictional games can be understood as contributing to the 'feedback oscillation' between familiarity and the unfamiliarity that is central to the experience of fiction and to its transformative effects.

Not all fictional games, however, serve the secondary, worldbuilding functions discussed in the above paragraphs. As already anticipated, some are of central significance in the work (or works) of fiction of which they are a part. This focality is often a consequence of the role these fictional games play in their respective fictional societies. In dystopian science-fiction works, for example, fictional games characteristically feature as tools of social control and misdirection. This is especially the case when the games are paired with pervasive communication technologies, as is observed in the configuration of televised 'game shows'. When compared with background fictional games, the games in this second group stand out as generally harder to associate with notions like freedom or playfulness. Novels such as *Solar Lottery* (Dick [1955] 2012) and *The Game-Players of Titan* (Dick [1963] 2001), and films such as *The Running Man*

---

[10] In the case of contemporary fiction, the reliance of modern chess on instrumental rationality has come to epitomize the dominant values of capitalist societies. This is far from a neutral representation of a societal orientation, however, as one can imagine different societal structures or values being typified by different kinds of games that may privilege, for example, postcolonial or indigenous points of view (see LaPensée 2020).

(Glaser 1987), *The Maze Runner* (Dashner 2009) and *The Hunger Games* (Collins 2008) can be considered exemplary of this second category.

A particular attention dedicated to fictional games within a work of fiction typically reflects a more central role of these games within its narrative. Their relevance, however, may not be uniquely dependent on their impact on the fictional society in which fictional games are (fictionally) played. Broadly speaking, we recognize two main narrative roles – or functions – that can grant a fictional game prominence within a work of fiction:

1. Fictional games as social instruments (either to maintain or to subvert the status quo).
2. Fictional games as contexts for the indirect characterization[11] of fictional characters.

Games that can be categorized under the first of these functions are typically designed to be persuasive and pervasive, and they often work on the basis of the coercion of players. Such games may serve the purpose of spreading and reaffirming hegemonic values and aspirations (see Chapter 2). The flipside of this dystopian role of fictional games in this group resides in their potential to function as utopian devices. In Chapter 3 of this book, 'Fictional Games as Utopian devices', we discuss this use of fictional games, examining their crucial and active role in transforming the sociopolitical relations within their respective fictional worlds. Examples of fictional games holding a more focal, relevant position within the narrative of a work of fiction can be found in Philip K. Dick's (1959) short story, 'War Game', in Ken MacLeod's (2011) novel *The Restoration Game* and in Cory Doctorow's *In Real Life* (2014). These works feature fictional games that have utopian qualities and direct transformative effects in the fictional worlds of which they are a part. We will return to some of these examples in the third chapter.

Fictional games in the second category (i.e. games serving as contexts for the indirect characterization of the main characters of a work of fiction) tend to have less political impact on the fictional world in which they are played. This is because their main narrative function is not to contribute directly to moving the plot

---

[11] This type of characterization is based on synecdoche, and it has also been referred to as 'implicit characterization'. Indirect or implicit characterization is not pursued directly (i.e. through a narrator's description of the character); rather, it is achieved through elements that are contiguous to the characters, such as their actions within their fictional world, their choice of words or their clothing style (Herman and Vervaeck 2019: 74). In this passage, we argue that a character's choice of which games to play and their in-game behaviour (e.g. their sportsmanship, slyness or competitive nature) can be a narrative device that complements what the audience already knows about the personality and the temperament of fictional characters.

forward (e.g. contributing to progress towards its resolution or to its transition from a dystopic stage to a utopian one) but rather to cast a new light on the present state of the fictional world. More specifically, such games add granularity and depth to how the fiction appreciator imagines and understands the main characters of a narrative and might be an occasion for their further development.

In *The Defense*, for example, Nabokov (1930) uses chess as a context in which salient traits of his chess-player protagonist are brought to the fore of the narrative. Similarly, the respective personalities of James Bond (Sean Connery) and Maximillian Largo (Klaus Maria Brandauer) are illustrated in the context of their playing a fictional game called *Domination* in the 1983 spy film *Never Say Never Again* (Kershner 1983). *Domination* is a tridimensional video game of reflexes, aiming accuracy and territorial strategy invented by Largo himself (see Figure 1.7). One particularly interesting aspect of the game is that the losing player receives a series of electric shocks of increasing intensity, with their strength depending on the amount of money wagered on the game. The scene in which the two characters challenge one another in a game of *Domination* has no bearing on the overall plot and merely serves the function of emphasizing their differences in attitude and personality. During gameplay, Largo proves sly and unsportsmanlike, which is revealed, for example, in his informing Bond of certain functionalities of the game only after he has already suffered their negative consequences. Bond, instead, faces the challenge with bravery and a quick intellect, also demonstrating an exceptionally high tolerance for physical pain.

To the list of games used in the pursuit of indirect characterization we might add a wide variety of examples including the fantasy deckbuilding card game

Figure 1.7 The fictional game *Domination* is played by James Bond (Sean Connery) and Maximillian Largo (Klaus Maria Brandauer) in this frame of the 1983 film *Never Say Never Again*, directed by Irvin Kershner © Taliafilm 1983. All rights reserved.

Card Wars played in the animated series *Adventure Time* (S4E14 – 'Card Wars'; Leichliter 2012), the board game Peg Game in Reynolds' 2021 novel *Inhibitor Space*, the fictional VR shooter video game in the television series *House M.D.* (also called *Bird Game* in S6E2 – 'Epic Fail'; Yaitanes 2009), the previously mentioned fatal game of Damage (see footnote 9) and the fictional action-strategy video game *Strategema* played in the television series *Star Trek: The Next Generation* (S2E21 – 'Peak Performance'; Scheerer 1989) by Lieutenant Commander Data (Brent Spiner) and a renowned alien strategist.

All the examples listed above show how fictional games can function as narrative devices that establish a new context for social interaction among fictional characters. In this playful context, fiction appreciators can glean new information about the characters in their roles as players and discover some of their previously inaccessible traits, such as how strictly they adhere to arbitrary rules, how aggressive they are in the pursuit of their objectives, how they take the feelings of other characters into consideration during gameplay or how they psychologically respond to moments of good or bad luck, victory or defeat. The context of fictional play is generally different from the main fictional world described in a work of fiction, but is also not entirely separated or separable from it. The boundary between these two realms is not always neatly defined and is often porous, allowing information and events that are shared during (fictional) play to transition into more narratively relevant aspects of the fiction.

This brief overview of the dichotomy between fictional games contributing to the 'ground' of a fictional situation and fictional games of central relevance to the narrative concludes the introduction to our object of inquiry in this book. The perspectives, theoretical frames and lexical specifications presented in this chapter are the foundation upon which the rest of *Fictional Games* is built. In the chapters that follow, the understanding of fictional games presented in this foundational chapter will be further expanded and discussed in terms of a variety of expressive possibilities, their cultural significance and – often – their potential uses as tools for philosophical inquiry.

References

Aarseth, E. J. (2007), 'Doors and Perception: Fiction vs. Simulation in Games', *Intermédialités: Histoire et Théorie des Arts, des Lettres et des Techniques / Intermediality: History and Theory of the Arts, Literature and Technologies*, 9: 35–44.

Aeschylus (2013), *Aeschylus I: The Persians, The Seven against Thebes, The Suppliant Maidens, Prometheus Bound*, trans. David Grene and Richmond Lattimore, Chicago, IL: University of Chicago Press.

Anderson, W. (2009), [Film] *Fantastic Mr. Fox*, 20th Century Fox Animation, 20th Century Fox.

Andrade, G. E. (2021), 'A Response to Cultural Arguments in the Renewed Disputes over the Ethics of Bullfighting', *Sport, Ethics and Philosophy*, 15 (5).

Aretino, P. ([1543] 1992), *Le Carte Parlanti*, Palermo: Sellerio.

Aso, H. (2010–16), [Manga series] *Alice in Borderland*, Tokyo: Shōnen Sunday S and Weekly Shōnen Sunday.

Atlus (2011), [Digital game] *Catherine*, directed by Katsura Hashino, published by Atlus.

Bachman, R. (1982), *The Running Man*, New York: Signet Books.

Banks, I. M. ([1987] 2012a), *Consider Phlebas*, New York: Orbit.

Banks, I. M. ([1996] 2012b), *Excession*, New York: Orbit.

Banks, I. M. ([1998] 2012c), *Inversions*, New York: Orbit.

Bateman, C. (2011), *Imaginary Games*, Winchester: Zer0 Books.

Berman, N. D. (1981), *Playful Fictions and Fictional Players: Game, Sport and Survival in Contemporary American Fiction*, Port Washington, NY: Kennikat Press.

BioWare (2012), [Digital game] *Mass Effect 3*, directed by Casey Hudson and published by Electronic Arts.

BioWare (2014), [Digital game] *Dragon Age: Inquisition*, directed by Mike Laidlaw and published by Electronic Arts.

Bizarre Creations (2003), [Digital game] *Project Gotham Racing 2*, directed by Craig Cook and Philipp Teschne, published by Microsoft Game Studios.

Björk, S. and J. Juul (2012), 'Zero-Player Games Or: What We Talk about When We Talk about Players', *Proceedings of the 2012 Philosophy of Computer Games Conference*, Madrid, 29–31 January.

Blanchot, M. ([1949] 1995), *The Work of Fire*, Stanford, CA: Stanford University Press.

Boccaccio, G. ([1353] 2003), *The Decameron*, New York: Penguin Books.

Bogost, I. (2007), *Persuasive Games: The Expressive Power of Videogames*, Cambridge, MA: The MIT Press.

Bogost, I. (2012), *Alien Phenomenology, or, What it's Like to be a Thing*, Minneapolis, MI: University of Minnesota Press.

Bould, M. and C. Miéville (2009), *Red Planets: Marxism and Science Fiction*, London: Pluto Press.

Braidotti, R. (2013), *The Posthuman*, Cambridge: Polity Press.

Brecht, B. (1964), *Brecht on Theatre*, trans. John Willett, London: Methuen.

Bright, K. S. (2002, 25 April), [TV series episode] 'The One with the Baby Shower', season 8, episode 20, in K. S. Bright, M. Kauffman, S. Silveri, S. Goldberg-Meehan, A. Reich and T. Cohen (executive producers), *Friends*, Bright/Kauffman/Crane Production, Warner Bros. Television.

CD Projekt RED (2007), [Digital game] *The Witcher*, directed by J. Brzeziński and published by Atari and CD Projekt.

CD Projekt RED (2015), [Digital game] *The Witcher 3: Wild Hunt*, directed by K. Tomaszkiewicz, M. Kanik and S. Stępień, and published by CD Projekt.

Clarke, A. C. (1973), *Profiles of the Future: An Inquiry into the Limits of the Possible*, New York: Harper & Row.

Clery, E. J. (1995), *The Rise of Supernatural Fiction, 1762–1800*, Cambridge: Cambridge University Press.

Collins, S. (2008), *The Hunger Games*, New York: Scholastic.

Cronenberg, D. (1999), [Film] *eXistenZ*, Alliance Atlantis, Scriptwriter: David Cronenberg.

Crosson, S. (2013), *Sport and Film*, London: Routledge.

Currie, G. (1990), *The Nature of Fiction*, Cambridge: Cambridge University Press.

Dashner, J. (2009), *The Maze Runner*, New York: Delacorte Press.

Davis, J. (1983), 'Three-Cornered Pitney', *Mad Magazine*, 241: 27–31. Scriptwriter: Tom Koch.

Detweiler, R. (1976), 'Games and Play in Modern American Fiction', *Contemporary Literature*, 17 (1): 44–62.

Dick, P. K. ([1955] 2012), *Solar Lottery*, New York: Houghton Mifflin Harcourt.

Dick, P. K. ([1959] 2002), 'War Game', in *The Minority Report and Other Classic Stories*, New York: Kensington Publishing, loc. 3913–4283.

Dick, P. K. ([1963] 2001), *The Game-Players of Titan*, New York: Harper Voyager.

Dixon, N. (2015), 'A Moral Critique of Mixed Martial Arts', *Public Affairs Quarterly*, 29 (4): 365–84.

Doctorow, C. (2014), *In Real Life*, New York: First Second.

Edwards, B. (2013), *Theories of Play and Postmodern Fiction*, London: Routledge.

Eidos Montreal (2016), [Digital game] *Deus Ex: Mankind Divided*, directed by Jean-François Dugas and published by Square Enix.

Farca, G. (2018), *Playing Dystopia: Nightmarish Worlds in Video Games and the Player's Aesthetic Response*, Bielefeld: Transcript Verlag.

Fassone, R. and W. Huber (2017), 'Game Studies in the Cinquecento. Prolegomena to a Historical Analysis of the Rhetorics of Play', *Ludica*, 21–2: 152–5.

Friedman, T. (1999), 'Civilization and Its Discontents: Simulation, Subjectivity, and Space', *On a Silver Platter: CD-ROMs and the Promises of a New Technology*: 132–50.

Friedman, T. (2005), *Electric Dreams: Computers in American Culture*, New York: New York University Press.

Glaser, P. M. (1987), [Film] *The Running Man*, TriStar Pictures, Scriptwriter: Steven E. de Souza.

Gualeni, S. (2011), 'What is it Like to Be a (Digital) Bat?' Proceedings of the 2011 Games and Philosophy Conference, held at the Panteion University in Athens, 6–9 April, 2011.

Gualeni, S. (2015), *Virtual Worlds as Philosophical Tools: How to Philosophize with a Digital Hammer*, Basingstoke: Palgrave Macmillan.

Gualeni, S. (2016), 'Self-Reflexive Videogames: Observations and Corollaries on Virtual Worlds as Philosophical Artifacts', *G A M E – The Italian Journal of Game Studies*, 5 (1): 11–20.
Gualeni, S. (2021), 'Fictional Games and Utopia: The Case of Azad', *Science Fiction Film & Television*, 14 (2): 187–207.
Gualeni, S. and D. Vella (2020), *Virtual Existentialism: Meaning and Subjectivity in Virtual Worlds*, Basingstoke: Palgrave Pivot.
Haraway, D. (1991), 'A Cyborg Manifesto: Science, Technology, and Socialist-Feminism in the Late Twentieth Century', in D. Haraway, *Simians, Cyborgs and Women: The Reinvention of Nature*, New York: Routledge, 149–81.
Harrison, W. (1973), 'Roller Ball Murder', *Esquire*, 1 September: 92–5, 20–11.
Hayles, N. K. (2008), *How We Became Posthuman: Virtual Bodies in Cybernetics, Literature, and Informatics*, Chicago, IL: University of Chicago Press.
Herman, L. and B. Vervaeck (2019), *Handbook of Narrative Analysis*, 2nd edn, Lincoln, NE: University of Nebraska Press.
Hesse, H. ([1943] 2000), *The Glass Bead Game*, trans. T. Winston and R. Winston, London: Vintage.
Holquist, M. (1968), 'How to Play Utopia', *Yale French Studies*, 41: 10–23.
Hook, A. (2019), 'Exploring Speculative Methods: Building Artifacts to Investigate Interspecies Intersubjective Subjectivity', *Alphaville: Journal of Film and Screen Media*, 17: 146–64.
Huizinga, J. ([1939] 1964), *Homo Ludens: A Study of the Play-Element in Culture*, Boston, MA: Beacon Press.
Hutchinson, P. (1983), *Games Authors Play*, London: Methuen.
Irrational Games & Looking Glass Studios (1992), [Digital game] *System Shock 2*, directed by Jonathan Chey and published by Electronic Arts.
Jewison, N. (1975), [Film] *Rollerball*, United Artists.
Johnston, J. (1995), [Film] *Jumanji*, Sony Pictures Releasing.
Kawabata, Y. ([1954] 2006), *The Master of Go*, New York: Penguin Random House.
Kershner, I. (1983), [Film] *Never Say Never Again*, Warner Bros.
King, S. (1982), *The Running Man*, New York: Signet Books.
Kishiro, Y. (1990–5), [Manga series] *Battle Angel Alita*, Tokyo: Business Jump.
Knowles, E., ed. (2006), 'Mornington Crescent', in *A Dictionary of Phrase and Fable*, Oxford: Oxford University Press.
Kosinski, J. (2010), [Film] *Tron: Legacy*, Walt Disney.
Kvalnes, Ø. (2015), *Moral Reasoning at Work: Rethinking Ethics in Organizations*, London: Palgrave Macmillan.
LaPensée, E. (2020), 'When Rivers were Trails: Cultural Expression in an Indigenous Video Game', *International Journal of Heritage Studies*, 26: 1–15.
Leichliter, L. (2012, 16 July), [TV series episode] 'Card Wars', season 4, episode 14, in C. Lelash, J. Pelphrey, B. A. Miller, R. Sorcher and P. Ward (executive producers), *Adventure Time*, Warner Bros. Television Distribution.

London, M. (2019), *Quidditch*, Minneapolis, MI: ABDO.
Lucas, G. (1977), [Film] *Star Wars: Episode IV – A New Hope*, Lucasfilm.
MacCallum-Stewart, E. (2018), 'The Gaming of Players: Jamming Azad', in N. Hubble, E. MacCallum-Stewart and J. Norman (eds), *The Science Fiction of Iain M. Banks*, London: Gylphi, 121–42.
MacLeod, K. (2011), *The Restoration Game*, Amherst, NY: Pyr.
Majkowski, T. Z. (2015), 'Grotesque Realism and Carnality: Bakhtinian Inspirations in Video Game Studies', in T. Bártek, J. Miškov and J. Švelch (eds), Proceedings of the Central and European Game Studies Conference. Brno: Masaryk University Press, 27–43.
Martin, G. R. R. (1996–present), [Novel series] *A Song of Ice and Fire*, New York: Bantham Books.
Matheson, R. (2011), *Steel and Other Stories*, New York: Tor Books.
McLuhan, M. ([1964] 1994), *Understanding Media: The Extensions of Man*, Cambridge, MA: The MIT Press.
Miéville, C. (2011), *Embassytown*, London: Pan Books.
Messenger, C. K. (1981), *Sport and the Spirit of Play in American Fiction: Hawthorne to Faulkner*, New York: Columbia University Press.
Midgeley, M. (1974), 'The Game Game', *Philosophy*, 49 (189): 231–53.
Möring, S., and O. Leino (2016), 'Beyond Games as Political Education – Neo-liberalism in the Contemporary Computer Game Form', *Journal of Gaming & Virtual Worlds*, 8 (2): 145–61.
Mortensen, T. E. and K. Jørgensen (2020), *The Paradox of Transgression in Games*, New York: Routledge.
Mortensen, T. E. and J. Linderoth (2015), 'Dark Play: The Aesthetics of Controversial Playfulness', in T. E. Mortensen and J. Linderoth (eds), *The Dark Side of Game Play: Controversial Issues in Playful Environments*, New York: Routledge, 3–12.
Murray, H. J. R. (1913), *A History of Chess*, London: Oxford University Press.
Nabokov, V. V. ([1930] 1990), *The Defense*, New York: Vintage.
Nagel, T. (1974), 'What is it Like to Be a Bat?', *Philosophical Review*, 83: 435–50.
Natale, S. (2016), *Supernatural Entertainments: Victorian Spiritualism and the Rise of Modern Media Culture*, University Park, PA: Pennsylvania State University Press.
Natali, V. (1997), [Film] *Cube*, Trimark Pictures.
Neveldine, M. and B. Taylor (2009), [Film] *Gamer*, Lionsgate.
Nguyen, C. T. (2020), *Games: Agency as Art*, Oxford: Oxford University Press.
Nickelodeon Animation Studio (2005–8), [Animated TV series] *Avatar: The Last Airbender*, created by M. D. Dimartino and B. Konietzko.
Nintendo (1986–present), [Digital game series] *The Legend of Zelda*, published by Nintendo.
Oku, H. (2000–13), [Manga series] *Gantz*, Tokyo: Shueisha.
Oriard, M. (1982), *Dreaming of Heroes: American Sports Fiction, 1868–1980*, Chicago, IL: Nelson Hall.
Oriard, M. (1991), *Sporting with the Gods: The Rhetoric of Play and Game in American Literature*, 45, Cambridge: Cambridge University Press.

Pajitnov, A. (1984), [Digital game] *Tetris*, published by Atari Games.
Patterson, S. (2015), *Games and Gaming in Medieval Literature*, Basingstoke: Palgrave Macmillan.
Payne, J. (2017), *The Book of the Thousand Nights and One Night*, vols 1–9, New York: Start Publishing.
Pedercini, P. (2014), 'Videogames and the Spirit of Capitalism', blog post, 14 February. Available online: https://www.molleindustria.org/blog/videogames-and-the-spirit-of-capitalism.
Pratchett, T. (1983–2015), [Novel series] *Discworld*, New York: Penguin Random House.
Reitherman, W. (1963), [Film] *The Sword in the Stone*, Walt Disney.
Reynolds, A. ([2002] 2004), *Diamond Dogs, Turquoise Days*, New York: ACE Books.
Reynolds, A. (2021), *Inhibitor Space*, London: Gollancz.
Robinson, J. A. (2013, 21 November), [TV series episode] 'The Cones of Dunshire', season 6, episode 9, in G. Daniels, M. Schur, H. Klein, D. Miner, M. Sackett, D. Holland and D. Goor (executive producers), *Parks and Recreation*, NBCUniversal Television Distribution.
Robson, J. and A. Meskin (2012), 'Video Games as Self-Involving Interactive Fictions', *Journal of Aesthetics and Art Criticism*, 74 (2): 165–77.
Rowling, J. K. (1997–2007), [Novel series] *Harry Potter*, London: Bloomsbury.
Saarikoski, P., A. Lindfors, J. Suominen and M. Reunanen (2022), 'The *Illuminatus* Space Game: From an April Fools' Joke to Digital Cultural Heritage', in K. Bonello Rutter Giappone, T. Z. Majkowski and J. Švelch, *Video Games and Comedy*, Basingstoke: Palgrave Macmillan, 13–51.
Scheerer, R (1989, 10 July), [TV series episode] 'Peak Performance', season 2, episode 21, in G. Roddenberry and R. Berman (executive producers), *Star Trek: The Next Generation*, Paramount Domestic Television, Paramount Domestic Television.
Schrank, B. (2016), 'Bust A Cup: Reclaiming Risk in Play', *GAME: The Italian Journal of Game Studies*, 5 (1): 47–58.
Schulzke, M. (2014), 'The Critical Power of Virtual Dystopias', *Games and Culture*, 9 (5): 315–34.
Schwimmer, D. (1999, 4 November), [TV series episode] 'The One on the Last Night', season 6, episode 6, in K. S. Bright, M. Kauffman, D. Crane, A. Chase and G. Malins (executive producers), *Friends*, Warner Bros. Television Distribution.
Sigler, S. (2009), *The Rookie*, San Francisco, CA: Dark Overlord Media.
Simon, R. L. (2001), 'Violence in Sports', in W. J. Morgan, K. V. Meier and A. J. Schneider (eds), *Ethics in Sport*, Champaign, IL: Human Kinetics Publishers: 345–54.
Slocombe, W. (2013), 'Games Playing Roles in the Fiction of Iain (M.) Banks', in K. Cox and M. Colebrook (eds), *The Transgressive Iain Banks: Essays on a Writer Beyond Borders*, 136–49, Jefferson, NC: McFarland Press.
Square (1999), [Digital game] *Final Fantasy VIII*, directed by Yoshinori Kitase, published by Square.

Stalder, F. (1998), 'From Figure / Ground to Actor-Networks: McLuhan and Latour', paper presented at the Many Dimensions: The Extensions of Marshall McLuhan Conference, Toronto, 23–25 October.

Suits, B. (1985), 'The Detective Story: A Case Study of Games in Literature', *Canadian Review of Comparative Literature / Revue Canadienne de Littérature Comparée*: 200–19.

Sulway, N. A. (2013), *Rupetta*, Leyburn: Tartarus Press.

Suvin, D. 2016, *Metamorphoses of Science Fiction*, ed. Gerry Canavan, Bern: Peter Lang.

Takahashi, K. (1996–2004), [Manga series] *Yu-Gi-Oh!*, Tokyo: *Weekly Shōnen Jump*.

Tasso, T. (1858), *I Dialoghi. Volume Secondo*, Firenze: Felice Le Monnier.

Tevis, W. (1983), *The Queen's Gambit*, New York: Penguin Random House.

Trammell, A. (2020), 'Torture, Play, and the Black Experience', *GAME: The Italian Journal of Game Studies*, 9: 33–49.

Van de Mosselaer, N. (2020), 'The Paradox of Interactive Fiction', PhD diss., University of Antwerp.

Van Dine, S. S. (1928), 'Twenty Rules for Writing Detective Stories', *American Magazine*, 26–30 September.

Waldrop, H. (1983), 'Man-Mountain Gentian', *Omni*, 60, September: 63–6, 152–6.

Walton, K. L. (1990), *Mimesis as Make-Believe: On the Foundations of the Representational Arts*, Cambridge, MA: Harvard University Press.

Wan, J. (2004), [Film] *Saw*, Twisted Pictures, Lions Gate Films.

Watterson, B. ([1990] 2005), [Comic book series] *Calvin & Hobbes*, Kansas City, MS: Andrews McMeel Publishers.

Whisp, K. (2017), *Quidditch through the Ages*, London: Bloomsbury.

Wildman, N. and R. Woodward (2018), 'Interactivity, Fictionality, and Incompleteness', in G. Tavinor and J. Robson (eds), *The Aesthetics of Video Games*, London: Routledge, 112–27.

Williams, R. (1980), 'Utopia and Science Fiction', *Problems in Materialism and Culture*, London: New Left Books.

Wolfe, C. (2010), *What is Posthumanism?*, Minneapolis, MN: University of Minnesota Press.

Yaitanes, G. (2009, 28 September), [TV series episode] 'Epic Fail', season 6, episode 2, in D. Shore (showrunner), *House M. D.*, Universal Television, Fox.

ZA/UM (2019), [Digital game] *Disco Elysium*, directed by Robert Kurvitz and published by ZA/UM.

2

Fictional Games and Ideology

In her highly influential book on interactive narratives, *Hamlet on the Holodeck*, Murray (1997: 142) describes games as 'symbolic dramas'. According to Murray, games synthesize and compress aspects of human experience into finite, regulated objects. Murray substantiates this claim through the analysis of popular games such as Monopoly (1935) ('an interpretation of capitalism, an enactment of the allures and disappointments of a zero-sum economy' [143]) and *Tetris* (1984). In discussing *Tetris*, Murray aims to demonstrate that even the most abstract games can be understood as representing more complex sociocultural phenomena. Murray argues that *Tetris* 'is a perfect enactment of the overtasked lives of Americans in the 1990s – of the constant bombardment of tasks that demand our attention and that we must somehow fit into our overcrowded schedules and clear off our desks in order to make room for the next onslaught' (144).

Within the game studies community, Murray's analysis of *Tetris* sparked a debate concerning the risk of overinterpreting non-representational games, and arbitrarily mapping their rules onto complex real-life processes and dynamics. Eskelinen (2001), in an article that reads as a direct response to Murray's claims, writes that 'instead of studying the actual game Murray tries to interpret its supposed content, or better yet, project her favourite content on it.'[1]

Although Murray's argument may be described as fallacious – not least because it describes a Russian game from the 1980s as emblematic of 1990s

America – its form warrants some discussion. Murray's concept of 'symbolic drama' refers to the fact that games tend to represent (or symbolize) various interlocking processes encountered in the actual world in a rarefied and often iconic fashion. Along the same line of thought, Murray also claims that games may facilitate systems thinking by allowing us to interact with highly abstracted versions of the complex, interacting systems that intervene in contemporary existence. Seen in this light, Murray's projection of 1990s American hyper-productivism onto a game developed in the Soviet Union is perhaps closer to a deliberate appropriation of a popular pastime as a means of making sense of her own predicament than to an act of fumbled hermeneutics. Murray's contested reading of *Tetris* helps us to advance a twofold claim that informs our reading of fictional games as narrative devices that communicate or reinforce certain ideological arrangements:

1. First, because games are specific types of systems produced under precise socio-technical conditions, they always replicate, at least in part, the systems that maintain and inform these conditions.[2] The claim that the rules, affordances and functional prescriptions of games more or less consciously represent or are inspired by real-world mechanics underpins a number of Marxist critiques of video games (e.g. Dyer-Witheford and de Peuter 2009; Kirkpatrick, Mazierska and Kristensen 2016).
2. Second, because we all possess some form of systems literacy because of our daily interaction with systems of varying complexity, we cannot help but project our knowledge of systems onto the games we play. A similar process of mapping real-world knowledge onto fictional artefacts can be observed in how fictional games are imagined by their authors.[3]

---

[1] Murray's book and the resulting polemic, along with other foundational texts in game studies, are often considered the beginning of the ludology vs narratology debate, an academic controversy that is frequently considered a foundational moment in the field of game studies. Although the relevance of this debate may have been overestimated – Frasca (2003) calls it 'a debate that never took place' – it is still widely considered a significant milestone in the history and development of the field.

[2] In Chapter 1, we discussed this process using the notion of 'apparatus' (Brecht 1964), but it should be noted that a similar approach characterizes numerous strands of work in media studies and in the philosophy of science and technology. Notable examples can be found, for instance, in the writings of Latour (1999) and Ihde (1990).

[3] A few remarkable exceptions notwithstanding, fictional games are almost invariably derivative of existing games. As explained in Chapter 1, this feature serves a double purpose: it is a way for authors to construct relatively complex fictional games without having to develop an entire formal system of rules and affordances from the ground up, and it offers an anchoring point for the reader, whose imagination, ideally, is aided by their pre-existing knowledge of or hands-on experience with the referenced game.

The fact that games can – and often do – represent stylized versions of actual processes and social practices is at the core of several studies addressing the political and social relevance of play. Flanagan and Nissenbaum (2014: 3), for example, claim that games can be understood as vessels for values that are found in a certain society and that 'games provide a compelling arena where humans play out their beliefs and ideas'. This does not mean that all games are consciously designed with the intention of promoting a certain set of values, but rather that games, 'like other technologies and like social practices, systems, and institutions – have values embedded in them' (Flanagan and Nissenbaum 2014: 8). The values 'embedded' in games are by no means univocal or universally shared, and they can be a source of disagreement and conflict. An example of incompatible values being inscribed in a game can be identified in the context of football, where fans' reactions against what they see as 'modern football' stem precisely from such a dispute around values. According to Numerato (2015), Italian football fans' uncompromising attitude towards the ills of contemporary football derives from a narrative in which the increasing commodification of the sport has emptied it of its traditionally established values of sportsmanship and loyalty.

The observation that the values inscribed in games can also be misapprehended and even deliberately subverted has an important consequence in terms of how we should approach the question of how meaning is attributed to games and fictional games. Even fictional games that have a clear and apparently inescapable ideological structure at the service of established power can be played in unexpected ways (i.e. when they are accidentally misunderstood or deliberately misplayed) and leveraged as countercultural tools. Given the relevance of this topic and the fact that it is central to the following chapter, here, we elaborate on the notion that games can incorporate shared or contested sets of values. Whereas Flanagan and Nissenbaum (2014) focus mostly on how specific characteristics and functions of games reveal certain beliefs and aspirations – claiming, for example, that symmetrical games, in which all players have access to the same means and tools, imply the desirability of fairness as a value[4] – there are other ways in which games can communicate ideas and social orientations. For instance, some games adopt an ethos of explicitness in their aesthetic and narrative components, making their political or ideological positioning unequivocal. The communicative strategy of games such as *Getting Over It with Bennett Foddy* (Foddy 2017) relies on this kind of redundancy. In this game, the

---

[4] The lineage of this mode of analysis can be traced back to the notion of 'procedural rhetoric', articulated by Bogost (2007) in *Persuasive Games: The Expressive Power of Videogames*.

player controls a chimeric figure – half man/half cauldron – who needs to climb a series of obstacles such as mountains, buildings and trees using only a two-handed hammer as a climbing tool. The extreme difficulty of this task is compounded by the deliberate inefficacy of the control scheme: players can only use a mouse to manoeuvre the hammer in a way that the player is likely to find counterintuitive and irritating. A voice-over track recorded by the designer of the game, Bennett Foddy, offers a semi-serious tirade on the nature of frustration, which further clarifies how the player should interpret the game experience. The precepts of sadistic difficulty and redemption through frustration found in *Getting Over It with Bennett Foddy* are made explicit in Foddy's commentary, which contributes to binding the explicitly intended values, aesthetic context and functioning of the game together into a consistent act of communication. In certain other cases, functional elements do not directly contribute to expressing a game's stated values. This is seen, for example, in the playable visual novel *Little Antifa Novel* (Vanetti, Colangelo and Gastaldo 2018), which tells the story of an antifascist demonstration in the Italian city of Pavia. In *Little Antifa Novel*, a political stance is expressed in the game not via its functionalities as an interactive system (the game is a rather minimal 'choose-your-path' interactive novel) but exclusively through the narrative components of the game, which explicitly promote antifascist views.

While the strategies described so far are based on a conscious and deliberate inscription of values within a game – be it via its mechanical, narrative or stylistic elements – one may claim that games, as social objects that are used and discussed within a certain community, are inevitably imbued with that community's shared values. In other words, one could take the radical stance that all games produced within a neoliberalist society somewhat reflect neoliberalism, regardless of their mechanical or narrative peculiarities. Using the words of Woodcock (2019: loc. 1748) on contemporary video games, 'We should therefore think of videogames as a technology that comes out of the conditions of existing society. Videogames, then, are played within those conditions, both shaping what kind of games we can play as well as how we play them'.

This kind of critique is often directed at a variety of expressive forms – including games and video games – by Marxist scholars, who usually refer to the shared sets of values discussed above as 'ideology'. According to Marxist philosopher Louis Althusser ([1970] 2020), the term 'ideology' refers to the sum of values that circulate within a certain society and that affect, among other aspects, social relations, economic transactions and political or legal arrangements. Ideological adherence is actively enforced by institutions such as the state or the juridical system, which 'ensure *subjection to the ruling ideology*' (ibid.: 7; italics in the original text), and reinforced by what Althusser describes as 'the ideological State apparatuses' (ibid.: 16). These apparatuses, which include institutions such as schools, media and cultural industries, do not act repressively (i.e. they do not *enforce* subjection to the ideology), but rather persuasively. In Althusser's theory, these apparatuses serve the purpose of reproducing the dominant ideology in at least two senses:

1. They reproduce it by representing it – that is, by offering content that underscores the necessity of the dominant ideology for the functioning of society. In contemporary Western societies, we may think of these apparatuses as serving the function of perpetuating what Fisher (2009) describes as 'capitalist realism': the belief that it is impossible to build a functioning society that is not underpinned by a capitalistic economic system.
2. The ideological state apparatuses reproduce the ruling ideology by ensuring its continuation. By being produced under the economic regimes of the ruling ideology – capitalism, in Althusser's case – these apparatuses ensure the perpetuation of such regimes. In other words, ideological state apparatuses benefit capitalism by producing goods and services that are exchanged within a capitalist economy. In the case of games, one may speculate that certain forms and styles of game design and game play gained popularity and were consequently replicated in multiple versions in a variety of social contexts on the basis of their being better suited than others to be produced, sold and marketed within that particular ideological context.

Games, at least in their commodified versions, can thus be said to participate in the functioning and perpetuation of the ideological state apparatus. Scholars such as Dyer-Witheford and de Peuter (2009) have claimed that video games can be appropriately understood as ideological tools adopted by what they describe, in the Marxist tradition of Hardt and Negri (2000), as 'the Empire' (i.e. globalized late-stage capitalism). Through a series of examples, Dyer-Witheford and de Peuter show how production strategies, work conditions, industrial cultures and issues of representation all contribute to making video games effective tools for the reproduction of the current ideological status quo. In a later commentary on their own work, these scholars conclude that 'digital gaming may prove to be a cultural practice so deeply mortgaged to an economy of technophilic, high-energy overconsumption, and to ideologically toxic memes of domination, that it must be jettisoned completely from any postcapitalist future (though we hope not!)' (Dyer-Witheford and de Peuter 2021: 377).

Despite the relevance and influence of these kinds of framing, several authors have questioned the applicability of such political analysis models to games. Although books such as Witheford and de Peuter's (2009) *Games of Empire* are arguably useful for presenting game scholars with refined tools for discussing the relation between games and ideology, the general applicability of an Althusserian theory of games as ideological state apparatuses can be challenged because of the theory's abstractness. The first issue one encounters when attempting such a reading is that of isomorphism: are games really able to accurately map the ideological status quo that produced them? Although deliberate attempts at doing so have proven relatively efficient in some cases – such as in *America's Army* (2002), a game produced by the US Army to portray its values and beliefs – the relation between the dominant ideology and other games is significantly less straightforward. Giddings (2018: 770) claims that a pretence of isomorphism derives from what he terms 'left pessimist assumptions', a prejudice that frames games and game makers as incapable of political self-determination and, at the same time, necessarily subservient to the status quo. Furthermore, assuming an isomorphic relation between ideology and games implies denying (or at least severely underplaying) the transformative potential of play. As demonstrated by several authors (see, e.g., Kafai 1995; Kafai, Franke, Ching and Shih 1998; Gualeni 2014; Gualeni and Gómez Maureira 2018), interacting with games as either a player or a designer has the potential to call into question and even transform one's world view by presenting an individual with various alternative possibilities to the current state of things, thus encouraging speculative and critical thinking. These kinds of cognitive effects are particularly evident when players find themselves interacting with a game that simulates a certain social or political situation being presented as unfavourable or uninhabitable. For example, Ruffino (2021) analyses how players of *AdVenture Capitalist* (2014), a game that simulates the incremental, frictionless accumulation of capital, find themselves frustrated with the endlessness of the game – so much so, in fact, that they end up devising their own solutions to break the infinite cycle of capital accrual in which they find themselves trapped. As we discuss in Chapter 3, such player practices, usually grouped under terms such as 'unplaying' (Flanagan 2009: 33) or 'counterplay' (Dyer-Witheford and de Peuter 2009; Meades 2015), aim at disclosing anti-hegemonic scenarios for the players by deliberately countering the game's intended use.

The correspondence between social processes and in-game dynamics described above can also be clearly recognized in fictional games. Often, the main role of a fictional game within a fictional world is to present a distilled and readily accessible version of some of the features and orientations of a fictional society. Whether they operate as focal points in a narrative or are utilized to provide background details in a process of worldbuilding, fictional games are frequently employed to convey to the appreciator the ideological paradigms that circulate in a certain fictional culture. The film *Rollerball* (Jewison 1975) is an exemplary case of this isomorphism. Adapted from a short story published two years prior (Harrison 1973), the film tells the story of a future society in which corporate capitalism has become a de facto substitute for the state. The world is governed by a series of corporations, one of which – Energy Corporation – has accrued enough power to significantly influence political, social and economic decisions on a global scale. The most popular sport in the fictional world of the film is Rollerball, a brutal combination of roller skating, American football and motorcycle racing (see Figure 2.1). In Rollerball, two teams compete on a banked skating track with the objective of scoring points by throwing a steel sphere into a specific hole. Some of the players are on skates, while others ride motorcycles that have been modified for the game. Rollerball is clearly a futuristic version of a gladiatorial contest, where major injuries and even deaths are common and where the audience seems to enjoy the brutal consequences of the sport. In the film, the most respected player in the game, Jonathan E. (James Caan), is asked by the president of Energy Corporation to retire, but the player decides to keep

Figure 2.1 A game of Rollerball: a ruthless sport combining skating, motorcycling and American football, played in the 1975 film with the same name, directed by Norman Jewison. © United Artists 1975. All rights reserved.

playing. To force Jonathan to comply, the corporation progressively introduces new rules into the game, making it increasingly more dangerous and, eventually, almost certainly lethal.

Scholars and critics have read the film as the Promethean struggle of a single man standing against imposed morals and behaviours and, ultimately, his own finitude (Marmysz 2009). Shifting the focus from the character of Jonathan E. to the game of Rollerball, it is possible to claim that the game and the world in which the film is set are bound by a symbiotic relationship. The world of *Rollerball* is described to the viewer through its imposing, ultra-functionalist architecture and the oppressive hierarchical relations among people of different social standings. Although we are not aware of the minute details of the political systems that regulate the world, the film communicates via aesthetic and narrative clues that the imperative of economic growth has been imposed on the population through strict social discipline. The game of Rollerball is one of these clues, as it appears to reproduce, in ludic form, some of the dominant values of the dystopian society in which it is played. The game's rules favour athletic prowess – or even brute force – over strategic thinking and cooperation, thus mimicking the functioning of the futuristic version of cutthroat capitalism portrayed in the film. Furthermore, the culture of the sport, which is revealed to the viewer through recurrent scenes set in locker rooms or at practices, is built around a hypermasculine competitiveness[5] that can be interpreted as a parallel for the ruthlessness of the global corporations fighting for domination.

Although the game of Rollerball can certainly be described as the focal point in the eponymous film, which goes to great lengths to depict the game's functioning and detailing its culture, a similar isomorphic function can also be observed in games that are only mentioned in passing and used as detail in worldbuilding efforts in other works of fiction. The novel *Zoo City* (Beukes 2010) tells the story of an alternative version of South Africa, where magic is common and people who have a criminal record or are otherwise guilt-ridden are assigned a magical animal that must stay with them at all times. The novel employs this narrative device to reflect on current societal issues such as the social marginalization of former convicts and other forms of class- or race-based

---

[5] It is particularly informative to observe that, in the film, women are invariably portrayed as performing ancillary tasks (serving as secretaries and receptionists, for example), with men occupying the top positions. The fictional world of *Rollerball* is built on competition, which is explicitly presented as an inherently masculine trait (e.g. in the competition for sexual partners). From this standpoint, it is telling that Jonathan E. hops from one female partner to the next, further emphasizing the fictional society's one-sidedness, as well as the systematic objectification of women as trophies.

stigmatization. A passage of the book describes the house of S'bu, a young musician, as follows: 'He waves a hand vaguely in the direction of the ashtray. There's a couple of video game boxes lying next to it, starring flesh-eating undead and aliens. One, *Grand Theft Auto VI: Zootopia*, features a badass in a hoodie, packing a shotgun with a snarling Panther by his side' (ibid.: loc. 1122).

This lone reference in the book to the fictional game *Grand Theft Auto VI: Zootopia* is a significant example of the use of fictional games to signify the wider cultural or social processes of a fictional world. The game's cover art, portraying 'a badass in a hoodie, packing a shotgun with a snarling Panther by his side' (ibid.), serves as a general reinforcement of the book's narrative premise – that criminals are assigned an animal familiar – but also performs a subtler task. In choosing to reference an existing series of games (*Grand Theft Auto*), Beukes implicitly informs the reader that some of the social and cultural traits of the real world can also be found in the novel's fictional world. The fetishization of crime insinuated in the passage cited above ('a badass in a hoodie') also resonates with some of the recurrent critiques of the *Grand Theft Auto* series. Furthermore, choosing to construct *Grand Theft Auto VI: Zootopia* as a fictional entry in the non-fictional canon of the *Grand Theft Auto* games may indicate an even more refined understanding of the function of fictional games. In game research and critique, the *Grand Theft Auto* series is generally understood as somewhat politically charged and is often associated with reactionary politics. Dyer-Witheford and de Peuter (2009: 157), for example, refer to *Grand Theft Auto: Vice City* (Rockstar North 2002) as a game that 'is informed by, and reinscribes, dominant relations of power'. Games in this series are thus generally perceived as replicating wider social tendencies (in the same book, the authors conduct a similar analysis of *Grand Theft Auto: San Andreas*, Rockstar Games 2004), and a fictional game such as *Grand Theft Auto VI: Zootopia*, rather than being a simple prop, may serve the same ideological function within the fictional world of *Zoo City*.

In the following sections, we introduce a variety of fictional games that can be understood as acting as proxies for certain ideological arrangements for the appreciator of the fiction. In section 2.1, we focus on the explicit use of fictional games as playable allegories of a moral kind, analysing a few games that are evidently meant as interactive ways to communicate and promote moral principles and desirable behaviours in a certain culture. Section 2.2 will analyse the game of Quintet, which is played in Altman's 1979 film of the same name. In Altman's film, participating in games of Quintet is the only social practice that is still pursued by the citizens of a dying society. Surviving as the phantasmal echo of the culture that produced it, Quintet still evokes the expired values and aspirations of its creators.

Notably, all the games analysed in this chapter are played by somewhat subservient players, who, with the exception of *Quintet*'s protagonist, do not question or transgress the games' rules and ideological orientations. The players' compliance in the selected works of fiction emphasizes these games' function as instruments of persuasion and also characterizes the players as passive recipients of ideological precepts.

2.1 The representation of virtues and vices in fictional games

Folk games are traditional games that are passed along informally and whose ruleset are subject to substantial variations that depend on the historical and cultural contexts in which those games are played. Folk games can be embraced as a particularly obvious example of how shared values, social orientations and aspects of a collective identity are condensed and manifest themselves in play. Like legends, folk songs and fairy tales, folk games typically serve the social function of signalling beliefs and behaviours that are considered proper and desirable. They are often, in other words, playable moral allegories. In this section we argue that the educational, moral and symbolic uses of folk games are similarly at work in fictional folk games. We begin with a brief historical analysis of the folk game snakes and ladders and then introduce two fictional games with similar characteristics and comparable functions in their respective fictional worlds.

Snakes and ladders is a board game for two or more players that is widely regarded as a folk classic. The first mentions of this game date back to second-century BCE documents from India, and historians believe the game may be a variation of the ancient game of Dasapada (whose name indicates a draughtboard with ten squares per side). More recent variations of the game that are still played in India and other South Asian countries are variously known by names such as Morsha Patamu (meaning the study of spiritual liberation), Gyan Chaupar (the dice game of knowledge), Parambada Sopanam (steps towards the highest place) and Golok Dham (journey to heaven) (Mukherjee 2020: 128). In its modern version, snakes and ladders is usually played on a square, gridded board with numbered tiles (usually ranging from 1 to 100, but grid sizes vary). Players of snakes and ladders take turns moving their pawns on the board by rolling a six-sided die and traversing the number of tiles corresponding to the number of pips on the die. The game is thus entirely reliant on chance, and there is no in-game interaction among the players; they are effectively playing a single-player game on a shared board. The winner of snakes and ladders is the first player to reach the end tile. A player's journey towards victory is aided by special tiles marked by drawings of ladders (that allow the players climb to a higher-numbered tile) and hindered by special tiles with images of snakes (which send the player back to a lower-numbered tile).

At the level of metaphorical representation, the historical forebears of snakes and ladders (introduced in the United Kingdom in the 1890s during the British Rule of India) are understood as allegories of a life virtuously lived – that is, walking the path towards knowledge and spiritual liberation. In contrast to snakes and ladders, however, the original goal of these games was not winning. In fact, Mukherjee (ibid.: 142) clarifies that understanding the game as a race towards the finish line is a relatively recent, Western development. Scholars of Sanskrit and Indian history are also careful to point out that, just like the karmic cycle of death and rebirth, a new game is always ready to begin and that the idea of rushing towards the end tile therefore did not make sense in the context of ancient Indian culture (ibid.: 136; Johari 2007). The objectives of these traditional games were, instead, pedagogical: to teach the different pathways and detect the various obstacles to reaching nirvana through the inevitable repetitions, ebbs and flows of karmic cycles.

One aspect that most modern versions of snakes and ladders share with their cultural predecessors is that each advantageous special tile (i.e. those depicting a ladder heading in the direction of the end tile) is named after a virtue, whereas each negative special tile (i.e. those showing a snake with its tail pointing in the direction of the beginning tile) corresponds to a vice. The explicit representation of virtues and vices and their association with positive or negative in-game events further reinforce the idea that all versions of the game are also (if not mainly) meant as a playable moral lesson.[6]

---

[6] Snakes and ladders' metaphorical and moral set-up also attracted the interest of Indian-born novelist and essayist Salman Rushdie, whose 1981 novel, *Midnight's Children*, describes the game as follows:

> All games have morals; and the game of Snakes and Ladders captures, as no other activity can hope to do, the eternal truth that for every ladder you hope to climb, a snake is waiting just around the corner, and for every snake a ladder will compensate. But it's more than that; no mere carrot-and-stick affair; because implicit in the game is unchanging twoness of things, the duality of up against down, good against evil; the solid rationality of ladders balances the occult sinuosities of the serpent; in the opposition of staircase and cobra we can see, metaphorically, all conceivable oppositions, Alpha against Omega, father against mother'.
> [1981] 2006: 160

In the case of snakes and ladders, the virtues and vices marking the special tiles have been components of the game since its early Victorian import (Mukherjee 2020: 129). The specific types of virtues or vices represented by the tiles, however, are irrelevant to the mechanical functioning of the game (or of its historical forebears). These special tiles iconically present values and character traits that are considered desirable or undesirable within a certain social group, but they do not organically participate in the fictional world of the game, merely functioning as abstract ideological tokens. The disconnection between the fictional aspects of the game and the kinds of virtues and vices represented on its special tiles has likely favoured various transformations and adaptations when snakes and ladders has been played in new historical and cultural contexts. What we are arguing here is, in other words, that virtues and vices are ideological icons serving as cues for the desired conduct that the game presents explicitly and reinforces behaviourally.

Similar to the abstract and tokenistic in-game representations of virtues and vices, the very snakes and ladders for which the game is named are elements that have often been changed to match the tastes and ideological aspirations of certain social groups. In the United States, for example, the game is usually sold as Chutes and Ladders, with images of less threatening and more familiar playground slides taking the place of the snakes. Aligning with local preferences, in Canada, the chutes are themselves often replaced by toboggan runs (see Vv. Aa. 2007). As another example of this ludic syncretism, the Christian version of the game (known as Bible Ups and Downs) indicates the positive and negative effects of the special tiles not by means of snakes and ladders, but by referencing biblical metaphors such as the punishing collapse of the Tower of Babel and an alluring stairway to heaven (ibid.).

As we have shown, in addition to having the ability to imply certain social values with the intent to promote and normalize them, games can also explicitly reference such values and ideals and mount overt rhetorical claims about them. The explicit representation (and labelling) of virtues and vices in games thus reflects the moral canons and aspirations of the society in which the games are played. In their obvious clarity, games that reference virtues and vices are typically used in teaching children through play. This remains the case regardless of the specific pedagogical aims in question, which may range from Indian cosmology to the Protestant work ethic illustrated in The Game of Life. The same overt representation of the moral orientation of a social group can be seen in fictional games. This is, of course, particularly cogent when fictional games pursue background thematic functions (or worldbuilding functions, as discussed in section 1.3), where the explicit invocation of virtues and vices is evidently meant to make the ideological context immediately clear for the fiction appreciator.

An example of this use of fictional games can be observed in Wicked Grace, a fictional card game reminiscent of poker that is played in the video game *Dragon Age: Inquisition* (BioWare 2014; see Figure 2.2). The game emphasizes deception and the matching of various hands of cards to achieve a numerically winning hand. The four suits in the Wicked Grace deck are Angels, Knights, Serpents and Songs, each containing cards that are explicitly either virtuous or vicious in the context of the game's fiction (with the Angels and Knights suits containing mostly virtuous cards, the Snakes suit comprising only vicious cards and the Songs suit featuring a combination of both). The game presents, for example, cards such as the Knight of Sacrifice, the Knight of Wisdom, the Angel of Fortitude, the Angel of Truth, the Serpent of Avarice, the Serpent of Deceit, the Song of Mercy and the Song of Temerity.

This obvious characterization of the moral (and, more broadly, ideological) orientations of a social group is not only seen in the representation and naming of in-game elements in fictional games; these values and traits are also communicated in how fictional games are titled, subtitled and illustrated, especially in the case of fictional games that are part of the thematic background of a work of fiction, briefly and superficially encountered as part of the experience

Figure 2.2 A screenshot of the 2014 video game *Dragon Age: Inquisition* (BioWare) in which some of the characters are playing a game of Wicked Grace. © BioWare 2014. All rights reserved.

of a fictional world. Suzerainty, the previously mentioned fictional board game that serves a thematic function in the dystopian fictional world of *Disco Elysium* (ZA/UM 2019), comes to mind here. In addition to referencing a particular political relationship (one that corresponds to the socioeconomic context and the absence of political autonomy that characterize the fictional settings of *Disco Elysium*), Suzerainty is described as having a star-shaped note on its box that informs the player that the newly updated version of the game now includes a completely new genocide option.

More instances of this superficial theme-reinforcing strategy can be seen in the previously mentioned science-fiction novel *Inversions* (Banks [1998] 2012). Apart from Monarch's Dispute (see section 1.2.1), which is the only fictional game in the novel that is more substantially involved in the development of the book's plot, *Inversion* simply alludes to other fictional games by their names. These names – Liar's Dice, Secret Keep, Subterfuge, Blaggard's Boast, Whiff of Truth, Travesty and The Gentleman Misinformant – arguably provide the audience with unambiguous clues about the hierarchically stratified and treacherous society in which the novel is set (Banks [1998] 2012: 110).

An exemplary work of fiction in which virtues and vices are explicitly featured in a fictional game is More's 1516 satirical novel, *Utopia*. Taking the point of view of fictional character Raphael Hythloday, a philosopher and world-traveller, in the second book of the novel, the author describes the leisurely after-supper activities of the Utopians. Hythloday reports that, aside from music and conversation, the Utopians also seem to enjoy a few games:

> They know nothing about gambling with dice or other such foolish and ruinous games, but they do play two games not unlike chess. One is a battle of numbers, in which one number captures another. The other is a game in which the vices fight a battle against the virtues. The game is ingeniously set up to show how the vices oppose one another, yet combine against the virtues; then, what vice oppose what virtues, how they try to assault them with open force or undermine them indirectly through trickery, how the defences of the virtues can break the strength of the vices or skillfully elude their plots; and finally, by what means one side or the other games the victory.
>
> More [1516] 2003: 50

Apart from this brief mention of the two games played by the Utopians, nothing else is written about games in the entirety of the novel. Interestingly, the description of the chess-like game of virtues and vices played by the Utopians does not provide any detail concerning what the two opposing sides of the game are like, how many virtues and vices are there or whether some virtues or vices have special in-game meanings or behaviours. Even more important for our point is the observation that the reader is not informed about *which* specific virtues and vices are represented in the game. In this, the use of this fictional game in *Utopia* differs from the role of Wicked Grace in *Dragon Age: Inquisition* (BioWare 2014). Although both fictional games are clearly fictionally incomplete, the incompleteness of the game played by the Utopians extends to its most obvious ideological markers. In other words, whereas Wicked Grace openly contributes to the characterization of the moral orientation of its fictional setting, the description of the game of virtues and vices merely presents a framework, a general structure of what a utopian game might look like. The fictional games in *Utopia* cannot, however, be said to be value-neutral: their chess-like qualities implicitly invite the reader to imagine them being played in a society that holds rationality and instrumental efficiency in high regard. The fact that the game reflects social preferences for competence and planning is also supported by the previously cited passage clarifying that chance-based forms of play do not exist in Utopia (More [1516] 2003: 107).

2.2 Play without labour in *Quintet*

As we have shown, several aspects of games – fictional or otherwise – can be understood as metaphors and/or proxies for certain societal or political conditions. They can be recognized as encapsulating and reproducing values that are dominant in certain contexts or offer playable alternatives to prevailing ideological arrangements (which will be the thematic focus of the next chapter). Games can also have a different – and more nuanced – relationship with the ideological context that produced them, allowing the fiction appreciator to recognize the extension and features of their own ideological or political standings. This is the case, for example, of games designed with critical, satirical or meta-reflexive intentions (see Flanagan and Nissenbaum 2014; Grace 2014; Gualeni 2016; Caselli et al. 2020). Several scholars contend that games and play serve this function in modern industrialized societies, highlighting the prevalence of a culture of productivity and the pervasiveness of labour by presenting themselves as a frivolous and unproductive activity, an alternative or an antidote to instrumental rationality.

In their book on the notion of fun and its political and existential ramifications, Sharp and Thomas (2019) claim that, by being unproductive by definition, games stand in stark contrast to the dominant values of productivity and efficiency. According to these scholars, 'if you buy into the Protestant-capitalist-rationalist complex, games and art are unproductive, trivial, useless, even harmful' (ibid.: 22). They further expand this claim by describing games as antithetical to the contemporary Western work ethos and reaffirming the relevance and formative potential of having (and crafting) experiences that fall outside the realm of productivity and teleology. Although a discussion of Sharp and Thomas' plea for fun as a political experience is beyond the scope of the current text, it may be useful to emphasize that the duality between games and work – or, more radically, between unproductive play and instrumental activities – is a preoccupation shared by most theorists of play. Suits' (1978: 41) famous definition of play as 'the voluntary attempt to overcome unnecessary obstacles' efficiently synthesizes this tension: play is voluntary, and its goals and means are unnecessary, which identifies playful activities as different from – and even antithetical to – work. Before Suits, pioneers of the study of games and play such as Roger Caillois and Johan Huizinga also alluded to this dualism. Caillois ([1958] 2001: 10) takes an explicitly economic stance on the unproductivity of play, writing that it '[creates] neither goods, nor wealth, nor new elements of any kind; and, except for the exchange of property among the players, [ends] in a situation identical to that prevailing at the beginning of the game'.

Caillois thus maps the notion of unproductivity onto the ideas of not producing goods or value, decoupling players from the generation and amassment of capital. Similarly, Huizinga (1955) adopts a 'distinctly modern ethos' (Fassone 2017) in describing the relationship between play and productive life. To Huizinga, playing implies carving out a niche within ordinary life – a distinct enclave that temporarily separates players from the preoccupations of productivity and work.[7] These theories, which more or less neatly distinguish between the seriousness of regular life and the frivolity of play, are categorized by Möring and Leino as 'romantic play theories' (2016: 145). According to these scholars, romantic play theories essentialize play as an exceptional activity that is autonomous and separated from one's ordinary roles and duties in everyday existence.

This analysis of the relationship between play and productivity helps us elucidate a claim made at the beginning of this section. Whereas Marxist theorists of play maintain that games entertain a quasi-isomorphic relation with the material and ideological conditions of their production, a different strand of

---

[7] For a modern interpretation of Huizinga's theory of play, we recommend to read Ehrman (1968).

game studies posits play as antithetical to labour. As noted by Sharp and Thomas (2019), this antithesis is often stigmatized, and play is frequently described as an idle waste of productive time and energy. However, play can also be the context in which the individual can access world views and possibilities for existential projectuality and self-realization that stand outside the prescriptive sphere of one's work (see Gualeni and Vella 2020). In a chapter devoted to games in his 1964 *Understanding Media*, McLuhan explicitly advances the idea that the unproductivity of games functions as an antidote to the 'grind' of productive life: 'Both games and technologies are counter-irritants or ways of adjusting to the stress of the specialized actions that occur in any social group. As extensions of the popular response to the workday stress, games become faithful models of a culture. They incorporate both the action and the reaction of whole populations in a single dynamic image' ([1964] 2001: 235).

In the same chapter, McLuhan also clarifies that games 'permit a respite from customary patterns' and that they are 'a kind of talking to itself on the part of society as a whole' (243). McLuhan's notion of play as a balm that soothes and heals the wounds of the stressful, hyper-regulated lives of subjects living under capitalism can also be adopted as a theoretical compass to use in navigating Altman's 1979 film, *Quintet*. The film allows viewers to reflect on the tension between work and play, presenting a society in which the latter seems to have taken the place of the former. The film, set in an unspecified, possibly future era, follows Essex (Paul Newman) as he returns home after years spent hunting seals in a distant region. Upon arriving, Essex finds the city he originally came from encrusted in a thick layer of ice, the result of Earth's progressive descent into an irreversible, eternal winter. Most of the city's infrastructure, including its advanced computerized directory of citizens, is in ruins, and the few inhabitants left live bleak and purposeless lives. The only social institution still active in the city is the game of Quintet, a board game for six players that is widely played in the city both in competitive tournaments and in recreational contexts. Quintet appears to be the only activity capable of shaking the citizens out of their radical apathy.

The game of Quintet, as described by Altman, 'is a game of survival' (Thompson 2011: 279). It is meant for exactly six players, who play on a pentagonal board and use personalized tokens to keep track of their moves. Five players are granted equal status and follow an identical set of rules, while the sixth player – called the sixth man – acts as a referee and a counsellor for the other players. In the game, players receive a kill list, which dictates their roles and the relations among them. Player A could, for example, be tasked with killing player B, while player B could be tasked with killing player C, and so on (see Figure 2.3). By moving their tokens around the board, the players must try to capture their prey by finding them alone in one of the board's five quadrants. At that point, a player can attempt the assassination of their intended victim by means of a die roll. When all but one of the players have been eliminated, the sixth man enters the game as an active player for a final showdown against the survivor. The sixth man acts both as one of the players and as a judge; the main strategy for the sixth man is to try to assist the weakest player in surviving until the final round, thus gaining a personal advantage in the final confrontation. The rules and materials of the game are depicted as imbued with the values and beliefs of the culture that produced them; in fact, the gameboard's division into five[8] sectors resembles the city's topography.

During his time in the city, Essex meets a cast of stereotypical characters – an innkeeper, a preacher and a referee for high-stakes games of Quintet – and realizes that the simulated assassinations that take place in games of Quintet are later carried out in real life, making the game into an instrument of a nihilistic

Figure 2.3 A frame of Robert Altman's 1979 film *Quintet*. The characters of the film play a game of Quintet on its five-sided wooden board using custom-made tokens. © 20th Century Fox 1979. All rights reserved.

---

[8] This number seems to hold significant value in the fictional world of the film. As mentioned, the game of Quintet has a five-sided board and is designed to be played by five players (plus the sixth man). During a sermon, the preacher, Saint Christopher, claims that life is divided into five stages, thus creating a clear numerological recurrence. The relevance of the number five extends outside of the film's diegesis, as Ness (2011: 39) notes in his analysis of the film's score: 'composer Tom Pierson reinforces the game that provides the film's title through the use of five-note clusters'.

and arbitrary form of justice. Appalled by the decadence of his own society, Essex decides to leave the city, rather than participating in its moral and social breakdown. After killing the city's preacher, Saint Cristopher (Vittorio Gassman), driven by his disdain for the decadence of the place that he once called home, Essex leaves the game of Quintet behind and disappears into an icy desert.

Quintet is one of Altman's less successful films. Shot in 1978, mostly in Montreal's semi-abandoned Expo 67 World's Fair building, and released the following year, the film was a commercial and critical disaster. Prominent critics, who had generally expressed enthusiastic views on Altman's previous films, did not pull any punches when writing about *Quintet*. Pauline Kael (1979: 101), a highly revered American film critic, characterized the film's pretentious dialogue, exhaustingly slow pace and angular, purposely alienating cinematography as 'a Monty Python show played at the wrong speed'. An interesting feature of most of *Quintet*'s film reviews is their general disinterest in the game of Quintet, which, despite being focal in the film's narrative, is treated by critics as little more than an eccentric prop.[9] It is also telling that different critics offer wildly varying descriptions of the functioning and characteristics of the game of Quintet. Delson (1979: 25), for example, dubs it a 'futuristic death [game]', clearly borrowing from the promotional language of 1970s science-fiction films such as *Rollerball* (Jewison 1975). Kagan (1982: 166), in contrast, highlights the game's anti-social traits, claiming that Quintet is 'an elaborate game of ritual murder'. Others, such as Kolker ([1980] 2000), describe the game as a form of gambling, which seems to be accurate both because the game features elements of chance and because the players exchange money during gameplay, although this is unclear and not explicitly addressed in the film.

In an interview for the short-lived magazine *Fantastic Films*, Altman claims that the game of Quintet as a pivotal narrative device remained central throughout the film's troubled production history. When asked about this point, Altman clarified that '[t]he game I'd started back in the original thing [the original treatment for the film] [...]. There was a game in this culture; it'd have been like backgammon or dominoes or one of those board games people played all the time' (Delson 1979: 27). During later stages of production, Altman decided to turn this general idea of a game into an actual, potentially playable game. He produced a rulebook for Quintet and went as far as contacting Parker Brothers

---

[9] Among the famed reviewers who wrote scathingly about the film and barely mentioned the game, *The Washington Post*'s Gary Arnold (1979) is possibly the fiercest. Arnold describes Altman's work as deserving 'a niche [...] in the '70s memory album of pseudo-profound fiascoes'.

about the possibility of releasing it commercially.[10] Quintet's status as a fictional game is thus liminal: it is a game that was developed specifically as a part of a fictional world, but the creator of the game itself devised a playable version of the game and even decided to print an abridged version of the rules of the game on some of the film's promotional posters. Here, our analysis is devoted to the version of Quintet found in the film, which is significantly underspecified in terms of its structure and formal components.

Despite Altman's efforts to develop a playable game, the film never fully informs the viewer of the rules of Quintet. Instead, the film adopts an allusive strategy, portraying the game as already being intimately known by all the characters and thus needing minimal explanation. Quintet is so pervasive in the film's frozen city that the characters often adopt game terminology to refer to common occurrences in their daily lives. As an example, Grigor (Fernando Rey), Quintet's main judge and referee, refers to himself as 'the sixth man' to Essex, implying both that he can play that role within the game and that he holds a similar position in the city's social hierarchy.

Quintet can be understood as having a twofold function in the film. First, Altman leverages games' oppositional relation to productivity as a tool to portray a decaying society. In the film, the role of Quintet in Essex's city seems to have undergone a profound change. The game went from originally serving as an antidote to the drabness of labour and everyday existence to being the only activity worth pursuing in a dying civilization. With the decay of the city's infrastructure and the dissolution of social relations – as noted, even the city's index of citizens no longer functions – the existence of the population is devoid of all purpose. In this sense, Quintet occupies a vestigial position in the city's social and political architecture. The supposedly generative friction between play and labour has ceased to exist following the extinction of all productivity; thus, playing Quintet has itself become an activity without of any meaning or purpose. According to Soares (2007: 75), 'in this dystopian world, the forces of production are frozen (literally, in this case), immobilized'. The association between the apocalypse that the city is clearly marching towards and the failure of all productive life – with play remaining as a habitual, semi-automatic activity – is compounded

---

[10] The productive history of the game of Quintet, along with its rules, have been published in a collection of interviews, where Altman also claims that Parker Brothers produced at least one copy of the game but never released it because of the film's poor performance at the box office (Thompson 2011). In this book, Altman also claims that groups of players in Minnesota produced a homemade version of the game for their own use. The board-game database BoardGameGeek reports the existence of a Portuguese-language version of the game released in Brazil as Quinteto (Origem 1979).

by Altman's choice to shoot the film in an abandoned pavilion from Montreal's 1967 World's Fair. For a viewer with knowledge about the Expo, which had the humanist, progressive theme of 'Man and His World',[11] Altman's apocalyptic narrative is likely to be perceived as ironic and even paradoxical. Furthermore, some of the dialogue in the film elucidates the situation of amputated dualism in which play has lost its 'natural' counterpart. In a very telling exchange, Vivia (Brigitte Fossey), Essex's partner, asks Essex's brother whether the city's inhabitants have hobbies. The man fails to understand the question, as, in the absence of productive purposes, the word 'hobby' seems to have lost all meaning.

The game of Quintet also plays a second function in the narrative. Earlier in this chapter, we discussed how games may be interpreted as miniaturized versions of a set of values or an ideology, but this map–territory relation seems to be reversed in the case of Quintet. Because the game is all that is left of the city's customs and social norms, its relevance is now totalizing. In other words, in a world where there is no ideology or set of values for a game to simulate, the simulation itself is all that is left. From this perspective, Grigor's tirade about the game is revealing: 'the only intelligent expression left is the game of Quintet: all things of value feed the game'. That is to say that the game has devoured its surroundings and taken the place of the very values it was supposed to represent with their corresponding ludic simulacrum.[12] The fact that capturing another player's pieces in the game leads to that player's death in the real world should not be seen as an indication of a morally abject game, but rather as a sign that the game has taken the place of all parts of the society.

2.3 Conclusions

In this chapter, we discussed how fictional games can encapsulate the ideological tenets, moral orientations and traits of the collective identity of a social group.

---

[11] For an analysis of the film's and the film set's relations with the history of Expo 67 and, more generally, with the city of Montreal, see Lyons (2009).

[12] Notably, Jean Baudrillard appears to have been one of the few admirers of the film. In his book *Cool Memories*, Baudrillard describes *Quintet* as 'that marvellous [sic] film made among the remains of the Universal Exposition in Montreal, where the human beings were like stalactites and played chess in the clear frosty light' (1990: 193–4). One may speculate that Baudrillard's interest in the film derives from the game of Quintet functioning as a fitting example of what the philosopher calls a simulacrum (1983): the imitation of a real-world process or system that, over time, grows to serve as its actual counterpart. Indeed, the game is a simulacrum of the social order before the onset of the eternal winter – a model whose origin, in the movie, is no longer present or attainable. This understanding of the game as the ghostly reappearance of lost meanings and functions is paralleled by the background of the Expo buildings, still standing and performing their function as movie locations long after the end of their role as symbols of human progress.

Whether they operate as thematic components of a general worldbuilding agenda or serve as focal elements of the narrative, fictional games function as interactive, condensed versions of the general values circulating in the fictional society in question. This is partially because of the regulated and systemic ways in which we understand games as social objects in general, as well as the fact that – as a consequence of the first observation – they can be mapped onto the rules and processes at work in a social context.

Section 2.1 focused on the explicit representation of a society's values, orientations and needs within games and fictional games. The examples we drew upon here (Wicked Grace in the video game *Dragon Age: Inquisition* and the game of virtues and vices in More's *Utopia*) reveal that the ideological functions of fictional games often mirror the social functions of actual folk games, which typically incorporate and signal shared values and aspects of social identity. Fictional folk games not only echo the social functions of folk games; they also often appropriate some of folk games' ludic and aesthetic aspects. In its vague and incomplete definition, the game of virtues and vices is presented as similar to the game of chess, and Wicked Grace is obviously inspired by poker. These associations serve as mental shortcuts, providing an immediately intuitive way to identify certain basic social orientations.

Section 2.2 offered a reading of Altman's 1979 film, *Quintet*, with a focus on its fictional game of the same name. The game of Quintet, arguably the protagonist of Altman's apocalyptic drama, acts as the last remaining vestige of a waning society, having evolved from simulating social relations in the fictional city portrayed in the film to being the only valuable activity after all values and ideologies are suspended by a climate catastrophe. In Altman's film, the game of Quintet thus serves a double function: the game is a manifestation of the values of the inhabitants of the city, but it also does more than communicating a certain ideological arrangement to the viewer. In Altman's film, the game becomes an active agent not only in describing but also in actually advancing the city's process of social and structural decay. On the basis of these observations, we framed Altman's experiment in (fictional) game design as both performing the abstraction or simplification of certain values and achieving a specific – and, in this instance, rather destructive – social function.

It is telling that the game of Quintet was actually inspired by a folk game, backgammon, which Altman has described as one of his main interests at the time of the shooting of the film (Delson 1979). Like backgammon, Quintet is heavily reliant on the use of dice to determine points. This reliance on chance correlates with the fascination with the indeterminate and the unknown expressed by the film's characters. In one of his sermons, Saint Christopher advances the belief in the unknown as life's engine, proclaiming 'only when you consider the unknown you have a hope, a chance to solve the dilemma'. While the characters living in the city and destined to die there can only experience the thrill of the unknown through play, Essex, the film's protagonist, eventually breaks free of this vicious, ludically enforced circle by leaving the city and venturing north in search of another, less ad hoc kind of unknown.

When fictional games are used as a synecdoche for the ideological tenets of a fictional society, they very often resemble existing games. Most of the cases we encountered, including those we used as focal examples in this chapter, are in fact variants or derivative versions of actual folk games. The game of Quintet is played on a board with tokens and dice, as is the case with most board games, the games found in More's *Utopia* are inspired by chess, and Wicked Grace obviously references poker. Above, we have alluded to the advantages of designing fictional games that resemble existing games: reduced design work for the author and pre-existing familiarity for the appreciator. Nevertheless, such a reliance on existing games may limit our ability to imagine other ludic forms or to spot the potential for playfulness in activities that are not immediately recognizable as games (e.g. formal practices that do not rely on competition among actors or the optimization of fictional resources). One of the most culturally valuable uses of fictional games in works of fiction is disclosing new ways of imagining play or encouraging appreciators to think beyond their prejudices regarding what a game is, can be or can do. The use of fictional games as tools for imagining different worlds is explored in detail in the next chapter, where we discuss the role of fictional games in suggesting alternative political arrangements, helping us to consider new social values and behaviours and, more generally, stimulating the fiction appreciator to entertain utopian aspirations.

References

Althusser, L. ([1970] 2020), *On Ideology*, New York: Verso Books.

Altman, R. (1979), [Film] *Quintet*, 20th Century Fox. Scriptwriters: Frank Barhydt, Patricia Resnick and Robert Altman.

Arnold, G. (1979), 'Meditation on Ice: A Frozen Allegory in Robert Altman's "Quintet"', *The Washington Post*, 12 February. Available online: https://www.washingtonpost.com/archive/lifestyle/1979/02/12/meditation-on-icea-frozen-allegory-in-robert-altmans-quintet/55b10c5b-8a46-48e3-8f1e-cd5d792f7052 (accessed 18 May 2022).

Banks, I. M. ([1998] 2012), *Inversions*, New York: Orbit.
Baudrillard, J. (1983), *Simulacra and Simulation*, Ann Arbor, MI: University of Michigan Press.
Baudrillard, J. (1990), *Cool Memories*, London: Verso.
Beukes, L. (2010), *Zoo City*, Nottingham: Angry Robot.
BioWare (2014), [Digital game] *Dragon Age: Inquisition*, directed by Mike Laidlaw and published by Electronic Arts.
Bogost, I. (2007), *Persuasive Games: The Expressive Power of Videogames*, Cambridge: The MIT Press.
Brecht, B. (1964), *Brecht on Theatre*, trans. John Willett. London (UK): Methuen.
Caillois, R. ([1958] 2001), *Man, Play, and Games*, Champaign, IL: University of Illinois Press.
Caselli, S., K. Bonello, K. Rutter Bonello Giappone, J. Schellekens and S. Gualeni (2020), 'Satire at Play: A Game Studies Approach to Satire', Proceedings of the 2020 FDG International Conference, Bugibba), 15–18 September.
Delson, J. (1979), 'Quintet', *Fantastic Films*, June: 24–35.
Dyer-Witheford, N. and G. de Peuter (2009), *Games of Empire: Global Capitalism and Video Games*, Minneapolis, MN: University of Minnesota Press.
Dyer-Witheford, N. and G. de Peuter (2021), 'Postscript: Gaming While Empire Burns', *Games and Culture*, 16 (3), 371–80.
Ehrman, J. (1968), 'Homo Ludens Revisited', *Yale French Studies*, 31: 31–57.
Eskelinen, M. (2001), 'The Gaming Situation', *Game Studies*, 1 (1).
Fassone, R. (2017), *Every Game is an Island: Endings and Extremities in Video Games*, New York: Bloomsbury.
Fisher, M. (2009), *Capitalist Realism: Is there No Alternative?*, London: Zero Books.
Flanagan, M. (2009), *Critical Play: Radical Game Design*, Cambridge (MA): The MIT Press.
Flanagan, M. and H. Nissenbaum (2014), *Values at Play in Digital Games*, Cambridge, MA: The MIT Press.
Foddy, B. (2017), [Digital game] *Getting Over It with Bennett Foddy*, published by Bennett Foddy, Noodlecake Studios, Humble Bundle, Inc.
Frasca, G. (2003), 'Ludologists Love Stories, Too: Notes from a Debate that Never Took Place', *Proceedings of the 2003 DiGRA International Conference: Level Up*.
Giddings, S. (2018), 'Accursed Play: The Economic Imaginary of Early Game Studies', *Games and Culture*, 13 (7), 765–83.
Grace, L. (2014), 'Critical Games: Critical Design in Independent Games', Proceedings of DiGRA Conference 2014: <Verb that ends in 'ing'> the <noun> of Game <plural noun>, 3–6 August, Salt Lake City, UT.
Gualeni, S. (2014), 'Freer than We Think: Game Design as a Liberation Practice', Proceedings of the 2014 Philosophy of Computer Games conference, held at the Bilgi University in Istanbul, 13–16 November.

Gualeni, S. (2016), 'Self-Reflexive Videogames: Observations and Corollaries on Virtual Worlds as Philosophical Artifacts', *G A M E – The Italian Journal of Game Studies*, 5 (1).

Gualeni, S. and M. Gómez Maureira (2018), 'Self-Transformative Effects of Designing Videogames and the Challenge of Capturing Them Quantitatively: A Case Study', *Proceedings of the international conference on the Foundation of Digital Games (FDG) 2018*, Malmo.

Gualeni, S. and D. Vella (2020), *Virtual Existentialism: Meaning and Subjectivity in Virtual Worlds*, Basingstoke: Palgrave Pivot.

Hardt, M. and A. Negri (2000), *Empire*, Cambridge, MA: Harvard University Press.

Harrison, W. (1973), 'Roller Ball Murder', *Esquire*, 1 September: 92–5, 208–11.

Huizinga, J. (1955), *Homo Ludens: A Study of the Play-Element in Culture*, Boston, MA: Beacon Press.

Hyper Hippo Productions (2014), [Digital game] *AdVenture Capitalist*, published by Kongregate Inc.

Ihde, D. (1990), *Technology and the Lifeworld: From Garden to Earth*, Bloomington, IN: Indiana University Press.

Jewison, N. (1975), [Film] *Rollerball*, United Artists.

Johari, H. (2007), *The Yoga of Snakes and Arrows: The Leela of Self-Knowledge*, Rochester, VT: Destiny Books.

Kael, P. (1979), 'The Altman Bunker', *The New Yorker*, 26 February: 100–1.

Kafai, Y. B. (1995), *Minds in Play: Computer Game Design as a Context for Children's Learning*, Mahwah, NJ: Lawrence Erlbaum Associates, Inc.

Kafai, Y. B., M. L. Franke, C. C. Ching and J. C. Shih (1998), 'Game Design as an Interactive Learning Environment for Fostering Students' and Teachers' Mathematical Inquiry', *International Journal of Computers for Mathematical Learning*, 3 (2): 149–84.

Kagan, N. (1982), *American Skeptic: Robert Altman's Genre-Commentary Films*, Ann Arbor, MI: Pierian Press.

Kirkpatrick, G., E. Mazierska and L. Kristensen (2016), 'Marxism and the Computer Game', *Journal of Gaming and Virtual Worlds*, 8 (2): 117–30.

Kolker, R. ([1980] 2000), *A Cinema of Loneliness: Penn, Kubrick, Scorsese, Spielberg, Altman*, Oxford: Oxford University Press.

Latour, B. (1999), *Pandora's Hope: Essays on the Reality of Science Studies*, Cambridge, MA: Harvard University Press.

Lyons, S. (2009), 'Memory of a Post-Apocalyptic Future: Whitening Skeletons and Frozen Time in Robert Altman's Quintet and Expo 67's Man the Explorer Pavilion', paper presented at the conference, Montreal as Palimpsest II: Hauntings, Occupations, Theatres of Memory, Montreal, 17 April.

Marmysz, J. (2009), 'Cultural Change and Nihilism in the *Rollerball* Films', in S. A. Lukas and J. Marmysz (eds), *Fear, Cultural Anxiety, and Transformation: Horror, Science Fiction, and Fantasy Films Remade*, Lanham, MD: Lexington Books, 85–105.

McLuhan, M. ([1964] 2001), *Understanding Media: The Extensions of Man*, Cambridge, MA: The MIT Press.
Meades, A. F. (2015), *Understanding Counterplay in Video Games*, New York: Routledge.
More, T. ([1516] 2003), *Utopia*, G. M. Logan and R. M. Adams (eds), Cambridge: Cambridge University Press.
Möring, S. and O. Leino (2016), 'Beyond Games as Political Education – Neo-liberalism in the Contemporary Computer Game Form', *Journal of Gaming & Virtual Worlds*, 8 (2): 145–61.
Mukherjee, S. (2020), 'Gamifying Salvation: Gyan Chaupar Variants as Representations of (Re)Births and Lives', in D. Brown and E. MacCallum-Stewart (eds), *Rerolling Boardgames: Essays on Themes, Systems, Experiences and Ideologies*, Jefferson, NC: McFarland.
Murray, J. (1997), *Hamlet on the Holodeck: The Future of Narrative in Cyberspace*, Cambridge, MA: The MIT Press.
Ness, R. R. (2011), '"Doin' Some Replacin"': Gender, Genre, and the Subversion of Dominant Ideology in the Music Scores', in R. Armstrong (ed.,. *Robert Altman: Critical Essays*, Jefferson, NC: McFarland, 38–58.
Numerato, D. (2015), 'Who Says "No to Modern Football?": Italian Supporters, Reflexivity, and Neo-liberalism', *Journal of Sport and Social Issues*, 39 (2): 120–38.
Origem (1979), [Board game] Quinteto.
Pajitnov, A. (1984), [Digital game] *Tetris*, developed by A. Pajitnov and V. Pokhilko.
Parker Brothers (1935), [Board game] Monopoly.
Rockstar Games (2004), [Digital game] *Grand Theft Auto: San Andreas*, directed by L. Benzies and published by Rockstar Games.
Rockstar North (2002), [Digital game] *Grand Theft Auto: Vice City*, directed by L. Benzies and published by Rockstar Games.
Ruffino, P. (2021), 'The End of Capitalism: Disengaging from the Economic Imaginary of Incremental Games', *Games and Culture*, 16 (3): 208–27.
Rushdie, S. ([1981] 2006), *Midnight's Children*, New York: Random House.
Sharp, J. and D. Thomas (2019), *Fun, Taste, & Games: An Aesthetics of the Idle, Unproductive and Otherwise Playful*, Cambridge, MA: The MIT Press.
Soares, M. (2007), 'A Note on the Regressive Side of Modernization in Relation to Two Films by Robert Altman', *Colloquy: Text, Theory, Critique*, 14: 74–80.
Suits, B. (1978), *The Grasshopper: Games, Life and Utopia*, Toronto: University of Toronto Press.
Thompson, D. (2011), *Altman on Altman*, London: Faber and Faber.
United States Army (2002), [Digital game] *America's Army*, developed by the United States Army and published by the United States Army.
Vanetti, M., C. Colangelo and D. Gastaldo (2018), [Digital game] *Little Antifa Novel*. Available online: https://maurovanetti.itch.io/lan (accessed 18 May 2022).
Vv. Aa. (2007), 'Snakes and Ladders', in the archives of Elliott Avedon Museum & Archive of Games, Waterloo, Canada. Available online: https://web.archive.org/

web/20080220175521/http://www.gamesmuseum.uwaterloo.ca/VirtualExhibits/Whitehill/snakes/index.html (accessed 4 April 2021).

Woodcock, J. (2019), *Marx at the Arcade: Consoles, Controllers, and Class Struggle*, Chicago, IL: Haymarket Books.

ZA/UM (2019), [Digital game] *Disco Elysium*, directed by Robert Kurvitz and published by ZA/UM.

3

Fictional Games as Utopian Devices

In the previous chapter, we discussed the use of games (and fictional games) as ideological tools, analysing games as being explicitly designed with the didactic and more generally rhetorical intention of signalling the values and orientations of a specific social group. In the cases we examined, the social group in question was the politically dominant one within the fictional world, meaning that the ideologies that were persuasively integrated into the various games we analysed were those of established power. Acting as a counterpoint to Chapter 2, this chapter elaborates on the possibility for games and fictional games to disavow and subvert dominant ideologies, rather than merely condensing and replicating them. The use of fictional games in the pursuit of alternative – and even utopian – sociopolitical arrangements is the focus of the present chapter. In exploring the utilization of fictional games as utopian devices, we draw on previously introduced notions such as that of fictional incompleteness.

Given the future orientation that typically characterizes utopian and dystopian fiction, this chapter will mostly discuss fictional games appearing in works of science-fiction. With their great variety of themes and media forms, the only trait that can perhaps be recognized as common to all works of science-fiction is their aspiration to stimulate their recipients to imagine future hypothetical scenarios and alternative possibilities of being (see Williams 1980: 198; Miéville 2009: 245; Canavan 2016: xviii). Understanding science-fiction as an imaginative gateway that allows the reader to speculate on the possible consequences of future political and technological developments dates back to the 'golden age' of classic science-fiction. In the 1930s, for example, H. G. Wells described his task as a writer of 'fantastic stories' as helping the reader 'play the game properly' – that is, to 'domesticate the impossible hypothesis' on the basis of a set of plausible assumptions (Wells 1933, as cited in Miéville 2009: 236).

Suvin's ([1979] 2016: 15) pioneering work in science-fiction literary history and criticism formalizes this perspective by defining science-fiction as 'the literature of *cognitive estrangement*'.[1] In his book *Metamorphoses of Science Fiction: On the Poetics and History of a Literary Genre* (originally published in 1979), Suvin advances the claim that, to be culturally relevant, science-fiction needs to be characterized by a degree of *novum* – aspects of the narrative world that are new and unfamiliar to the reader. According to Suvin (ibid.: 88), the *novum* in science-fiction literature is typically found in the narrative presentation of a scientifically plausible alternate reality – 'one that possesses a *different historical time* corresponding to different human relationships and sociocultural norms [. . .]'. The specific mode of existence of these alternate realities is described as a 'feedback oscillation that moves now from the author's and implied reader's norm of reality to the narratively actualized *novum* to understand the plot-events, and now back from those novelties to the author's reality to see it afresh from the new perspective gained' (ibid.). For Suvin, the sociocultural relevance of science-fiction, thus, is not found in its often bizarre settings, ray-guns, hyperdrives or mysterious alien civilizations, but rather in 'its vision of a radically different social order that, in the end, is always a critique of our own very flawed one, alongside the dream of our flawed order supersession' (Canavan 2016, xxiv). Accordingly, Suvin ([1979] 2016: 59) proposes an understanding of utopian literature as a subgenre of science-fiction literature 'in which human relationships are described as more desirable and better organized than they are in the author's actual community'. Lucy Sargisson similarly wrote that utopia is first and foremost an *act of imagination* that revolves around the principle of hope and is forward-looking towards the prospect of a better world (Levitas and Sargisson 2003: 17).

---

[1] Suvin's idea of estrangement relies on a cultural tradition first articulated by the Russian Formalists in the context of literature through, for example, Viktor Shklovsky's idea that a sense of unfamiliarity and uncertainty could be elicited through aesthetic experience (Crawford 1984). In explaining his ideas about 'a theatre for the scientific age', Brecht (1964: 64) similarly included the aspiration of 'distancing' the audience from familiar beliefs and values to encourage them to see things (including themselves) from new perspectives.

Our approach to the notion of utopia is in line with the authors and perspectives discussed above, especially in terms of the concept's future orientation and hopeful aspirations for a fairer, freer and more sustainable existence for all. As such, our approach to utopian fiction and utopian thinking also aligns with the dominant interpretation offered by social theory, in that we understand utopia as a critical device that prompts its recipients to rethink their political and moral contexts and to imagine attainable alternatives.[2]

The anticipative dispositions of utopian thinking (and utopian fiction) must, however, be recognized as a relatively recent development in the fiction genre. We believe that this point deserves further elaboration before we discuss the relationship between utopian thinking and games or – even more to the point – the utopian potential of fictional games. According to Gundolf S. Freyermuth (2019: 9), the forward-looking approach (as well as its frequent reliance on technological advancements) is the result of cultural transformations that began in the Renaissance. In Greek and Roman antiquity, Freyermuth argues, the ideals of a better world and a fairer society were not something that people could aspire to and work towards; rather, they were understood as belonging to the Golden Age, a mythical past that was forever bygone.[3] Similarly, he continues, in the Christian Middle Ages, one could hopefully anticipate eternal life in paradise or bemoan the expulsion from the Garden of Eden, but it was not possible to harbour utopian hopes like those seen in the modern age – the belief that there could be salvation in our future as a society and as a species, a future that we might not live to see and experience but that our descendants might (ibid.). More specifically, according to Freyermuth, the kinds of utopias that could be encountered in pre-modern literature – for instance, in Plato's *Republic* (c. 375 BCE), Virgil's *Eclogues* (c. 38 BCE) or More's previously discussed satirical novel, *Utopia* (1516) – used the toolkit of fiction to propose and explore alternative social values and more desirable forms of political arrangement. By using the fictional device of (dis)placing such unfamiliar prospects at a reasonable distance

---

[2] We thus understand utopia as a mode of thinking (and a genre of fiction) that is typically oriented towards potentiality rather than practicality. After all, a utopia that is realized quickly becomes the status quo and, as such, inevitably loses its critical, countercultural and hopeful functions (see Mannheim 1985; Labuschagne 2011). Very much like fictional games, utopias must thus be constituted by unrealized possibilities, and, if they are ever actualized, this can only be in a temporary fashion.

[3] The longing for a mythical past as a sort of unattainable utopia became one of the rhetorical tools of twentieth-century reactionary politics, usually inspired by traditionalist thinking. As observed by Jesi (1979) and Staudenmaier (2020), among others, the racial politics of Italian fascism were informed by this sort of aspirational 'passatism'. In this case, one could argue that a weaponized version of pre-modern utopias existed alongside modern technological utopias and was employed as a tenet of reactionary political discourses.

in terms of either space or time (e.g. in a fabled past, on a remote island or in distant lands yet to be discovered), these authors encouraged readers to treat their fictional worlds as objects of critical reflection and philosophical speculation. The hopeful desires and the critical attitudes these authors of utopian literature aimed to elicit in their readers clearly targeted the moral and political set-up of the societies in which they were living. Later, spurred by the processes of enlightenment and industrialization, the focus of these hopes and desires shifted from morals and politics to technological innovations and the cultural and anthropological consequences thereof (Freyermuth 2019: 27). To be sure, we do not see the transformation of utopian thinking emphasized by Freyermuth as a radical departure from the themes and methods of classical utopian fiction; rather, we interpret it as a shift in focus that, while not excluding reflections and aspirations that are specifically political, frames those thoughts and aspirations in specific (and often specifically technologically involved) perspectives. Clearly, political and moral issues, new social possibilities and related threats to our well-being all emerge from (and are co-constitutive of) the wider socio-technical context of the fictional world in question, especially in science-fiction.

We thus understand utopian thinking as forward-looking, hopeful and always permeated with what Jameson (2005) calls the 'utopian impulse'. Building on the work of Ernst Bloch, Jameson examines the idea of utopian impulse as a reaction to a certain status quo. More specifically, the 'utopian impulse' is a reaction that attempts to transform or overcome established political and cultural conditions deemed unfair or otherwise dissatisfactory (Jameson 2005: 53). This impulse, according to Jameson, is deeply rooted in the human psyche and manifests itself in several ways, such as in social struggle, communitarian projects and works of fiction. In the specific context of utopianism in games and video games, Farca (2018: 120) similarly emphasizes that, through the interactive experience of utopia, the player is likely 'to see empirical reality for what it is, and may be inclined to work towards Utopia in real life'.

Regardless of the specific media configuration taken by utopian fiction (i.e. thought experiments, literature, film, animation, comics, theatre, radio shows, podcasts, games or video games), its defining trait is the intention to stimulate our moral and political imagination, along with a critical disposition towards the status quo. Broadly speaking, utopian fiction pursues such cultural effects in two often concomitant ways:

1. As a call to action: indicating a virtuous path towards a better future (in works specifically labelled as utopias); and

2. As a warning: presenting nightmarish visions of possible tomorrows (in the fictional genres of dystopia and anti-utopia).[4]

The genre of dystopia is by far the most common of these two approaches, especially when it comes to interactive fiction. Despite the dire and oppressive future that works in this genre typically outline and take place in, and against the odds, in works such as games and choose-your-own-adventure books, the player/appreciator is presented with a chance to change their fictional world, which also constitutes a clear and compelling motivation to act.

By interactively engaging in an unjust and almost hopeless world, players are given the opportunity to actively oppose and potentially overcome the dystopian situation in which they find themselves and to actively contribute to bringing about a new, more desirable socio-political arrangement.[5] During the experience of dystopian fiction (regardless of interactivity), the appreciators are often indirectly warned about undesirable tendencies and potential dangers that are already present in their actual society. By presenting a potential undesirable projection forward from the current situation, dystopian fiction tends to implicitly suggest to the audience that they still have time and that they can still act in their own world to prevent the actualization of the nightmarish future presented. The interactive and ergodic qualities of games and video games set them apart from the classical dystopias of literature, theatre and film, and these qualities can be particularly efficient in leveraging feelings of hopelessness; games are particularly well suited to present what are often referred to as 'dystopias of resignation' and anti-utopias – oppressive, dark futures that the protagonists can never redeem or reverse (see footnote 4). This capability can be seen as a consequence of how games are currently understood, designed and used as (playful) systems of control and interdiction where the freedom afforded

---

[4] The difference between the dystopian and anti-utopian genres of fiction has historically been rather vague and confusing, to the point that they are often used interchangeably in academic literature. In a general sense, and for the sake of using these terms in a clear and operational manner, dystopian works can be understood as negative forms of fiction that, despite their darkness, still harbour hope for the future and urge their characters and appreciators to work towards a less dreadful and unfair future. In the genre of the anti-utopia, in contrast, works of fiction, which usually present themselves as reflections on the impossibility of utopia and the unchanging and uncaring essence of human beings, advance to the point where there are no possibilities for a better future. To put it simply, there is no hope in an anti-utopian work, but there is always hope in a dystopian work.
[5] It should also be noted that players' interactive engagement in a dystopian scenario is not sufficient to prompt the player's utopian impulse. For instance, Schulzke (2014) argues that the need for players to acquire in-game resources and to survive in an unjust and violent gameworld may lead to their conforming to its dystopian social norms. In other words, the risk highlighted by Schulzke here is that players might accept the dystopian situation and adapt to it, rather than developing an urge to fight it and work to build a better world.

to the player is carefully apportioned by the game designers. This fundamental quality of our relationship with games was already emphasized in the Introduction to this book, where games were broadly presented as artefacts characterized by both spatial (and, more generally, interactive) limitations and prescribed criteria for success. The imposition of criteria for success, the limitations of players' interactive possibilities and the scarcity of in-game resources are arguably among the most salient and frequently used rhetorical tools in these hopeless games and video games. These qualities are typically complemented by narrative and aesthetic design choices such as presenting gameworlds that are dark and inhospitable, or putting players in desperate situations such as facing an ecological crisis, being among the few survivors of a cataclysm or being oppressed and marginalized by hegemonic power structures (see Farca 2018).

Dystopian games of resignation and anti-utopian games tend to make players face circumstances where they are frustratingly disempowered. This game design strategy is meant to emphasize the helplessness of the individual and to instil the feeling that, regardless of the player's most valiant efforts, it is too late to act. In other cases, players of dark dystopian games are given what would appear to be sufficient resources and interactive possibilities to work towards a utopian outcome, only to discover that the prospect of change was an illusion and that they never really stood a chance. Examples of these designed situations of hopeless and ineffectiveness can be identified in digital games such as *Every Day the Same Dream* (Molleindustria 2009; see Figure 3.1) and *Cart Life* (Hofmeier 2010).

The design strategy of making players active participants in creating or perpetuating the problems that make the gameworld dystopian is often used in

Figure 3.1 In the 2009 digital game *Every Day the Same Dream*, the player experiences various episodes within the monotonous life of a white-collar worker in a short, playable reflection on existence, alienation and the refusal of labour. © Molleindustria 2009. All rights reserved.

these games (see Schulzke 2014: 324–30). This design intention typically materializes in games as constraints and goals that mirror the problems the dystopia in question is designed to express. For example, the player may be forced to engage in violent behaviours in gameworlds pervaded by violence or hoarding behaviours in game situations defined by resource scarcity (ibid.). This design purpose can be pursued further by putting players in the insufferable role of social actors that the players would ideally side against (e.g. high school shooting murderers, Nazi officers, whale harpooners or evil corporations). Games of this kind are thus meant to shock, irritate and provide simplified insight into the motives and the modus operandi of forces within society that can be considered dystopian from the implied point of view of the player. Examples of this design strategy can be seen in the interactive dystopias in *The McDonald's Videogame* (Molleindustria 2005), *Harpooned: Japanese Cetacean Research Simulator* (O'Kane 2008) and the Second World War-themed tabletop game Train (Romero 2009). Through interactively experiencing games of this kind, 'the player comes to see empirical reality for what it is and may be inclined to work towards Utopia in real life' (Farca 2018: 120).

As we have seen, actually existing games can use the lack of interactivity and the futility of in-game players' efforts as components of their dark dystopian and anti-utopian strategies. However, it is rare for fictional games to be used in such hopeless and oppressive scenarios, likely because of the inherent unplayability of fictional games, which makes the lack of meaningful input and interaction possibilities in the fiction less remarkable as an expressive element. When they are utilized as narrative elements that are central within a certain dystopian world, fictional games can typically be recognized as either a utopian element or one that echoes and promotes hegemonic values. In their utopian function, fictional games are often used to suggest the potential for change, to incite a shift in mentality and political orientations or even to directly spark a revolutionary cultural shift within a work of fiction. But how can fictional games transcend the boundaries of play and affect the spheres of morality and politics in the fictional worlds of which they are a part? How can artefacts that were previously defined as fictional systems of control and interdiction become utopian elements? This can happen through one or more of the following three expressive possibilities:

1. Structural indeterminacy: The characteristic flexibility and under-specification of fictional games discussed in Chapter 1 are often leveraged to produce unexpected in-game behaviours, strategies and meanings. These

new ways of playing can, by extension, reveal new possibilities to understand and shape one's relationship with power and to organize social groups.
2. The possibility of transgression: Games, understood as rigid and inescapable systems of control and interdiction, can nevertheless be transgressed, broken away from and revealed to be not only arbitrary but also imperfect and unjust. This revelation can then apply, as synecdoche, to the social structure and the system of power in which the games are played, typically leading to revolutionary acts and the eventual collapse of established power in the fictional world.
3. Rhetorical and transformative effects: Game boundaries and interdictions can be designed to communicate and reinforce values and ideologies that differ from those underpinning the ruling hegemony, and can propose new and more desirable forms of political arrangement, effectively functioning as a rhetorical tool to persuade and transform players.

The following sections introduce the focal games selected for this chapter on the theme of utopia. Specifically, section 3.1 focuses on Azad, a fictional game that has a centrally important role in Banks' 1988 science-fiction novel, *The Player of Games*. We consider Azad exemplary of the first kind of utopianism (the one stimulated by a game's indeterminacy). In section 3.2, we analyse the deadly game show in *The Running Man* (both the original novel and its movie adaptation) as representative of the second kind of utopianism (the one emerging from transgressing the game's seemingly unbreakable boundaries and rules).

Although examples of the third kind of utopianism also abound. One example of this third expressive use of fictional games is the game of Syndrome – a counter-hegemonic fictional board game described by Dick in his 1959 short story 'War Game'. Within its fictional world, Syndrome is a Monopoly-inspired game designed by the economically exploited Ganymedeans to be played on Terra, the home of their economic and political oppressors. As playable propaganda, Syndrome rewards non-colonial and non-consumerist player behaviours and leads to a shift in the Terrans' capitalist mindset. Similar cases can be found in MacLeod's 2011 science-fiction novel, *The Restoration Game*, and in Reynolds' 2001 space opera, *Chasm City*. In *The Restoration Game*, the protagonist creates a multiplayer online digital game that becomes both the ideological basis and the organizational linchpin of a popular rebellion. In the epilogue of *Chasm City*, the novel's protagonist devises a newer, fairer version of 'The Game', which is a technologically enhanced, ritualized manhunt where the ruling class of Chasm City hunt selected individuals from the lower class.

Together with a new media coverage system, the new version of 'The Game' – called *Shadowplay* – is described as having led to the collapse of the dehumanizing, hierarchical status quo and to the emergence of a new social equilibrium (Reynolds 2001: 630–3).

3.1 The game of Azad and indeterminacy

The science-fiction novel *The Player of Games* is part of the Culture series, a sequence of ten loosely related books written by Banks from 1987 to 2012. The shared background of these books is 'the Culture', a functioning anarchist, utopian, post-scarcity, galaxy-spanning society of pan-humans, nonhuman species and advanced artificial intelligences. The Culture has been discussed by literary critics as 'a sprawling, inter-galactic left-libertarian thought experiment' (Suderman 2013). *The Player of Games* (1988) stands out from the other novels in the series because it addresses, with a degree of self-reflexive irony, the limitations and contradictions of utopian thinking in the context of science-fiction (Gualeni 2021).

As noted in the previous chapters of this book, games are frequently found in Banks' fictional worlds, where they mostly function as ready-made symbols operating in the background. They are presented as structured systems of rules that replicate certain ideologies, moral orientations and ways of living in the societies in which they are played (Cobley 1990: 26; Slocombe 2013: 136; Caroti 2015: 64; Kincaid 2017: 17). In this chapter, we focus on Azad, a fictional game that has a central narrative role in the novel *The Player of Games*. We selected Azad as it is particularly suitable for exemplifying the utopian function of indeterminacy as a prominent feature of fictional games as narrative devices.

The protagonist of *The Player of Games*, Jernau Morat Gurgeh, is a game scholar and professional player recruited by the Culture's 'Special Circumstances' branch to infiltrate a gaming event planned to take place two years later in the distant, space-faring Empire of Azad. *The Player of Games* presents Gurgeh as one of the most brilliant and accomplished players in the entire Culture, a civilization in which games play an important role, as demonstrated by their frequent occurrence in the series. In these novels, games and sports feature as sources of discomfort and uncertainty for space-faring societies that have managed to eradicate both from all other aspects of the existence of their members. The Culture's interest in games, together with its more general hedonistic take on utopia, is possible because of scientific and technological advancements and because of the work of 'the Minds' – artificial, conscious superintelligences that constitute the logistical and political backbone of the interstellar civilization. Having been blackmailed by his recruiters and falling victim to the existential tedium that plagues many in the Culture, Gurgeh decides to accept the infiltration job.

Gurgeh's two-year outbound journey to the Empire of Azad is spent learning the game that he will play in the tournament. Banks deliberately obfuscates the rules and processes governing the game of Azad but leaves tantalizing clues about its set-up and functioning throughout the novel (see MacCallum-Stewart 2018: 128). *The Player of Games* presents the game of Azad as a staggeringly complex and nuanced turn-based military strategy board game that also features several aspects of chance. Banks describes Azad as having a preliminary phase where players are expected to make decisions concerning the strategic and political orientations that will structure the game. This initial phase also includes a few minigames in which players gather and develop their resources to be used in the main part of the game. These small, preparatory games are exclusively played with special cards and dice. The main phase of Azad, in contrast, takes place on enormous three-dimensional boards of various shapes and sizes. The boards are described as 'at least twenty metres to a side' and can be walked on when players need to move their pieces (Banks [1988] 2012a: 75). The game can be played with two or more players, depending on the situation, and can give rise to temporary in-game alliances that usually reflect the shared interests of certain factions of Azadian society. The game is played with a variety of pieces that represent in-game resources and military units. Some of these pieces are genetically engineered constructs called 'biotechs' that are particularly difficult to master because they change and mature during the game depending on how they are used. During his two years of ludic and linguistic preparation, Gurgeh is encouraged by the artificial intelligence training him to hold some of the particularly important biotechs while sleeping, as this will somehow help him understand them better in the context of play.

As suggested by its name, the game of Azad is intricately connected to the political functioning of the empire. The reader is informed that, in the Eächic language used on the home planet of the Empire of Azad, the word 'Azad' has a multitude of meanings generally relating to complex, interconnected systems and mechanisms and that the term is also applied to entities such as animals, plants and machines. Although the study of games and the study of philosophy are sharply distinguished in the Culture, the links between a civilization, its languages and its games are of particular interest to Gurgeh, whose scholarly work is motivated by a fascination with 'the way a society's games revealed so much about its ethos, its philosophy, its very soul' (Banks ibid.: 30). In *The Player of Games*, we read that the game of Azad was 'developed over several thousand years, reaching its present form about eight hundred years ago, around the same time as the institutionalization of the species' still extant religion. [...] [The game] is used as an absolutely integral part of the power-system of the empire. Put in the crudest possible terms, whoever wins the game becomes emperor' (ibid.: 76).

There is thus a correspondence between the game's system of rules and the functioning of Azad's sociopolitical system in which 'whoever succeeds at the game succeeds in life; the same qualities are required in each to ensure dominance' (ibid.). Accordingly, Azadians who perform well in the official tournaments (held at regular intervals reminiscent of present-day political elections) take up institutional roles with levels of importance that match their tournament performance. Notwithstanding its political structure matching that of a game, the social organization in the Empire of Azad is neither playful nor free: *The Player of Games* is not set in an anarchistic or liberal society, but rather in a totalitarian one. The main ideological paradigm underpinning both the empire and the game is that of instrumental rationality, which is particularly recognizable in the gameplay's focus on activities such as resource management, territorial control and military tactics.

Banks' space opera *The Player of Games*, like Dick's novel *Solar Lottery*, uses a game as a social tool to justify and maintain the hegemonic power in a fictional society. The transgression of the boundary between the artificiality of a ludic structure and the reality of social organization constitutes the most striking aspect of *novum* in both books. In this aspect, *The Player of Games* and *Solar Lottery* have an obvious predecessor in Jorge Luis Borges' 1941 short story, 'The Lottery in Babylon' ([1941] 1962). In *Solar Lottery*, absolute power wears the mask of chance. In *The Player of Games*, power is solely distributed within 'an economically privileged class retaining its advantages through – usually – a judicious use of oppression and skilled manipulation [...]' (Banks [1988] 2012a: 74). Members of the ruling classes of the Empire of Azad maintain their status through their in-game performance, which is ensured by a social system that grants them higher-quality education and mentorship. Their privileged position in society is further protected by a planet-wide programme of genetic manipulation aimed at suppressing the intelligence (and, consequently, the in-game performance) of the rest of the population. This programme includes selective birth-control and sterilization, area-specific starvation and mass deportation (ibid.: 80).

Against this dark background, Banks introduces a utopian aspect that sets *The Player of Games* apart from the resigned dystopianism that characterizes both *Solar Lottery* and 'The Lottery in Babylon'. In his novel, in addition to leveraging the ideological conformity between the game and society to emphasize the durability and pervasiveness of the hegemonic power structures in place, Banks also shows that, by understanding relationships of power through a game (and, ultimately, *as a game*), one can reveal their fragility and contingency. The aspects of interaction and uncertainty that define many fictional games, including Azad, can thus be used as tools for stimulating utopian thought in works of fiction: if a player can challenge the empire's established assumptions and ideologies within the game, then it is possible for the whole system to be questioned and potentially destroyed. The uncertain interactions in the game of Azad (evident, for example, in the uses of secret units and resources and the presence of biotechs in the game) and its elements of randomness are precisely the aspects of the fiction that offer a glimmer of hope that the future can be changed and that things can take an unexpected turn. Uncertainty features in these games as the faint possibility for players to overturn dystopias from within (see Gualeni 2021).

One could argue that the main structural difference between the game of Azad and Dick's and Borges' lotteries is that Azad is not purely a game of chance. Although chance is an important component of Azad, Banks' fictional game requires its players to understand and interpret dynamic situations and respond in ways that allow them to pursue strategic objectives. *The Player of Games* describes the game of Azad as an interactive system that is so complex, subtle and flexible that it is the most precise and comprehensive a model of life that it is possible to construct (Banks [1988] 2012a: 76). Thus, its players are not simply taking part in a ludic activity defined by aspects of randomness and strategic thinking; rather, they are proposing competing political claims that are implied in their in-game interactions. As the book explains, the game of Azad 'is used not so much to determine which person will rule, but which tendency within the empire's ruling class will have the upper hand, which branch of economic theory will be followed, which creeds will be recognized within the religious apparat, and which political policies will be followed' (ibid.).

Discussing the possibility of expressing and manipulating ideological positions through the activity of play, Flanagan's work is again important (see Chapter 2). In *Critical Play*, Flanagan (2009) discusses several ways to play games (and play *with* games) that can incite critical and subversive attitudes in players. Among these approaches, the idea that players can decide to act according to their own beliefs and inclinations, disputing the values and objectives imposed on them by a game's rules and affordances, is of particular interest. Also relevant for the scope of this chapter is the practice she labels as 'unplaying', which consists of configuring unanticipated and often absurd in-game situations. The game's objective resistance to players' subversive intentions is of central importance in Flanagan's work, as it demonstrates how games are often designed to enforce and uphold norms and existing power structures. Examining *The Player of Games* with Flanagan's critical perspectives, the aspects of randomness and indeterminacy that characterize the game of Azad can be understood as elements of fragility in the Empire of Azad's political structure. Given the correspondence between the game and the empire, Banks' novel presents the uncertainty inherent to the game and player behaviour as a potential threat to the stability of Azad's sociopolitical status quo. The utopian function of the game of Azad is thus to show that power relationships are ultimately indeterminate and potentially subject to change, even in the darkest dystopian and most oppressive of scenarios.[6] In other words, because of its elements of chance and indeterminacy (which is also reflected in how the game is presented in the novel), Azad stimulates the reader's political imagination, which is likely to make them more receptive to social change in their actual life.

Addressing the critical (and even utopian) uses of indeterminacy in games requires a brief explanation of how we apply the term in this context. Many types of indeterminacy can exist – and coexist – in games. The most common are those related to aspects of randomness, unexpectedness and ambiguity (for a more complete treatment of this topic, see Costikyan 2013). In games and fictional games, these features are generally encountered in three non-mutually exclusive ways. First, they can be experienced as deliberate components of a game's formal or technical set-up (i.e. designed randomness). Second, indeterminacy can emerge from players' choices and actions – that is, from how they understand and react to what a game situation means and how they are allowed (and expected) to act within it. Finally, indeterminacy in games can occur because of unanticipated malfunctions of the game itself, as technical problems, material failures or the game's design not being fully resolved.

---

[6] Game studies have often tackled the critical implications of gameplay and the ability of a player to subvert the game's political or cultural assumptions. From this perspective, the game of Azad can have a double meaning. On the one hand, it can be understood as a 'complicit political' game (Schrank 2014: 113) – a utopian projection of the aspirations of the ruling class. On the other hand, the way in which Gurgeh decides to play the game configures a new kind of political programme in which the Azadian ruling class' aspirations are exposed and challenged.

In discussing playful uncertainty, it is also relevant to mention how modernist artistic practices systematically embraced aspects of chance, nonsense and uncertainty to stimulate reflections on the arbitrariness and contingency of the status quo and to facilitate the imagination of alternative sociopolitical configurations. Of the modernist avant-gardes, the currents of Dada, Surrealism and Situationism most obviously embraced chance and interactivity in artistic production as expressive ways to oppose instrumental rationality, the dominant paradigm of Western thought. In addition to having the explicit intention to 'militate against means/end rationality' (Laxton 2003: 34), these movements' playfulness and reliance on chance also aspired to reveal that it is always possible to question established social canons. Several groups in these movements sharing leftist, anti-war and anti-capitalistic political positions systematically adopted playfulness and the use of games as part of their insubordinate and utopian artistic strategies (see Gooding and Brotchie 1995; Flanagan 2009: 88–94). In its interactive, participatory mode of engagement, the Surrealists' use of games in the context of artistic production challenged the traditional understanding of authorship, which they saw as echoing feudal-capitalistic relationships of production.

There are many parallels between the rhetorical use of games in utopian fiction and modernist artistic practices. The following passage from *The Player of Games* (Banks [1988] 2012a: 41), in which Gurgeh gives his account of the philosophical importance of indeterminacy, is helpful in highlighting these correspondences:

> All reality is a game. Physics at its most fundamental, the very fabric of our universe, results directly from the interaction of certain fairly simple rules, and chance; the same description may be applied to the best, most elegant and both intellectually and aesthetically satisfying games. By being unknowable, by resulting from events which, at the sub-atomic level, cannot be fully predicted, the future remains malleable, and retains the possibility of change, the hope of coming to prevail; victory, to use an unfashionable word. In this, the future is a game; time is one of the rules. [...] The very first-rank games acknowledge the element of chance, even if they rightly restrict raw luck.

Unlike artists participating in currents such as Dada, Surrealism and Situationism, Gurgeh already lives in a socialist utopia: a post-scarcity civilization that is kept economically viable and politically stable by technological means. The artificial, conscious superintelligences mentioned above ('the Minds') are at the core of the strategic and logistical functioning of the Culture. The politically prominent role played by the Minds' machine network in the Culture, along with its aspirations for functional efficiency and political stability, have often led science-fiction critics and literary scholars to speculate about why the Culture did not opt at some point to get rid of its 'flesh sentient' members (i.e. pan-humans and nonhuman animal species). It seems that their expulsion would be the most stable and cost-effective way to rationally run an interstellar civilization. After all, the unpredictability and irrationality of biological creatures (both inside and outside the Culture) are often directly responsible for the complications and the conflicts treated in each book in Banks' series.

The pivotal function of indeterminacy in the game of Azad may be seen as a clue about its relevance within the whole of Banks' Culture cycle, and acts as an interpretative tool for larger-scale features of the Culture's history. One could, in fact, argue that getting rid of biological sentients would contradict the principles on which the Culture was founded, such as inclusiveness and non-discrimination, but one also needs to consider that values and orientations may change over the millennia. In our view, it is particularly interesting to explore the presence and permanence of biological sentients (and biological life in general) in the Culture in relation to aspects of the Minds' characters that make them more similar to ancient Greek gods than to rational supercomputers (see also Banks [1996] 2012b: 219–20). *The Player of Games* ([1988] 2012a), *Excession* ([1996] 2012b) and *The Hydrogen Sonata* (2012c) exemplify Culture novels in which the Minds are presented as having unique personality traits, specific interests, quirks and dispositions. In Banks' books, the Minds continuously express what could be considered genuine curiosity and even existential care towards the affairs of sentient biological beings (both inside and outside the Culture). The continued presence of biological sentients in the Culture can thus be justified as one of the 'noble goals' of the pan-galactic civilization, rather than an obstacle to its political stability and resource efficiency. From this perspective, biological sentient beings would constitute inherent sources of uncertainty, interest and existential meaning for the Minds. This seemingly holds true throughout the Culture series, where humanoids are featured both as creatures capable of creative and surprising new approaches to complex problems (e.g., Gurgeh in *The Player of Games* and Fal 'Ngeestra in *Consider Phlebas*) and as elements of disequilibrium and amusement for the Minds in what would otherwise be a fully predictable existence. Biological sentients might thus be what keeps the Culture interesting for the Minds in the same way that complexity and indeterminacy are the aspects of games that motivate Gurgeh's enthusiasm as both a scholar and a player (Banks [1988] 2012a: 21). *The Player of Games* overtly describes the Minds as 'tricky. Devious. They're gamblers, too; and used to winning' (ibid.: 22). The unpredictability of biological sentient beings might thus be traits that are evolutionarily essential to the Culture. In Banks' utopian civilization, indeterminacy features as an interesting, desirable resource that can be harnessed to keep the Culture's future malleable, preserve its possibility to adjust and permit it to keep nurturing – at least to a degree – utopian aspirations. In this sense, we can understand the ambiguities and contradictions within the Culture, as well as their fascination with games, as 'possibility spaces' in which the Culture's own utopian aspirations can reflect onto themselves and allow them to re-assess their own possibilities and incongruities. As already mentioned, such spaces afford a utopian project the capability to continue to change – and the possibility to remain utopian (see Gualeni 2021).

3.2 Thinking outside the game in *The Running Man*

Gurgeh, the protagonist of Banks' novel analysed in the previous section, is an exceptionally skilled player who decides to accept the challenge of playing the game of Azad according to its formal rules and its established conventions. Gurgeh is a professional player who leverages his cognitive inclinations, his vast knowledge of games and multiple drugs synthesized by his technologically enhanced body to master the game of Azad. His mission consists of mastering the game's unique, cruel and complicated gameplay and gaining information – by proxy as well as first-hand – about the structure and aspirations that characterize the Empire of Azad. In its isomorphism with the structure of the hegemonic power and values that permeate Azadian society, the game of Azad was clearly designed as an ideological device. Its oppressive, instrumental logics, however, are never absolute or completely inflexible, and, as Gurgeh demonstrates, they can be interpreted and repurposed to serve alternative (and potentially utopian) projects.

Gurgeh adopts a compliant approach in *The Player of Games*, but the drive towards a fairer, better future is pursued through fictional games in very different ways in other works of fiction. In some fictions, the protagonists, forced to take part in game shows or blood sports, decide to push back against the game's interdictions and prescribed performativity. These rebellious acts against hegemonic power (hypostatized in the established game rules, boundaries and goals) reveal the arbitrariness and fragility of a system that, up to that point, had been deemed unshakable and beyond question. In this section, we provide an example of how subversive players, by disobeying the rules of a fictional game, can negate the game's authority, reveal the arbitrariness and fragility of power and actualize utopian aspirations. In his fundamental work on play, *Man, Play, and Games*, Caillois ([1958] 2001: 7) describes two types of subversive players: the 'cheat' and the 'nihilist'. The cheat violates the game's rules while pretending to respect them, thus operating under a pretence of loyalty to the rules and prescriptions of the game. The nihilist, in contrast, acts as an apostate, openly denouncing the senselessness of the game's rules and ethos, thus refusing to participate in play. Both types of players – the cheat and the nihilist – may be stigmatized by players who are competent and respectful, as the subversive players' actions highlight the precariousness of the game. This is due to the fact that the rules of any game are valid only as long as players are willing to voluntarily subject themselves to them.

For the sake of simplicity, in this book, we collapse acts of cheating and challenging a game's authority over its players into the category of 'counterplay'. This term, introduced in game studies by Dyer-Witheford and de Peuter (2009) and analysed in depth by Meades (2015),[7] is generally used to characterize the political implications of questioning, subverting or negating the rules and boundaries of a game. According to Dyer-Witheford and de Peuter, whose work centres on digital games, counterplaying means recognizing and questioning the late-capitalist production modes under which video games are produced and distributed, thus adopting an anti-capitalist political stance. From this perspective, to denounce a game as politically or ethically problematic, it is necessary for the player to understand – and eventually refute – its rules. This critical relationship to games as structures of power is supposed to raise political awareness and, as we discuss later in this chapter, kickstart a utopian project.

Forms of counterplay that are political (and often explicitly utopian) have become a recognizable narrative trope in twentieth-century science-fiction, as the relevance of both fictional games and utopian speculation in the genre has led to inevitable hybridizations. From this perspective, it may be argued that fictional games present themselves as effective tools for utopian formulations. As observed in Chapter 2, the regulated, self-contained and prescriptive nature of games allows them to encapsulate certain ideologies and sets of values; consequently, players can devise methods and tactics for utopian counterplay.

[7] A similar concept can be found in Myers' (2010) term of 'bad play'. However, whereas counterplay explicitly refers to the political implications of subverting the prescriptions of a game, 'bad play' characterizes forms of play that are performed outside a framing of play as beneficial (e.g. because it encourages socialization or serves as an educational tool), without necessarily involving an explicit political or ideological implication.

The popular *The Hunger Games* series of novels (Collins 2008–20) and films (Lawrence and Ross 2012–15) employs this narrative technique to showcase the resoluteness of its protagonist, Katniss Everdeen. Set in a dystopian future where a cynical ruling elite is entertained by an annual competition in which young boys and girls are pitted against each other in a deadly game of survival, *The Hunger Games* centres on the character of Katniss, a young girl who, by refusing to submit to the game's cruel and individualistic rules, ends up spearheading an anti-establishment movement. Similar narrative dynamics – a resolute protagonist who imagines or creates a better future for themselves and others by rebelling against the inhumane rules of a game – can also be found in earlier works of fiction.[8]

In Elio Petri's film *The 10th Victim* (1965), which is based on a short story by Robert Sheckley (1953), characters portrayed by Marcello Mastroianni and Ursula Andress participate in a deadly game called *The Big Hunt*. In this state-sanctioned, televised game, players are divided into 'hunters' and 'victims'. The hunters must try to locate the victims and kill them, whereas the victims must try to escape. The hunters and victims trade places after each session, and those who survive for ten sessions win a cash prize and other privileges. Although the film offers an ironic take on totalitarian social engineering – the existence of *The Big Hunt* is said to have rendered wars and other conflicts completely useless – its main focus is on the hunt as a metaphor for dysfunctional interpersonal relationships (Cardone 2005). Marcello Poletti (Marcello Mastroianni) and Caroline Meredith (Ursula Andress) end up sidestepping the game's rules and goals by using prop guns and bulletproof vests to flee and continue their love affair. In an ironic final twist, Marcello, who had been trying to avoid remarrying after a failed first marriage, finds himself on a 'marriage plane' and is forced to marry Caroline. In the fiction, bourgeois social conventions are thus presented as more difficult to overcome than the rules of a deadly game imposed by the powers that be. Accordingly, *The Big Hunt* can be interpreted as a sardonic commentary on human nature.

Similar plots can be found in many other works of fiction, including the 2021 survival drama streaming television series *Squid Game*, the original version of 'The Game' in Alastair Reynolds' 2001 novel *Chasm City* and the film *Series 7: The Contenders*, directed by Daniel Minahan (originally released in 2001). In the last of these examples, six contenders who are randomly selected from the

---

[8] See Boschi (2017) for an in-depth analysis of the subgenre of science-fiction that involves televised or otherwise mediated deadly games.

general population are given a gun and instructed to hunt each other down. Whereas *The 10th Victim* uses a fictional game as a way to reflect on power dynamics in human relations in contemporary society, *Series 7: The Contenders* serves as a critique of a morally bankrupt form of entertainment. The film is shot in the style of a television show belonging to the genre of 'tabloid TV' (Glynn 2000), reality-based television programs that aim to provoke the audience by portraying gruesome or shocking aspects of contemporary life. Building on the wave of moral panic that accompanied the broadcast of reality TV shows in the United States (Biltereyst 2004), the film offers a critique of a perverse application of the notion of a game show. In the final sequence, the two remaining players decide to try to sidestep the game's rules by forming an alliance and taking hostages; again, as is seen in *The Hunger Games*, imagining an alternative to the game implies taking a nihilistic attitude towards its rules, which must be transgressed to restore the value of human solidarity.

An accomplished and elaborate take on the utopian potential of cheating or nihilistically refusing to accept a game's rules is offered by Stephen King's[9] 1982 novel *The Running Man* ([1982] 2012) and the film adaptation of the same name directed by Paul Michael Glaser (1987). Although the film's plot diverges significantly from that of the novel, both works of fiction can be used to discuss the relevance of dissent and opposition in relation to a fictional game as triggers for a character's utopian impulse. In both cases, the protagonist is the victim of an oppressive state apparatus that constantly reasserts itself and its values by forcing the marginalized and the downtrodden to participate in a potentially deadly game. Both the novel's protagonist and the character played by Arnold Schwarzenegger in the film transition from aiming to be competent players – and thus to potentially defeat the state – to stepping outside the game completely, symbolically denying its (and the state's) authority.

King's novel introduces its protagonist, Ben Richards, as a man living a destitute existence in a near-future dystopian North America. Unable to keep a job and needing to provide for his wife and his sick daughter, Richards signs up to participate in one of the many state-approved game shows that provide entertainment and excitement for the upper class. In exchange for physical and psychological humiliation, the players of these games are promised substantial cash prizes and, consequently, access to a higher social echelon. King ([1982] 2012: 708) describes one of these games as follows:

---

[9] The novel was first published under the pseudonym Richard Bachman. King adopted this penname to publish more material without saturating the market. The novel was written in 1971 but published in 1982. Here, we refer to King as the author of *The Running Man*.

This wasn't one of the big ones, of course, just a cheap daytime come-on called *Treadmill to Bucks*. They accepted only chronic heart, liver, or lung patients, sometimes throwing in a crip for comic relief. Every minute the contestant could stay on the treadmill (keeping up a steady flow of chatter with the emcee), he won ten dollars. Every two minutes the emcee asked a Bonus Question in the contestant's category (the current pal, a heart-murmur from Hackensack, was an American history buff) which was worth fifty dollars. If the contestant, dizzy, out of breath, heart doing fantastic rubber acrobatics in his chest, missed the question, fifty dollars was deducted from his winnings and the treadmill was speeded up.

Richards is selected for the most dangerous and rewarding game produced by the network: *The Running Man*. The rules of the game presented in the novel are simple: released into the world after a battery of tests, Richards must survive for as long as possible with professional manhunters on his track. The whole world acts as a playground, so, to some degree, regular citizens participate in the game by providing information on Richards' whereabouts. Every bit of information is rewarded by the network, with Richards earning money for each hour he is not caught. After thirty days, the hunt is over, and, if he manages to survive, Richards is compensated with a grand prize, but he is informed by the network executive in charge of *The Running Man* that 'to date, we have no survivals. To be brutally honest, we expect to have none' (King [1982] 2012: 750). Richards manages to run from the hunters for a few days, eventually setting a new record for *The Running Man*; badly hurt and out of resources, he resorts to hijacking a plane and tries to strike a deal with the producers of *The Running Man*. When he finds out that his family has been killed, he crashes the plane into the television network building.

Although he shares the name Ben Richards with King's protagonist, the character played by Schwarzenegger in the 1987 film finds himself in a significantly different predicament. In the film, Richards is an ex-policeman who was removed from the force after refusing to shoot at an unarmed mob. After escaping from jail, Richards tries to flee the country – a dark near-future version of the United States, like in the novel – but is apprehended and forced to compete in a game show called *The Running Man*. After managing to kill some of the hunters sent to pursue him, Richards joins a group of rebels and jams the television network signal, allowing the broadcast of the rebels' anti-establishment message. In the final climax of the film, Richards kills the host of the game show (see Figure 3.2).

The differences between the source text and its adaptation – together with a certain degree of suspicion of Hollywood narratives – led some commentators

Figure 3.2 The final confrontation between Ben Richards (Arnold Schwarzenegger) and the show host Damon Killian (Richard Dawson) in the 1987 film *The Running Man*, directed by Paul Michael Glaser. © Olive Films, Paramount Pictures 1987. All rights reserved.

to describe the film as a disappointing dilution of what is generally considered one of King's most politically charged novels. Texter (2007: 45) laments the fact that 'a very Marxist-oriented interrogation of the American superstructure' was turned into 'the very thing it both predicted and criticized' (ibid.: 43) – an action-packed, hypermasculine spectacle produced by Hollywood, which Texter implicitly equates with the cynical television network presented in King's text. This neo-Adornian take on contemporary American cinema belongs to an established tradition in film criticism and film studies (see, e.g., Ryan and Kellner 1988) that rests on the idea that Hollywood's industrial machine eventually trivializes and mitigates any dissent by turning it into spectacle. Our interpretation of both versions of *The Running Man* takes a different direction from Texter's, as it focuses on the function of the fictional game, *The Running Man*, in triggering a utopian impulse in the protagonist. While we agree with Texter that the film somewhat downplays some of King's most aggressively anti-capitalist stances,[10]

---

[10] Although this is not the place to offer a complete account of the ways in which Glaser's film is significantly less politicized than King's novel, turning Richards from a struggling blue-collar worker into a somewhat superhuman ex-policeman who systematically takes matters into his own hands rather than deferring to collective strategies can be read as an explicit adherence to what Bordwell (2008) describes as the 'murky' politics of contemporary American cinema, which frequently straddle the line between regressive and progressive politics in a 'strategically ambiguous' (ibid.) manner.

we argue that a comparative analysis of the utopian uses of the fictional game in these works of fiction may help us to offer a more comprehensive theory of the relations between fictional games and utopia.

To this point, we have discussed *The Running Man* as a fictional game found in a novel and a film. This apparently simple assumption should nevertheless be questioned. One can understand *The Running Man* as two different fictional games, each with its own rules and conventions and each requiring different strategies to be transgressed. Both in the novel and in the film, *The Running Man* is played on two levels: the game show, which is televised and follows some of the conventions of contemporary television, and the game itself, which is played by Richards and his pursuers in a way that is relatively autonomous from broadcasting needs and policies. In King's novel, the duality of *The Running Man* as a game show and a deadly manhunt is rendered fairly explicitly by the fact that most of the events described in the novel are not witnessed by the viewers of the game show. The rules of the game dictate that Richards must provide the network with daily recordings of his activities. To avoid being caught, he decides to provide minimal information about his whereabouts and resorts to recording in neutral locations. In these recordings, Richards goes on extended tirades on topics such as social inequalities and air pollution, but his words are systematically drowned by the jeering disapproval of the audience or edited and manipulated by the network. The game show and the deadly manhunt are, however, not separate contexts for Richards. On several occasions, for example, Richards leverages his understanding of network policies by spending long stretches of time in crowded spaces, well aware of the fact that the network will not allow an execution that may involve or harm other civilians.

The fact that *The Running Man* is inextricably embedded in a mass-media ecosystem is even more apparent in Glaser's film. In the final scenes of the film, after having escaped from his hunters, Richards finds his way back to the television studio where *The Running Man* is produced. There, Richards kidnaps the host of the show, straps him to the device used to catapult players into the playground of the game, and, as a response to the man's pleas for mercy, utters a laconic 'I don't take requests.' While belonging to the canon of Schwarzenegger one-liners, a recurrent feature of his films during the 1980s, this deliberate use of television jargon also signals the final collapse of the two games.

Both the novel and the film feature a protagonist who, after having played the game according to its hegemonically imposed rules for some time, decides to abandon his role as a dutiful player in an attempt to break away from these rules. In both versions of *The Running Man*, this utopian impulse manifests itself fairly late in the narrative. In the film, Schwarzenegger's character joins a group of rebels, whereas, in the novel, Richards decides to commit suicide by crashing a plane into the television network building, symbolically destroying the power apparatus that had held him prisoner for his whole life. For the film's protagonist, the recognition of his own utopian impulse takes place through a long process. Richards meets the group of rebels early in the film but refuses their offer to join them, saying, 'I'm not into politics; I'm into survival' (another Schwarzenegger one-liner). The rebel group, a ragtag gang of what look like near-future socialists, clearly has a plan to topple the state. Tapping an unforeseen political drive, Schwarzenegger/Richards finally resolves to oppose the values and behaviours inscribed in the game and to embrace those embodied by the rebel group's political agenda. In the novel, in contrast, Richards' utopian transition is much quicker and more personal. When he is informed of the death of his wife and daughter, Richards, who – up to that point – had played the game obediently and masterfully, decides to abandon the game and indulge in his suicidal-utopian impulse. Richards' rejection of the game's rules and ideologies can be said to correspond to what Jameson (2005: 170) refers to as the 'moment of truth' – the instant in which one is able to recognize a precise utopian impulse and act upon it. Furthermore, the radical nature of Richards' decision exemplifies what Jameson describes as the moment of truth's main function – presenting the satisfaction of a utopian impulse as the only viable option (ibid.: 175). The death of Richards' family reveals to him a potential alternative to the frame of both the game and hegemonic power, which, up until that point, had been totalizing and unquestionable. It is clearly a moment of profound transformation.

The two events – joining the rebels and deciding to commit suicide – may seem different in terms of their relationship to society. Schwarzenegger/Richards' utopian impulse involves sharing a political objective with others, whereas the protagonist of King's novel appears to be driven solely by personal feelings of grief and resentment. Other aspects of the narrative accompanying the emergence of the utopian impulse in both protagonists, however, might tell a different story. In the film, Richards helps the group of subversives achieve something they had not been able to accomplish before. This, according to Browning (2009), is the onset of a process aimed at turning the filmic Richards from a relatable everyman into the superhuman hero who single-handedly takes on an army of network security guards. In this sense, Schwarzenegger/Richards is not a mere component of the rebels' collective utopian program but assumes the paradoxical role of their leader. Conversely, while escaping from his pursuers, the literary Richards is helped by people who share his marginalized social status. In this perspective, we may think of Richards' final act as a way of actualizing the collective aspirations of the downtrodden, which had been expressed to him by Bradley, a young man who had helped him along the way, as follows: 'A bad day is comin, though. A bad day for the maggots with their guts full of roast beef. I see blood on the moon for them. Guns and torches. A mojo that walks and talks' (King [1982] 2012: 835).

3.3 Conclusions

This chapter addressed the uses and potential roles of fictional games in the pursuit of sociopolitical arrangements alternative to the status quo. Section 3.1 focused on the utopian potential that emerges from aspects of fictional games such as indeterminacy and chance, discussing fictional games' particular suitability for revealing the instability and contingency that ultimately characterize all social situations, gameful or not. From this standpoint, fictional games were presented as tools for revealing the 'possibility spaces' (or the 'play') where hope can germinate even under the most repressive and dystopian conditions. This section of the chapter leveraged a positive, playful and generative approach to the notion of indeterminacy – one that does not resonate with notions such as arbitrariness and meaninglessness, but rather constitutes the possibility space in which utopian projects can be pursued.

As we observed in section 3.1, in the game of Azad, utopian possibilities are discovered and pursued in new and unprecedented ways of playing, thus imbuing old rules and interdictions with new meanings. Section 3.2, in contrast, examined the liberatory potential of intentionally acting against such rules and interdictions. In this part of the chapter, we examined the utopian possibilities emerging from going against the explicit rules and/or the (implicit) ethos of a game. This examination was pursued through the combined analysis of the novel *The Running Man* and its film adaptation, as particularly interesting cases. In both the novel and the film, the idea of counterplay is clearly at work as a utopian strategy; a defiant attitude towards the authority of the game reveals and opposes the values and ideological orientations underpinning the game's functioning. In *The Running Man* and other similar titles such as *The Hunger Games* and *The 10th Victim*, players who are forced by the establishment into a deadly competition eventually resort to counterplay as a means to liberate themselves and actualize their utopian impulses. Ben Richards, the protagonist of *The Running Man*, exemplarily realizes that the only way to escape his condition as an oppressed individual is to refuse to obey the rules of the game and – by synecdoche – to transgress and symbolically destroy the social order that underpins its cruel gameplay.

We conclude this reflection on the utopian potential of fictional games with a discussion of a 1968 paper entitled 'How to Play Utopia', written by comparative literature scholar Michael Holquist. In this paper, Holquist observes that, like games, fictional utopias are typically presented as taking place in an imaginary context that is separate from our actual, everyday experience of the world, yet plays out against the backdrop of that experience. Moreover, according to Holquist, utopias are models: they are the representations of enormously complex processes and dynamics that are rendered manageable and clear through a process of simplification. This process is also obviously at work in games that are modelled on actual events or practices. Just as chess is a distilled version of war, a utopia is a condensed and intuitively graspable representation of a new and desirable sociopolitical arrangement; the game of chess has rules, whereas a utopia has laws (Holquist 1968: 110).

An analogy between games and utopias that Holquist did not explicitly discuss (but that is implicit in his writing) is the idea that utopias are always utopias for somebody in particular.[11] Understanding utopia through a game (and, ultimately, as a game) is helpful for revealing that a better reality for someone often corresponds to a less desirable outcome for someone else. Like the game of chess (or the game of Azad, for that matter), the pursuit of utopia is a struggle, where, for someone to be on the winning side, there must be someone else who loses.

Anticipating a potential criticism of the parallel between utopian fiction and games he proposed, Holquist concedes that one could argue that chess is free and indeterminate in a way that a text is not. Even if one considers, he continues, the limitless possibilities available to the author of a utopian work of fiction before they present their imaginary society, once the work of fiction is complete, the shape of that society is fixed; it cannot be played and replayed in the way that chess can (ibid.: 119). Writing in the 1960s, it would have been difficult for Holquist to seriously consider the possibility for fiction to ever become as interactive and flexible as a game of chess. Notwithstanding the cultural success of digital games and other ergodic forms of fiction over the last four decades, his

---

[11] The 'somebody' for whom a utopia is actually utopian (within a work of fiction) is always a rationally competent and benevolent being. We cannot recall a work of fiction that offers a utopian perspective framed in the desires and ambitions of the mad or the deranged. Speculatively, this may be simply because the moral sensitivity of fiction appreciators would likely perceive these things as profoundly dystopic. To put it in simpler terms, a utopia is always for someone, and – for the utopia to be recognized as such – that someone must have moral and political orientations that are compatible with those of the implied fiction appreciators.

own point of criticism remains valid when applied to classic, non-interactive utopian fictions. If this is true, then how could we ever compare non-interactive works of fiction to games, when the former are rigidly defined by an author and cannot in any way be played, replayed or counterplayed? To this potential objection, Holquist's response is that the author of a (classic, non-interactive) work of fiction plays the game of utopia when developing and hypothesizing about imaginary societies, and the readers of utopian texts are also somehow playing. Elaborating on the last point, he argues that utopian fiction may be interpretatively and speculatively 'played' again and again – every time it is experienced. Holquist identifies a key component of this 'replayability' in the fact that most utopian fictions have open endings onto which appreciators can project their own hypothetical scenarios: upholding a close correspondence between utopian fiction and games, Holquist (ibid.: 120) pointed out that 'the utopist leaves it up to the reader to decide who lost, who won.'

References

Banks, I. M. ([1988] 2012a), *The Player of Games*, New York: Orbit.
Banks, I. M. ([1996] 2012b), *Excession*, New York: Orbit.
Banks, I. M. (2012c), *The Hydrogen Sonata*, New York: Orbit.
Biltereyst, D. (2004), 'Media Audiences and the Game of Controversy: On Reality TV, Moral Panic and Controversial Media Stories', *Journal of Media Practice*, 5 (1): 7–24.
BioWare (2012), [Digital game] *Mass Effect 3*, directed by Casey Hudson and published by Electronic Arts.
Bordwell, D. (2008), 'Superheroes for Sale', *Observations on Film Art*, 16 August. Available online: http://www.davidbordwell.net/blog/2008/08/16/superheroes-for-sale/ (accessed 3 May 2021).
Borges, J. L. ([1941] 1962), *Ficciones*, ed. Anthony Kerrigan, New York: Grove.
Boschi, A. (2017), 'Let the Games Begin! – La figura del gioco distopico nel cinema e nella letteratura fantascientifica', *Cinergie – Il Cinema e le altre Arti*, 12: 269–80.
Brecht, B. (1964), *Brecht on Theatre*, trans. John Willett, London: Methuen.
Brown, C. (2001), 'Special Circumstances: Intervention by a Liberal Utopia', *Millennium*, 30 (3): 625–33.
Browning, M. (2009), *Stephen King on the Big Screen*, Bristol: Intellect.
Caillois, R. ([1958] 2001), *Man, Play, and Games*, Champaign, IL: University of Illinois Press.
Canavan, G. (2016), 'Introduction: The Suvin Event', in G. Canavan (ed.), *Metamorphoses of Science Fiction: On the Poetics and History of a Literary Genre*, by Darko Suvin, Bern: Peter Lang: xi–xxxvi.

Cardone, L. (2005), *Elio Petri, Impolitico. La Decima Vittima (1965)*, Pisa: ETS.
Caroti, S. (2015), *The Culture Series of Iain M. Banks: A Critical Introduction*, Jefferson, NC: McFarland Press.
Cobley, M. (1990), 'Eye to Eye: An Interview with Iain M. Banks', *Science Fiction Eye*, 6: 22–32.
Collins, S. (2008–20), [Novel series] *The Hunger Games*, New York: Scholastic.
Costikyan, G. (2013), *Uncertainty in Games*, Cambridge, MA: The MIT Press.
Crawford, L. (1984), 'Viktor Shklovskij: Différance in Defamiliarization', *Comparative Literature*, 36 (3): 209–19.
Dick, P. K. ([1955] 2012), *Solar Lottery*, New York: Houghton Mifflin Harcourt.
Dick, P. K. ([1959] 2002), 'War Game', in *The Minority Report and Other Classic Stories*, New York: Kensington Publishing, loc. 3913–4283.
Dyer-Witheford, N. and G. de Peuter (2009), *Games of Empire: Global Capitalism and Video Games*, Minneapolis, MN: University of Minnesota Press.
Farca, G. (2018), *Playing Dystopia: Nightmarish Worlds in Video Games and the Player's Aesthetic Response*, Bielefeld: Transcript Verlag.
Flanagan, M. (2009), *Critical Play: Radical Game Design*, Cambridge, MA: The MIT Press.
Freyermuth, G. S. (2019), 'Utopian Futures: A Brief History of Their Conception and Representation in Modern Media – From Literature to Digital Games', in B. Beil, G. S. Freyermuth and H. C. Schmidt (eds), *Playing Utopia: Futures in Digital Games*, Bielefeld: Transcript Verlag: 9–66.
Glaser, P. M. (1987), [Film] *The Running Man*, scriptwriter S. E. de Souza, Tristar Pictures.
Glynn, K. (2000), *Tabloid Culture: Trash Taste, Popular Power, and the Transformation of American Television*, Durham, NC: Duke University Press.
Gooding, M. and A. Brotchie (1995), *A Book of Surrealist Games*, Boston, MA: Shambhala Redstone Editions.
Gualeni, S. (2021), 'Fictional Games and Utopia: The Case of Azad', *Science Fiction Film & Television*, 14 (2): 187–207.
Hofmeier, R. (2010), [Digital game] *Cart Life*. Available online: https://hofmeier.itch.io/cartlife (accessed 18 May 2022).
Holquist, M. (1968), 'How to Play Utopia', *Yale French Studies*, 41: 106–23.
Jameson, F. (2005), *Archaeologies of the Future: The Desire Called Utopia and Other Science Fictions*, London: Verso.
Jesi, F. (1979), *Cultura di destra*, Milano: Garzanti.
Kincaid, P. (2017), *Iain M. Banks*, Chicago, IL: University of Illinois Press.
King, S. ([1982, as R. Bachman] 2012), *The Running Man*, in *The Bachman Books*, London: Hodder & Stoughton: 707–978.
Labuschagne, D. (2011), 'Deconstructing Utopia in Science Fiction: Irony and the Resituation of the Subject in Iain M. Banks's *The Player of Games*', *Journal of Literary Studies*, 27 (2): 58–76.

Lawrence, F. and G. Ross (2012–15), [Film series] *The Hunger Games*, Color Force, Lionsgate.

Laxton, S. (2003), 'The Guarantor of Chance: Surrealism's Ludic Pactices', *Papers of Surrealism*, 1: 31–47.

Levitas, R. and L. Sargisson (2003), 'Utopia in Dark Times: Optimism/Pessimism and Utopia/Dystopia', in R. Baccolini and Tom Moylan, *Dark Horizons: Science Fiction and the Dystopian Imagination*, New York: Routledge: 13–27.

MacCallum-Stewart, E. (2018), 'The Gaming of Players: Jamming Azad', in N. Hubble, E. MacCallum-Stewart and J. Norman (eds), *The Science Fiction of Iain M. Banks*, London: Gylphi: 121–42.

MacLeod, K. (2011), *The Restoration Game*, Amherst, NY: Pyr.

Mannheim, K. (1985), *Ideology and Utopia: An Introduction to the Sociology of Knowledge*, Orlando, FL: Harcourt Press.

Meades, A. F. (2015), *Understanding Counterplay in Video Games*, New York: Routledge.

Miéville, C. (2009), 'Afterword: Cognition as Ideology: A Dialectic of SF Theory', *Red Planets: Marxism and Science Fiction*, ed. M. Bould and C. Miéville, London: Pluto Press: 231–48.

Minahan, D. (2001), [Film] *Series 7: The Contenders* (2001), directed by Daniel Minahan, Blow Up Pictures, Killer Films, October Films.

Molleindustria (2005), [Digital game] *The McDonald's Videogame*, developed by Paolo Pedercini. Available online: http://www.molleindustria.org/mcdonalds/ (accessed 18 May 2022).

Molleindustria (2009), [Digital game] *Every Day the Same Dream*, developed by Paolo Pedercini. Available online: https://molleindustria.org/everydaythesamedream/everydaythesamedream.html (accessed 18 May 2022).

More, T. ([1516] 2003), *Utopia*, ed. G. M. Logan and R. M. Adams, Cambridge: Cambridge University Press.

Myers, D. (2010), *Play Redux: The Form of Computer Games*, Ann Arbor, MI: University of Michigan Press.

O'Kane, C. (2008), [Digital game] *Harpooned: Japanese Cetacean Research Simulator*, developed by Conor O'Kane. Available online: http://www.harpooned.org/ (accessed 18 May 2022).

Pedercini, P. (2014), [Blogpost] 'Videogames and the Spirit of Capitalism', published on 14 February. Available online: https://www.molleindustria.org/blog/videogames-and-the-spirit-of-capitalism (accessed 18 May 2022).

Petri, E. (1965), [Film] *The 10th Victim* [*La decima vittima*], C. C. Champion, Les Films Concordia.

Reynolds, A. (2001), *Chasm City*, London: Orion.

Romero, B. (2009), [Analogue game] *Train*, tabletop game developed by Brenda Romero and Ian Schreiber.

Ryan, M. and D. Kellner (1988), *Camera Politica: The Politics and Ideology of Contemporary Hollywood Film*, Bloomington and Indianapolis, IN: Indiana University Press.

Schrank, B. (2014), *Avant-Garde Video Games: Playing with Technoculture*, Cambridge, MA: The MIT Press.

Schulzke, M. (2014), 'The Critical Power of Virtual Dystopias', *Games and Culture*, 9 (5): 315–34.

Sheckley, R. (1953), 'The Seventh Victim', *Galaxy Science Fiction*, 6 (1): 38–50.

Slocombe, W. (2013), 'Games Playing Roles in Banks's Fiction', in M. Colebrook and K. Cox (eds), *The Transgressive Iain Banks: Essays on a Writer Beyond Borders*, Jefferson, NC: McFarland Press: 13–49.

Staudenmaier, P. (2020), 'Racial Ideology between Fascist Italy and Nazi Germany: Julius Evola and the Aryan Myth, 1933–43', *Journal of Contemporary History*, 55 (3): 473–91.

Suderman, P. (2013), 'The Endless Lives of Iain M. Banks', *Reason*, 15 September. Available online: https://reason.com/2013/09/15/the-endless-lives-of-iain-m-banks/ (accessed 18 May 2022).

Suvin, D. ([1979] 2016), *Metamorphoses of Science Fiction: On the Poetics and History of a Literary Genre*, ed. G. Canavan, Berlin: Peter Lang.

Texter, D. W. (2007), '"A Funny Thing Happened on the Way to the Dystopia": The Culture Industry's Neutralization of Stephen King's *The Running Man*', *Utopian Studies*, 18 (1): 4–72.

Vieira, F. (2010), 'The Concept of Utopia', in G. Claeys (ed.), *The Cambridge Companion to Utopian Literature*, Cambridge: Cambridge University Press, 3–27.

Williams, R. (1980), 'Utopia and Science Fiction', in *Problems in Materialism and Culture*, London: New Left Books: 196–212.

4

Fictional Games as Deceptions and Hallucinations

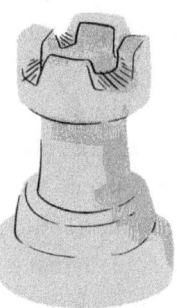

In the previous chapters, we discussed examples of the use of fictional games as proxies for complex ideological arrangements and as narrative tools to trigger and/or reinforce a fictional character's utopian drive. In these analyses, we often argued that fictional games can perform these political functions by virtue of their being clearly distinct and distinguishable from the social and existential contexts that the fictional characters consider to be their 'real lives'.[1] Put in simpler terms, by allowing players to take a step back from their everyday duties and customary engagement with the actual world, games may help to disclose alternative world views or render certain ideological constructs evident. Building on these premises, this chapter examines instances in which fictional games seek to blur or even erase the line that separates the fictional characters' actual lives from their experiencing being in a gameworld. This is pursued by some fictional games via deceptive design strategies that make them not only alluring and often

---

[1] In scholarly discussions concerning the differences between play and 'real life', we argue that the notion of 'real life' is often taken for granted or inadequately defined. On the one hand, it could be claimed that, because play takes place in the actual world (in the sense that it is a component of our actual lived experience), it cannot be said to take place 'outside' of real life. On the other hand, for various authors, 'real life' is synonymous with 'productive life', where the idea of production refers to activities with measurable outcomes such as work. For a more detailed overview of this issue, see Fassone (2017: 38).

addictive, but that can make them in some extreme cases perceptually indistinguishable from everyday existence.

The degree to which play is a context that is removed from what we call 'real life' has been the object of several contributions to our understanding of games from disciplines such as game studies and game philosophy. In this regard, a passage from Salen and Zimmerman's (2003) book, *Rules of Play*, has become a staple in the discussion of the issue of play as a separate, or even insular, pursuit. According to these scholars, 'In a very basic sense, the magic circle of a game is where the game takes place. To play a game means entering into a magic circle, or perhaps creating one as a game begins' (ibid.: 95). They trace the expression 'magic circle' back to Huizinga's ([1938] 1955) foundational treatise, *Homo Ludens*, implicitly arguing for its historical importance in the field of game studies. In Salen and Zimmerman's book, play is discussed as a unique kind of activity that establishes a special, separate context within the player's ordinary existence. The authors use the metaphor of the 'magic circle' to indicate that play happens in a social and semiotic domain that is removed and different from real life in the same way rituals are. This understanding of play has sparked a lasting debate within game studies and has often been challenged for essentializing play and games, partially disconnecting them from the larger contexts of society and culture and almost turning them into ineffable concepts. This argument, articulated by scholars such as Consalvo (2009), considers the notion of the magic circle to be unusable in its abstraction because all play practices coexist with – and often incorporate – elements from the players' ordinary existence. Zimmerman (2012) himself felt the need to revisit the concept almost ten years after the publication of *Rules of Play*, claiming that a passing reference in a very substantial game design manual turned into '[what] seems to have become a rite of passage for game studies scholars: somewhere between a Bachelor'sdegree and a Master's thesis, everyone has to write the paper where the magic circle finally gets what it deserves' (Zimmerman 2012).

A useful re-evaluation of the concept is offered by Schrank (2014), who claims that the magic circle is better understood as a non-serious context where real-life issues and tensions are brought to the fore and engaged, rather than exorcized or kept at bay. In other words, for Schrank, the magic circle of play does not segregate players from their ordinary existence; rather, it allows them to confront and revisit this existence in a somewhat safe – or even 'sacred' – context. To him, play is a sort of incantation – an invitation to summon certain forces – rather than an effort to separate oneself from them. Indeed, we adopted a similar stance in the previous chapters when discussing fictional games as ideological proxies and catalysts for utopian realizations and impulses.

In this chapter, we specifically explore what happens when the magic circle becomes so large that it conquers and encompasses the entirety of one's actual existence. What happens to the idea of a magic circle when the player is no longer able to identify the conceptual and existential boundaries separating play from non-play? In considering this question, we analyse fictional games that aim to temporarily or permanently invade or even take the place of a player's ordinary life. These radically immersive games, which are often phenomenologically indistinguishable from ordinary existence, can be considered deceptive technologies that are designed to disguise their nature as artificial, unserious activities. In some of the discussed cases, the characters are unaware of their situation as players and are tricked into believing that the game they are playing corresponds to their actual existence (or a grotesque distortion of it). In other cases, the characters are aware that they are playing a game and consciously choose to be deceived by the immersive experiences to enjoy the aesthetic and experiential pleasures they provide.[2] In both types of cases, the superimposition of a deceptive game onto one's actual experience constitutes the starting point for narratives in which the characters' sanity or sense of themselves is at risk. In works of fiction, fictional games of this type tend to act as malignant parasites, exploiting the characters' difficulty in distinguishing an artificial world from the actual one.

The notion that play can be a deceptive activity that affects and modifies one's sense of self or reality is not a new philosophical theme. In his foundational book, *Truth and Method*, Hans-Georg Gadamer ([1960] 2013) relies on the idea of play to structure a philosophical theory of art. Although we do not have the space to fully articulate Gadamer's stances on art and artists, his understanding of play is important to explore here because it advances a position that goes against the common-sense framing of this activity as inherently vital, joyful or liberating. According to Gadamer, play can also be understood as a hypnotic force that entrances players and encourages them to drift away from other aspects of their existence. In Gadamer's (ibid.: loc 3098) words, 'The structure of play absorbs the player into itself, and thus frees him from the burden of taking

---

[2] Gualeni and Van de Mosselaer (2021) argue that deception can also be a deliberate game design strategy. Game designers can decide to mislead or deceive players with the intent of generating experiential effects and emotional responses that are not necessarily malicious or abusive; rather, these responses can actually be in the interest of the player. Most of the radical varieties of ludic deception presented by the fictional games analysed in this chapter can be said to pursue a positive experiential outcome for the player.

the initiative, which constitutes the actual strain of existence. This is also seen in the spontaneous tendency to repetition that emerges in the player and in the constant self-renewal of play, which affects its form (e.g. the refrain)'.

Here, Gadamer hints at the fact that play can act as a hallucinatory drug of sorts, relieving players of the burden of their ordinary existence by compelling them to perform repetitive, essentially meaningless tasks. Later in the same text, he adds further emphasis to this idea by claiming that: 'All playing is a being-played. The attraction of a game, the fascination it exerts, consists precisely in the fact that the game masters the players. [...] What holds the player in its spell, draws him into play, and keeps him there is the game itself' (ibid.: loc. 3128–31).

Gadamer thus advances an understanding of games as spellbinding devices capable of disclosing alternative realities that attract and eventually subjugate the player. A similar process is evidently at work in a number of contemporary play practices; consider how casinos and other gambling facilities actively seek to retain players by amplifying and weaponizing play's endless cycles to extract value from their customers (see Dow-Schüll 2014). So-called 'casual video games', relatively short and simple games that are usually played on mobile devices, are also known for adopting a variety of behavioural methods to condition players to replay the game, compelling them to spend increasing portions of their time and money in the game (see Neely 2021). Some of these predatory practices exploit or seek to reinforce a cognitive status loosely defined as 'flow' (Csikszentmihalyi 1990), which describes instances in human consciousness where one is deeply absorbed in an activity, to the point of losing track of time and largely ignoring stimuli that are not pertinent to the task at hand.[3]

Games found in works of fiction often demonstrate this potential, especially in the case of dystopian or moralistic narratives in which a game is narratively employed as a disturbing agent that lures and threatens an otherwise virtuous community. One such case is found in an episode of the television series *Star Trek: The Next Generation* (1987–94) entitled 'The Game' (S5E06; Allen 1991). In this episode, most of the crew of the United Federation of Planets starship USS *Enterprise* (Enterprise-D) falls into the thrall of a highly addictive augmented reality game. The fictional game in question is a single-player game of skill that is played via an advanced technological interface directly connected to the

---

[3] In describing the concept of flow, Csikszentmihalyi (1990) adopts a largely non-politicized view on the matter and barely touches on the potential downsides and dangers of designing activities that might lead to the emergence of flow (e.g. addiction, tendency to overwork and alienation). A socially engaged criticism of the notion of flow is offered by Soderman (2021), however, who claims that the understanding of this cognitive state as unproblematic, or even beneficial, conflicts with real-world examples where a state of flow has been used as part of exploitative design strategies.

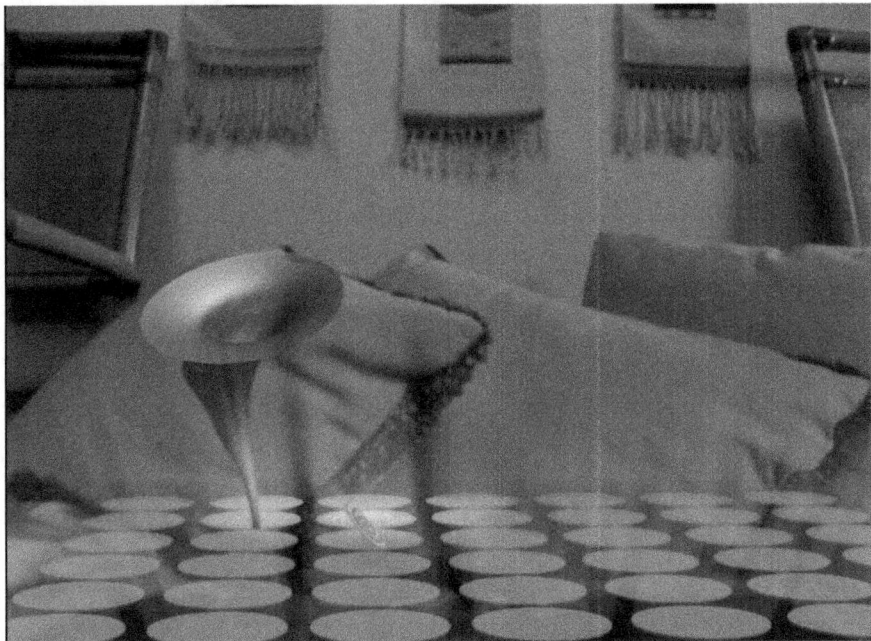

Figure 4.1 The entrancing game found in *Star Trek: The Next Generation*'s episode 'The Game'. The characters' addiction to the game is so profound that they eventually put their own survival (and that of their ship) at risk. © Paramount Pictures 1987–1994. All rights reserved.

player's synapses (see Figure 4.1). The game is part of a plan devised by Etana Jol (Katherine Moffat),[4] a Ktarian woman seeking to enslave the crew and take over the ship. In the episode, the presentation of the game resonates with Gadamer's understanding of games as instruments to master their players: this game is shown to be a non-conventional weapon deployed by Jol to sedate and control the minds of every humanoid on the spaceship. It is particularly interesting to observe that, for Jol's plan to work, it is essential that Data (Brent Spiner), a sentient robot, is deactivated. In the episode, it is explained that Data's artificial intelligence would not be captivated by the game in the way that a regular human (or humanoid) mind would. Data would therefore be able to see through and neutralize Jol's devious plan. Implicit in this plot device is the assumption that

---

[4] Jol's manipulation of the crew of the Enterprise through a malicious game could also be understood as a variation on the trope of the deceitful and manipulative woman. This narrative cliché is also recognizable in *The Game*, a film that is going to be discussed in this chapter, in which a woman is hired to seduce and beguile the protagonist (Cerny, Hatters Friedman and Smith 2014).

the possibility of becoming addicted to play is a weakness found in non-artificial creatures – a trait that is absent in the otherwise very much human-like Data (see Figure 4.1).

Although we have no proof that the authors of the episode had read Gadamer's work, an understanding of (specifically digital) play as an activity with potentially negative effects such as addiction and misdirection may have been fuelled by a set of coinciding historical circumstances. In the early 1990s, the debate around video game addiction began to emerge in popular discourses as part of a larger set of concerns over the influence of video play on children and adolescents (Cover 2006; Griffiths, Kuss and King 2012). In the same period, the publication of popular studies on virtual reality (see Rheingold 1991) – a technology that is clearly referenced in the *Star Trek* episode discussed above – both as a technological wonder and as the potential cause of a variety of phenomena connected to mental dissociation and social isolation – injected concerns about technology into popular discourses.

Illustrating a Gadamerian understanding of play as entrancing and beguiling, the game in the *Star Trek: The Next Generation* episode described above is presented as deliberately capturing and fully occupying the attention of players, with a clear negative effect on the Enterprise crew. The game is shown to be a meaningless, addictive pastime that poses a threat to these individuals' capability to function as crew members and perform their duties. Notably, however, despite being engrossed in the augmented reality game, the crew members remain capable of distinguishing one plane of reality (the minimalistic shapes and sounds projected by the game) from another (their experience of being aboard a spaceship). The characters are not incapable of maintaining their social roles through interpersonal communication or performing their assigned tasks, such as manoeuvring the spaceship. Although they are under the 'spell' of the game, no confusion arises over the status of reality: the environment of the game and that of the Enterprise coexist as two separate experiential contexts. The game breaks the will of the players – who may be said to be clinically addicted, despite suffering no withdrawal symptoms when Data frees them from the spell – but leaves their basic sense of reality intact.

Other fictional games are more radically deceptive, infiltrating and eventually becoming indistinguishable from the players' empirical reality. In these cases, players experience the game as their sole experiential and existential context. In some works of fiction, such as Carrie Vaughn's (2021) novel *Questland*, where a team of engineers is hired to construct a high-tech immersive fantasy park, this process of substitution is the result of a deliberate act by the designers of the game. This is also the case in David Fincher's (1997) film *The Game*, one of the focal fictional games in this chapter (see section 4.2). In other instances, it is the game itself that, reflecting the subconscious desires of its designers or exhibiting an autonomous technological intentionality of its own, 'infects' and eventually overtakes the player's conscience.

Moving towards an analysis of these radically deceptive types of games requires clarification regarding *who* is supposed to be deceived. In some cases, the superimposition of play and real life is not experienced by the characters of a work of fiction but is used as a narrative device to surprise or disorient the fiction appreciator. A remarkable example of this strategy is found, again, in the *Star Trek* universe. The feature film *Star Trek II: The Wrath of Khan* (1982) opens with a dramatic sequence: following the receipt of a distress signal, the crew of the Enterprise is called to rescue the Kobayashi Maru, a Federation vessel found drifting in a sector of space that is presented as inaccessible to Federation ships because of a war treaty. When approaching the Kobayashi Maru's location, the Enterprise is attacked, and, eventually, all its crew members, including beloved characters such as Spock (Leonard Nimoy) and Sulu (George Takei), are killed. Less than ten minutes into the film, with most members of the cast dead, the audience is supposed to be at a loss. Suddenly, Captain Kirk (William Shatner) appears from behind a steel door and reveals that the sequence was only a simulation. The crew was merely playing along with aspiring captain Saavik (Kristie Alley), who was facing the 'Kobayashi Maru test', a complicated training scenario designed to test the mettle of Space Academy cadets and prepare future Federation captains. The unwinnable Kobayashi Maru test is never explicitly referred to as a game, although it clearly alludes to the prisoner's dilemma,[5] the foundational experiment of mathematical game theory. In *Star Trek II: The Wrath of Khan*, this initial scene offers a clear example of a narrative strategy where the audience is tricked into thinking that what they are seeing is actually occurring within the fictional world, while the characters are in fact consciously taking part in a role-play scenario. An example of a similar, although possibly less unsettling, narrative device can be found in Banks' novel *The Player of Games* ([1988] 2012; see section 3.1), which opens with a battle scene that is later revealed to be a safe and leisurely activity that some of the protagonists of the novel conversationally refer to as a game.

In contrast, there are also deceptive fictional games where the characters of the narrative are not aware of having been enraptured in an artificial gameworld.

---

[5] The Kobayashi Maru test is portrayed as a problem-solving experiment in the fictional universe of Star Trek. In her 1989 novel *The Kobayashi Maru*, Ecklar presents four possible solutions to the problem posed in the test.

Whether through an impossibly elaborate performance or the use of deceptive technologies, several works of fiction feature characters that are trapped within a gameworld – characters that, in other words, are unaware that their existence has shifted and that they have become players of (or are being played into) an illusory scenario. In other cases, players become aware of the game's deception but – due to its consequences in terms of existential dread and epistemological instability –perceive themselves not as players but rather as subjects dealing with a distorted and unintelligible version of what was once their everyday existence. From this perspective, games assume a hallucinatory quality: what the characters see and experience is somewhat veridical in the sense that it is consistent with the phenomenological qualities of reality, but it is unexpected, incomprehensible or even monstrous. A parallel can thus be drawn between these deceptive fictional experiences and the experience of virtual reality. The work of philosopher Fiona MacPherson (2020) investigates the hallucinatory qualities of virtual reality environments and explicitly posits the veridical quality of virtual reality experiences in the sense that they, like the fictional games we investigate in this chapter, are supposed to be indistinguishable from actually lived experiences. The frequent association of deceptive fictional games with virtual reality technologies may be interpreted as reflecting the anxieties and fears found in popular discourses regarding the radical immersion offered by these technologies.

The episode 'Playtest' (Trachtenberg 2016) of the television series *Black Mirror* (2011–19) offers an example of this relationship between virtual reality technologies and deceptive games. In the episode, Cooper (Wyatt Russell), a young American tourist stranded in London, is unable to use his credit card to book a flight back to the United States. Therefore, to earn some money, he decides to participate in a playtest for the latest horror video game created by the elusive Japanese game designer Shou Saito (Ken Yamamura). The playtest begins with a neurotransmitter being embedded into the nape of Cooper's neck and directly wired to his synapses. He is then led into an abandoned manor and left there to confront his nightmares, which will manifest in the form of increasingly realistic and threatening holograms. The game pushes Cooper to the brink of insanity, causing him to be unable to distinguish reality from fiction and eventually trapping him in a spiral of nested, nightmarish realities. In the final sequence of the episode, the audience discovers that Cooper's test lasted only a fraction of a second because of a malfunction caused by interference from his phone. Cooper's nightmare playthrough, spanning the majority of the episode, was only a hallucination triggered by the game's powerful experimental technology – a neural interface capable of latching onto the player's memories and turning them into monsters that appear to be actual – and actually present – threats.

As is often the case with episodes of *Black Mirror*, 'Playtest' addresses a number of debates and anxieties concerning current technologies, with a particular focus on digital play and the blurring of the boundaries between virtuality and actuality. A face-value interpretation of 'Playtest' might frame the episode as a commentary on the digital games industry's obsession with realism. Notably, game industry professionals or commentators generally use 'realism' to denote the possibility for games to become indistinguishable from filmed images of the actual world. Thus, the creators of video games can be seen as striving for photo-realism rather than realism tout-court.[6] In 'Playtest', the fictional game seems to allude to the aspiration to provide a sense of phenomenological realism within virtual environments by creating artificial worlds in which physical sensations, social relations and, more generally, the user's bearing in the world are precisely mapped and rendered effectively indistinguishable from empirical reality. The fact that this creation is presented as a video game rather than as an experimental virtual reality experience serves as an intuitive shortcut linking the themes of the episode to the audience's existing knowledge about the tropes and expressive conventions of horror video games. The fictional video game that is being tested in 'Playtest' thus offers a proxy through which the episode can articulate a series of concerns over the inextricable meshing of the virtual and the actual, as well as the possibility for technology to fool our cognitive apparatus. This effect is achieved by leveraging a common-sense, if not precisely Gadamerian, understanding of games as deceptive and potentially addictive technologies. A similar discourse, although with notable differences, is showcased in a fictional game in the *Rick and Morty* episode 'Mortynight Run' (S2E02). This game, called *Roy: A Life Well Lived*, is the focus of our analysis in the following section.

4.1 *Roy: A Life Well Lived* (within the Machine)

Imagine a large vat on the table in a futuristic laboratory. Inside the vat, a disembodied human brain floats in some kind of liquid. The scientists running the laboratory use advanced computer technology to keep the brain alive and to

---

[6] Alexander R. Galloway (2006: 70–84) presents a convincing deconstruction of the notion of realism as it is currently applied to video games in his book, *Gaming: Essays on Algorithmic Culture*.

provide it with artificial input and sensations. For the brain in the vat, these artificial stimuli are indistinguishable from the ones that regular human bodies experience in their everyday engagement with the actual world. Additionally, in this hypothetical set-up, the laboratory's technology feeds the brain's output back into the advanced computer, giving the brain the possibility to interact with the simulated environment it perceives. In this imaginative scenario, the brain floating in the vat can be understood as effectively inhabiting a persistent, interconnected whole – an artificial world in the phenomenological sense. How can one know if the world one experiences on a daily basis is an artificial construct of this kind?

Hypothetical situations analogous to this one are common throughout the history of Western thought. The Socratic dialogues and the texts of the sceptics feature allegories and questions that are conceptually very similar to the thought experiment presented in the previous paragraph. In the Western tradition of thought, these propositions are often referred to as the 'brain-in-a-vat hypothesis' (or as the 'evil genius hypothesis', after René Descartes' ([1641] 2013) infamous argument in *Meditations on First Philosophy*). To be sure, comparable ideas have also emerged in non-Western cultural contexts such as Chinese Taoism and Vedic literature, where they also function as tools for thinking that assist people in maintaining a degree of suspicion towards the emotions and sensations we experience in our daily lives as embodied beings. They are philosophical fables that prompt us to question what we mean by 'reality' and what qualifies as an actual experience (Chalmers 2005).

Most of the imaginative scenarios mentioned to this point in the chapter invite us to consider whether the world of sensations and relationships that we experience on a daily basis could be an artifice or a hallucination of sorts. However, not all thought experiments that feature our brains being fed artificial or deceitful data and sensations serve this purpose. Philosopher Robert Nozick, for example, proposed the *Gedankenexperiment*, which is meant to raise questions concerning what we value in our existence and why. Nozick (1974) originally proposed this mental exercise, called 'The Experience Machine', in *Anarchy, State, and Utopia*, where he hypothesized the existence of a computer device capable of disclosing persistently immersive virtual experiences for the human being using it. In analogy with 'brain-in-a-vat' scenarios, one of the fundamental premises of 'The Experience Machine' is that Nozick's fictional machine is capable of producing sensations and feelings that are completely indistinguishable from those we experience in our everyday dealings with the actual world as human beings. More specifically, the fictional device imagined by

Nozick challenges the reader to envision having the technological possibility to override their everyday experiences with artificial ones designed to maximize their pleasure and satisfaction.

An important feature of Nozick's fictional machine is its requirement of existential commitment – the decision to plug into the experience machine is presented as irrevocable. One cannot, in other words, return to one's normal life after having plugged into the experience machine. This feature is obviously meant to add *gravitas* to the choice of whether to use the machine, which could otherwise be approached with the light-heartedness with which one decides to start playing a role-playing video game. Plugging into Nozick's machine, to put it simply, is not meant as technological escapism or temporary entertainment; rather, it is a decision with lasting existential implications and profound ethical repercussions. 'Plugging into the machine', Nozick (1974: 43) writes, 'is a kind of suicide'. Following the tradition of philosophical thought experiments, the part of *Anarchy, State, and Utopia* dedicated to 'The Experience Machine' culminates in Nozick (ibid.: 42) raising a focal question: if such a machine existed and if you could choose to permanently opt in to its solipsistic, pleasurable, artificial world, would you plug in and abandon the actual world?

In Nozick's text, plugging into the experience machine is presented as a voluntary decision – one that is related to one's perspectives and preferences on themes such as pleasure, satisfaction, self-realization and relatedness. Given the crucial existential significance and the irrevocability of the choice made concerning the experience machine, it might be counterintuitive and even problematic to conceptualize the fantastic contraption as a game. Similarly, we suspect that many would resist considering the 'brain-in-a-vat' thought experiment a playful scenario, especially in light of its deceitful set-up. In relation to the enthralling and deceitful capabilities of games discussed in the introduction to this chapter, following Gadamer's construction of games as beguiling devices, it is relevant to mention several works of fiction in which reality-supplanting technologies are explicitly presented as instruments of control, misdirection and abuse. Here, one cannot help but think of the experience-supplanting devices in Dick's 1969 science-fiction novel *UBIK* and in films like *Strange Days* (Bigelow 1995) and *The Matrix* (Wachowski and Wachowski 1999). Along with these dystopian works, there are also fictions in which experience machine-like devices feature as rather innocuous technologies for entertainment and escapism. Particularly worthy of mention among these are Green Peyton Wertenbaker's 1929 pioneering science-fiction short story 'The Chamber of Life', where the chamber in question is a fantastic experience-supplanting machine and the film

Total Recall (Verhoeven 1990), where the memory machines built by Recall Inc. are usually used to implant false recollections of vivid, pleasurable experiences in the minds of human subjects. Another similar case involves the fully immersive virtual reality pods in the fictional world of the video game *Fallout: New Vegas* (Obsidian Entertainment 2010).

Some experience-supplanting devices that are designed for entertainment and escapism are explicitly presented as games in their respective fictional worlds. This is the case, for example, for the video game *eXistenZ* in the film of same title (Cronenberg 1999; more on this in Chapter 5) and for *Roy: A Life Well Lived*, a virtual life-simulation video game that is played in the second episode of the second series of the animated television show *Rick and Morty* (Polcino 2015). Before specifically homing in on *Roy: A Life Well Lived*, we describe three particularly relevant examples of experience machines that are explicitly presented as fictional games:

1. American Cowboy Suit in Dick's ([1959] 2002) science-fiction short story 'War Game' – American Cowboy Suit is a prototype for an experience machine that is being tested in a laboratory to assess its safety and commercial suitability as a toy for children. When one of the lab technicians manages to squeeze into the child-sized suit, the game experientially dislocates him to the ancient American West. While wearing the suit, not only is he able to experience an interactive and life-like recreation of the American frontier – he is convinced that he is actually there. Moreover, he is convinced that he is a 10-year-old boy who lives in the Old West. To maintain this technologically enforced illusion, the suit feeds his brain with artificial experiences and edits and rearranges the dialogues he has with other technicians during the tests.

2. The Mind Game in Orson Scott Card's ([1985] 1994) science-fiction novel *Ender's Game* – The Mind Game is a fictional game that involves a highly advanced artificial intelligence. It is played at the Battle School in *Ender's Game* to analyse the personality and psychological traits of the students in a number of immersive, interactive scenarios. Through futuristic technology, the game is played directly in the mind of the player, with the settings of the game and the characters in the various scenarios changing depending on the player's in-game behaviour. Among the many minigames in The Mind Game package is the notoriously unfair and unwinnable 'Giant's Drink', which serves to test the player's perseverance in the face of an obviously impossible quest.

3. The *OASIS* in Ernest Cline's (2011) science-fiction novel *Ready Player One* – The *OASIS* (Ontologically Anthropocentric Sensory Immersive Simulation) is a massively multiplayer online simulation infrastructure that is part of the fictional world of *Ready Player One*. Advanced virtual reality gear allows an immersive life-like simulation of a shared immersive virtual reality universe.[7] The novel clarifies that, while the *OASIS* was initially devised as an online gaming platform, it gradually transitioned into being a multi-purpose, multi-user alternate universe that most of humanity (i.e. those who can afford to access it) inhabit and explore on a daily basis.

Like Nozick's experience machine, these three fictional devices are designed to be used in a way that is voluntary. Playing these fictional games presupposes awareness of the artificiality of the worlds to which they give interactive experiential access. In other words, none of those imaginative technologies is presented as beguiling in terms of how they supplant experiences from the actual world, even if phenomenological deception is clearly the central feature of their intended functioning. Unlike the device in Nozick's thought experiment, however, American Cowboy Suit, The Mind Game and the *OASIS* do not impose an all-or-nothing kind of existential commitment on their users. One does not need to opt in to these virtual worlds for the rest of their biological life; these fictional games can be enjoyed in a temporary and often carefree fashion. In analogy with pastimes, games and video games, the minigames in The Mind Game package and the interactive worlds and sub-worlds of the *OASIS* can be accessed and exited at will. In contrast to Nozick's machine, in other words, The Mind Game and the *OASIS* are always experienced predominantly as devices. Regardless of how immersive and phenomenologically granular the experiences afforded by these technologies are, the characters plugged into them are constantly aware of their virtual constitution.[8]

As a fictional device, American Cowboy Suit falls in the conceptual space between Nozick's experience machine and the playful use of experience-supplanting technology that characterizes the *OASIS* and The Mind Game. The

---

[7] A similar case and in many ways a progenitor of the *OASIS* can be found in the idea of the 'metaverse' in Neal Stephenson's 1992 science-fiction novel *Snow Crash*, which offers a vision of how a virtual reality-based Internet might evolve in a technologically advanced future. Resembling a massively multiplayer online video game, the virtual world of the metaverse is populated by avatars controlled by human users and by artificial intelligences known as 'daemons' (jargon drawn from the UNIX operating system).

[8] For a detailed treatment of this 'double perspectival stance' of the player, see Gualeni and Vella (2020: 12–19, 26).

artificial experience of being a child on the American frontier is supposed to be voluntarily chosen and impermanent, but one is not aware of the artificiality of the situation (and cannot remember who one actually is) after being 'plugged in'. *Roy: A Life Well Lived* occupies the same ambiguous position as American Cowboy Suit, and this ambiguity is particularly interesting for us in the context of this book. We chose the fictional game of *Roy: A Life Well Lived* for in-depth analysis over American Cowboy Suit here simply because of the popularity of *Rick and Morty*; we believed that this selection would be more likely to resonate with our readers compared with a relatively obscure short story written in the 1950s.

As mentioned above, *Roy: A Life Well Lived* is a single-player virtual life simulation video game that appears in the animated television series *Rick and Morty* (S2E02 – 'Mortynight Run'). In the game, the player assumes the role of Roy Parsons, a male human child living in middle-class American suburbia in the 1960s. To be more accurate, the player does not just *assume the role* of Roy Parsons; the player *is* Roy Parsons. In a way that is analogous to American Cowboy Suit, the machine providing the experience in *Roy: A Life Well Lived* is capable of convincing the user that they are in fact a child (Roy, in this case) and that their previous existence was nothing more than a long, vivid dream from the night before.

The status of *Roy: A Life Well Lived* as a game in the fictional world of *Rick and Morty* is made obvious by its being played in an intergalactic arcade and by its being directly addressed as a game within the fiction. It also shares a number of traits that are typically associated with arcade video games, further clarifying the context of leisure and unseriousness in which the machine is encountered. Specifically, *Roy: A Life Well Lived* is coin-operated, it invites spectatorship by means of its otherwise unnecessary display (see Figure 4.2) and it features a score that gives some measure of player performance (partially quantified in the number of years that the player manages to live as Roy). It is also revelatory that players are rewarded for their in-game performance with arcade redemption tickets.

In *Roy: A Life Well Lived*, players interactively experience Roy's life from childhood to death, making all kinds of decisions for their new, artificial self and overcoming difficulties along the way. The duration of a lifetime in the machine seems to correspond to only a few minutes in the wider fictional world of *Rick and Morty*. In the process, the arcade machine adjusts the simulated, fictional world to account for the decisions of the player. However, the criteria for in-game success and victory conditions for *Roy: A Life Well Lived* are not explicitly presented in the episode.

Figure 4.2 A frame taken from the episode 'Mortynight Run' of the animated series *Rick and Morty* capturing Rick Sanchez playing *Roy: A Life Well Lived*. The social context of the pan-galactic arcade hall and its orientation towards entertainment and performativity is evident in this figure, with the spectator-friendly screen showing the game progress while the active player lies unconscious in their seat. © Cartoon Network, Inc 2013. All rights reserved.

In which sense does *Roy: A Life Well Lived* fit in between Nozick's hypothetical machine and the playful fictional devices conceptualized by Card and Cline? Like The Mind Game and the *OASIS*, *Roy: A Life Well Lived* is presented in *Rick and Morty*'s fictional universe as a playful technology. What we mean here is that after engaging with any of these machines the player returns to their ordinary experiential context (i.e. the 'actual' world) without the burden of serious or long-lasting psychological or existential consequences. *Roy: A Life Well Lived* even appears to be potentially educational and could possibly lead to the development of new skills, perspectives and critical capabilities. Plugging into the playful machine shown in the 'Mortynight Run' episode thus cannot be considered 'a kind of suicide'. Instead, it could more fittingly be compared to other voluntary activities that have the potential to lead to personal revelations and developments, such as practicing meditation, mountaineering, taking music lessons or undergoing psychotherapy, for instance.

Although *Roy: A Life Well Lived* does not require the totalizing kind of commitment that characterizes Nozick's experience machine, commonalities between the two machines can nevertheless clearly be identified. To achieve their intended experiential effects, for example, both fictional devices must rely on the suppression and reframing of past memories. Nozick is not forthcoming about what happens to one's actual memories when they are plugged into his machine, but it is only logical to conclude that the machine's technology must temporarily suppress and alter a significant portion of an individual's own past recollections to allow the machine to produce the desired effects. These memories must include, among other things, the knowledge that one decided to use the machine, walked up to the machine, input one's own preferences and plugged in. As mentioned above, in the case of *Roy: A Life Well Lived*, memories and experiences leading up to plugging into the machine are experientially framed as a vivid dream the player had the night before waking up as Roy (thus making them unreliable and ultimately irrelevant). Notably, however, similar to the case with Nozick's machine, the player's experience of being Roy is not lived as a playful or unserious situation while the experience itself is unfolding. Both machines deceive their users, causing them to believe that they are experiencing a genuine lifeworld when they are actually in an artificial, single-player playground (see Gualeni 2017). In this sense, *Roy: A Life Well Lived* is an interesting compromise – an experience machine that neither allows for the awareness of an external world nor requires a long-term existential commitment. It thus offers the best of both archetypes of experience machines, as a device that – from the outside – invites a playful approach while – from the inside – is existentially and experientially totalizing.

Roy: A Life Well Lived, we believe, does not qualify as a particularly effective thematic device for the series in which it appears. It does not add crucial detail to the context of the narrative, as the *Rick and Morty* series is already bursting with fictional, advanced technological devices of all kinds (e.g. time-reversing machines, dimension-crossing portals, memory-supplanting apparatuses and cloning vats). In the fictional world of *Rick and Morty*, the encounter with the machine is not central to the plot; the segment where the game is shown is tangential to the episode and is inconsequential to the plot development. In short, the game is narratively trivial. Interpreted as a philosophical thought experiment, *Roy: A Life Well Lived* is also rather vapid; the question of 'How would you conduct your existence as a middle-class teenage boy in 1960s American suburbia?' is at the same time broad to the point of intractability and painfully narrow, being confined to the possibilities of a specific individual – Roy Parsons. It is not necessary to go out on a limb to qualify this scenario as rather uninteresting in terms of the development of philosophical thinking. If all our observations concerning the game are correct and agreeable with, what good is *Roy: A Life Well Lived* as a fictional device and a fictional game? What purpose does it serve?

In Chapter 1 of this book, we discussed the idea that fictional games can play a relevant role in a work of fiction in a number of different ways. Among the various functions that these games can fulfil, we listed their use for 'indirect characterization' (i.e. as narrative devices that allow the audience to observe and increase their familiarization with certain fictional characters). As indirect characterization tools, games played in works of fiction (and fictional games in particular) offer the audience new information about characters in their roles as players. In this context, fiction appreciators can discover previously inaccessible traits of fictional characters such as how strictly they adhere to arbitrary rules, how aggressive they are in the pursuit of their objectives, how much they take the feelings of others into consideration during gameplay or how they psychologically respond to luck, victory and defeat.

Thus, the narrative function of *Roy: A Life Well Lived* is duplicitous. As mentioned above, this fictional game reaffirms the fact that *Rick and Morty* is set in a universe full of wildly imaginative contraptions where anything is possible. It also casts new light on character traits of the two protagonists in their unusual roles as players of a life-simulation game. In this new context, the audience is exposed to information about aspects of these characters' personalities that might rarely come through in other circumstances. The way Morty plays Roy is for the most part successful in terms of outcomes such as athletic accomplishments, job stability and quality of relationships, but Rick criticizes Morty's approach for being too attached to social norms and canons. Rick's game, in contrast, is as eccentric and caricatural as Rick himself and provides additional detail regarding the character's nihilistic traits and self-destructive tendencies.

As a final note, it should be noted that *Roy: A Life Well Lived* is played in the fictional universe of *Rick and Morty*, where time and space can be technologically manipulated, the boundaries between universes are permeable and the continuity of personal identity is often no more than a formality. The fictional game's role within the fiction can thus be also understood as one of ironic reversal – in the technologically advanced universe of *Rick and Morty*, the escapist fantasies of fictional characters are about living the conventional and mundane life of a regular man in a technologically primitive world.

4.2 Being played by *The Game*

Most of the examples of deceptive games presented so far in this chapter involve the use of advanced technology. In works of fiction, virtual worlds are often used as narrative devices that tap into our anxieties regarding an increasingly technologically mediated existence. These technologically advanced games imply that our empirical reality could one day be smoothly and perhaps deceptively replaced by digital alternatives. These new realities could, then, be maliciously harnessed as tools for manipulation and oppression. Futuristic virtual reality gear, fictional neurological implants and persistently habitable digital spaces often contribute to projecting a future in which a technologically enforced magic circle could constitute a threat to our present understanding of personal identity, sense of reality and existential autonomy.

The film *The Game* is an interesting exception to the use of gameworlds in works of fiction outlined above. Fincher's film does not rely, in fact, on futuristic brain interfaces or computer-generated deceptions. Set in contemporary San Francisco, *The Game* portrays an expansive and pervasive game that subverts its sole player's sense of reality by making him unable to distinguish between the game and his ordinary life. In the film, Nicholas Van Orton (Michael Douglas), heir to a financial empire, lives an overindulged, risk-free existence. Nicholas is presented to the audience as a self-centred and emotionally detached middle-aged man – in the opening scenes, he purposely avoids responding to people wishing him a happy birthday. He is shown to be extraordinarily effective in his job of administering his family's enormous wealth. Nicholas' brother Conrad (Sean Penn), in contrast, is a former drug addict who is presented throughout the film as unreliable and manipulative. As a birthday gift, Conrad signs Nicholas up for a 'game' organized by a mysterious company known as Consumer Recreation Services (CRS). From that moment onwards, Nicholas faces an increasingly unexpected and dangerous series of events. He interprets some of these events – for example, finding a mysterious key in the mouth of a puppet – as part of CRS' game, but others – such as being drugged and shipped to Mexico without money or his passport – convince him that he has fallen prey to an elaborate con aimed at depriving him of his wealth. In the final scene of the film, feeling hopelessly trapped, Nicholas jumps off a building, only to fall through a fake-glass window and land on a safety mattress. The whole of Nicholas' existential nightmare is revealed to have actually been a baroquely elaborate game, organized by Conrad with the intent of reconnecting with his estranged brother.

The Game is often cited as an example of a puzzle film, a relatively successful sub-genre of Hollywood cinema in the 1990s and the early years of the twenty-first century. The notion of puzzle films was introduced by Buckland (2009: 1) to describe films, usually psychological thrillers, that 'reject classical storytelling techniques and replace them with complex storytelling'. By 'complex storytelling',

Buckland refers to stories that involve elements such as multiple planes of reality, several interwoven narrative threads and unreliable or dishonest narrators. These films also often present protagonists who, because of permanent mental issues or temporary altered states, tend to see reality as malleable and uncertain, thus forcing the viewer to question the reliability of what is being presented as true and accurate within the narrative. In *Memento* (2000), for example, Leonard Shelby (Guy Pearce) suffers from short-term memory loss. The character's condition, coupled with the film's narrative, which proceeds in reverse, starting with the final climax and moving towards the beginning of the plot, forces the viewer to perform significant cognitive labour to reconstruct a semblance of narrative consistency. Although Nicholas Van Orton does not suffer from mental illness, the effects of the combination of traumatic events – which include having being drugged – render his world view unstable and unreliable, placing him in the canon of 'central characters whose mental condition is extreme, unstable, or pathological' (Elsaesser 2009: 14). Seeing the fictional world through the eyes of Shelby or Van Orton, the viewer needs to split their effort in terms of making coherent sense of the situation by interpreting the film's narrative (e.g. by decoding the characters' motivations and following plot threads) while simultaneously engaging with the complexities of the narrative structure engendered by the presence of a fundamentally unreliable protagonist (Kiss and Willemsen 2017). These films are known as 'puzzle films' precisely because they ask the viewer to find and arrange the pieces of a disjointed, reticent, contradictory or overly complex narrative.

The success of films such as *The Game*, as well as critics' and audiences' general approval of their unconventional narrative strategies, has been ascribed by some commentators to these films' kinship with the forking narratives of contemporary video games. Puzzle films, the argument goes, are geared towards consumption by an audience that has absorbed complex, multi-threaded narratives by playing video games. According to Elsaesser (2021), puzzle films or 'mind game films', as they are called in his texts, share with video games the notion of assigning a degree of agency to the appreciator. In the case of video games, this manifests in the player being able to intervene in the game's plot, whereas puzzle films make this process closer to engaging with a thought experiment (see ibid.: 247; Elgin 2007). In other words, the audience is invited to interpret puzzle films such as *The Game* as a specific type of logic-based game played by mentally tying together the threads of a complex and enigmatic narrative. As we argued in Chapter 1, playful interaction between the author and the appreciator of a work of fiction is typical of literary genres such as the detective or espionage story, where untangling the complexities of the plot or avoiding narrative distractions such as red herrings and MacGuffins can be framed as a game of logic played by the reader.

The fictional game in *The Game*, interpreted as a game of this kind, offers some degree of resistance; it asks the viewer to 'solve' it but often fails to provide the clues necessary for them to do so, eventually casting the viewer into a position of self-doubt akin to that of the protagonist. In Elsaesser's (2021: 24) words, 'these films play with our perception of reality, which connects with manipulation and deception: an important aspect of narration, but also a feature that creates scepticism and (self-)doubt at an epistemological level, while alternating between trust and cynicism on a moral level'.

It is unsurprising, then, that *Sight and Sound*'s review of *The Game* defined Fincher's film as 'a rewarding spectator sport' (Strick 1997: 42), acknowledging the playful engagement required of the viewer of this and similar puzzle films. In the case of *The Game*, however, the viewer is not the only subject playing. According to Elsaesser (2009: 14), among puzzle films, 'there are films where it is the audience that is played games with, because certain crucial information is withheld or ambiguously presented', but there are also 'films in which a character is being played games with, without knowing it or without knowing who it is that is playing these (often very cruel and even deadly) games with him (or her)'. *The Game* is a rare case of a film that is puzzling in both senses: the viewer is invited to play with the film's perplexing narrative, and the protagonist himself is trapped in a deceptive game that progressively takes over his existence. Whereas the literature about puzzle films usually focuses on the viewer's experience or on the narrative devices and strategies used to create complex narratives, in this book about fictional games, we analyse the game that the fictional character of Nicholas Van Orton is playing (or being played by). In other words, we are not trying to describe or interpret the experience the film designs for its viewer; rather, we aim to analyse the characteristics of the fictional game found in *The Game* and its effects on its single fictional player.

Another game-like feature of Van Orton's nightmarish journey is the establishment of a ludic contract of sorts between Nicholas and CRS. After receiving the gift of a game organized by CRS from his brother Conrad, Nicholas, as instructed, drives to CRS' offices and learns that to be able to participate in the game he needs to sign a consent form and then take a series of physical and cognitive assessments. Nicholas is asked questions about his attitudes and habits, undergoes medical checks with a physician and is asked to watch a montage of disturbing and apparently unrelated images. This battery of tests, whose seeming futility baffles Nicholas, will eventually be revealed to already be part of the game.

Fictional Games as Deceptions and Hallucinations 137

Figure 4.3 In this frame, Nicholas Van Orton (Michael Douglas) signs the contract that initiates the game that will lead him to the brink of insanity in David Fincher's 1997 film *The Game*. © Propaganda Films 1997. All rights reserved.

At this point, Nicholas is unaware that, by signing a contract with CRS, he has participated in establishing a magic circle whose boundaries will be constantly challenged and reassessed throughout the film. In fact, a few days after completing the tests, Nicholas receives a phone call from CRS to inform him that he did not pass the tests and that his game will therefore not take place. That same night, when arriving home from work, Nicholas finds an ominous puppet in his backyard and a key marked with the CRS logo. This set of ambiguous messages reinforces Nicholas' epistemological confusion over the extent of CRS' game. Has it started or not? How far will it reach into his life? The game played by Nicholas (or, again, by which Nicholas is played) is properly Gadamerian, as discussed in the introductory section of this chapter: it holds the player under its 'spell', stripping him of his agency to leave the game at will (see Figure 4.3).

Unbeknownst to him, Nicholas is entering into a new relationship with the actual world presented in the fiction. By participating in the game, he is forced to take on several different social roles, all of which differ significantly from his usual role of successful businessman. Gary Alan Fine (1983: 205), who was among the first scholars to discuss the cultural and social implications of role-playing, describes this activity as 'role-taking'. According to Fine, when starting a role-playing session, players enter a mental and social frame[9] that is constructed

---

[9] In using the term 'frame', Fine refers to the theoretical approach proposed by Goffman (1956), who claims that social interactions among humans happen within frames that orient and inform behaviours and attitudes. One is supposed to behave differently within the frame of a party and within that of a work meeting. Similarly, role-playing games can be said to establish specific types of temporary frames, whose social rules and norms are negotiated by players in advance and then upheld in their interpretation of the various characters.

ad hoc for the play session (refer also to the notion of 'en-roling' proposed by Gualeni and Vella 2020: 25–36). Within the frame proposed by the game, players are asked to take up certain roles that can be (and often are) shaped by very different constraints and needs compared with their customary roles in everyday social life. Under normal circumstances, players of role-playing games voluntarily choose to adopt a ludic subjectivity (see Vella 2015), but Nicholas is forced, through the game's deception, to become someone else.

Throughout the game, he progressively loses his self-confidence and becomes more doubtful of his ability to think rationally. Eventually, Nicholas finds himself destitute when all his savings are withdrawn from his bank accounts and he is stranded in Mexico. This transformation is signalled in the film by Nicholas constantly needing to change outfits; his usual suit and tie are replaced by increasingly more casual – and less explicitly class-signalling – clothing. Later in the film, Nicholas ends up wearing the same stained and worn-out suit for days. The change in outfits and demeanour is a clear indication that the protagonist is moving away from his usual role and gradually (albeit unwillingly) taking up a new one as the game progresses.

The Game's peculiar brand of role-playing, rather than being played around a table or in front of a computer, is enacted in real life. What Fine described as the frame of the game is not a cognitive construct that players uphold via an improvised narrative, but a situation generated by a series of rules and prescriptions imposed upon Nicholas' empirical reality. Nicholas the businessman and Nicholas the victim exist in the same reality, and this superimposition of selves prompts feelings of confusion and profound self-doubt. Conrad's intent to mitigate his brother's aloofness and elitism, revealed in the film's finale as the goal of the game, is obtained through a process of traumatic role-taking. 'I had to do something. You were becoming such an asshole,' Conrad reveals to Nicholas in the closing sequence of the film, but what makes this traumatic change effective is the fact that the game takes place within (and gradually substitutes for) Nicholas' ordinary life. From this perspective, CRS' game can be described through the lens of a particular kind of pervasive game (Montola, Stenros and Waern 2009) generally defined as a live action role-playing game (LARP). LARPs[10] are role-playing games played in the real world, with players generally assuming specific roles and performing these roles for the length of the game, which can last from a few hours to several days. In Fincher's film, everyone except Nicholas is effectively LARPing – all the characters

---

[10] An account of the history and characteristics of LARPs, especially those played in Scandinavia and other Nordic countries, is offered by Stenros and Montola (2010).

that Nicholas encounters are in fact actors hired to play a role within the game – with Nicholas left unable discern whether what he is experiencing is part of a game or not.[11] The specific kind of deception enacted by the game forces Nicholas to consider whether he is the player of a pervasive game that 'appropriate[s] objects, vehicles, and properties of the physical world' (ibid.: 12) or whether he is literally being played by the game. Nicholas initially tries to solve this epistemic conundrum by anchoring his notion of what a game is (or should be) to it being physically safe for the players. In a pivotal sequence in the film, Nicholas is dumped into the sea while locked in a taxi; as the car sinks and he tries desperately to break free, he keeps repeating to himself 'It's just a game'. The implication here is that games – no matter how extreme or scary – must ensure some degree of physical safety for their players. Nicholas intuitively seems to subscribe to a somewhat classical theory of play that frames it as a safe activity, free of consequences and essentially innocuous;[12] such an assumption is often challenged, or at least deconstructed, in pervasive role-playing games such as LARPs. While rarely putting the players at risk of substantial physical harm, LARPs often seem to tread the line between safety and danger. LARPs can engender radical emotional distress by putting players into traumatic situations. This is referred to by Stenros and Sihvonen (2019) as the 'affective labor' of a LARP. As they are enacted in the real world, LARPs also inevitably put players at risk of physical harm. This is generally perceived as one of the specific pleasures of this form of play for players, who willingly engage in a style of play that may involve real-life consequences. Mochocki (2020: 186) describes this tendency towards potentially dangerous play as the predisposition of LARP players towards 'embracing the risk'.[13] Despite not actively or voluntarily

---

[11] One may speculate that Van Orton's brother and ex-wife are not paid as actors to be part of the game. Nevertheless, these individuals are tasked with playing roles that, at least to some degree, are distorted versions of their actual selves. Conrad must act as if he is spinning out of control, although the film suggests he has actually gotten his life back on track; Nicholas' ex-wife is supposed to be surprised when he appears at her door, even though it is safe to assume that, being part of the game, she would have been informed of this eventuality.

[12] Nicholas repeating to himself that no physical harm can come from the experience is a way to ground the viewer's perception of the events as being part of a game. Throughout the film, this perception is alternatively reinforced and questioned to exacerbate ambiguities in the narrative and to magnify the epiphanic effects of the final scene. This narrative strategy is often articulated by using the possibility of bodily harm as the deciding factor for the nature of the events. In a scene in the film, Nicholas finds himself trapped in a room while a hail of bullets fly through the windows. This escalation of potential physical harm is supposed to tilt the viewer's perception of Nicholas' predicament towards it being real.

[13] Mochocki attributes this paradoxical interest in physical harm within a ludic context to a current in LARPing culture that is generally described as 'immersionism'. This current argues in favour of the idea that LARPs should provide as high a degree of immersion as possible and maximize the psychological – and potentially physical – effects of the game on its players. Immersionist LARPs often portray traumatic situations as a way of encouraging the player to reflect on their own traumas or on certain political or social situations.

embracing the risk of physical harm, by being subjected to physical abuse – which, we will later learn, was always mitigated by a series of invisible measures to protect Nicholas' safety – Nicholas experiences the peculiar ludic pleasures of LARPing (or, more aptly, being 'LARPed'), which consist of not being able to tell where the game ends and where actual social interaction begins.

In the final scenes of *The Game*, Nicholas is trapped on the roof of a building, holding a loaded handgun, convinced that he is being pursued by armed security guards. When the door to the rooftop finally opens, potentially allowing the guards to capture or kill him, Nicholas shoots, in a desperate attempt to fight back, only to find that behind the door is his brother Conrad, holding a bottle of champagne to celebrate the end of the game. Overwhelmed by guilt, Nicholas jumps off the roof but finds himself on a mattress in the middle of a ballroom, where his friends – and Conrad, still dripping with fake blood – are waiting for him. This event marks the actual end of the game for Nicholas, and the scenes that follow this revelation, in which Nicholas talks with his friends, congratulates the actors on their performance and splits the exorbitant bill with Conrad, act as an instance of 'de-roling' for the character. Gualeni, Vella and Harrington (2017; see also Gualeni and Vella 2020: 25–36), describe de-roling as a set of techniques for cooling down and removing one's fictional subjectivity that can be beneficial after experiences that involve a form of role-taking (such as acting, professional training, dramatherapy or long sessions of role-playing). In other words, at the end of a game in which players must maintain a role, it is useful, these scholars claim, to establish a distance from that role through a series of debriefing and disrobing techniques. This is particularly relevant in LARPs, in which players enact a fictional role for a long stretch of time and with a significant degree of psychological investment, without the ability to temporarily step out of character.

The final scenes of *The Game* show Nicholas undergoing a sort of de-roling process that involves revisiting some of the events of the game with the actors who were present in them and using this action as a way to signal his personal evolution (or becoming 'less of an asshole') triggered by the traumatic experience of the game. When Nicholas steps out of the role of the victimized, powerless object of an elaborate con, he regains some of his original demeanour (despite having just fallen through a glass ceiling), but he also shows traits that were not present in his pre-game persona. He reconnects with his brother, promises to call his ex-wife more often, apologizes to a former business partner and pursues one of the performers in the game with what seem to be authentic romantic intentions. Although these conventions fall into the canon of a traditional happy ending to a moral tale of sorts, they also signal the re-establishment of the safety and discernibility of the game. The borders of the magic circle are now clearly delineated, and play is once again separated from 'real life'.

4.3 Conclusions

In this chapter, we looked at fictional games that act as deceptive devices and that *play their players* rather than being played by them. We analysed various examples, distinguishing them on the basis of the degree to which they take over their players' lives. Games such as the simple augmented reality video game in the *Star Trek: The Next Generation* episode discussed in the introduction to this chapter can be described, employing a metaphor first used by Gadamer, as spellbinding machines. These games, without performing a totalizing takeover of the lived experience of their players, captivate the players' attention to the point of controlling their will. The players of these games are often absorbed in them to a pathological degree, but they are still fully capable of sensorily distinguishing their own empirical reality from the one disclosed by the game. Other deceptive fictional games fully replace the reality of their players through radical immersive strategies. The interactive experiences with games such as the one described in the *Black Mirror* episode 'Playtest' are not perceived by their players as ludic, as the borders separating play and real life are blurred to the point of indistinguishability. Within works of fiction, these games are generally portrayed as insidious technologies, but there are cases, such as that seen in the novel *Ready Player One*, where the complete sensory engagement with an artificial reality is a desired effect of advanced game technologies.

As the first focal game for this chapter, we discussed *Roy: A Life Well Lived*, a single-player virtual life-simulation video game that appears in the animated television series *Rick and Morty*. In this game, the player assumes the role of Roy Parsons, a male, human child living in middle-class American suburbia in the 1960s. This game was used as an example of a deceptive technology that, in the narrative of the episode, is openly and exclusively used for entertainment purposes. This discussion also allowed us to explore different examples of leisure-focused 'experience machines' and to compare their roles in works of fiction on the basis of the existential investment they demand from their players.

The second focal game for this chapter was in Fincher's film *The Game*, where a wealthy man is trapped inside an apparently deadly pervasive game. In this case, the synthetic reality projected by a deceptive game is not found within a virtual reality environment but is produced by manipulating the player's empirical reality through an elaborate series of schemes and plots. To analyse the characteristics of *The Game*'s deceptive game, we used some of the theoretical tools developed to understand LARPs, a kind of pervasive role-playing game that may involve upsetting – and even traumatizing – experiences. The protagonist of *The Game* is the object rather than the player of this pervasive game and is thus played by the labyrinthine machinations of its creators.

References

Allen, C. (1991, 28 October), [TV series episode] 'The Game', season 5, episode 6, in G. Roddenberry and R. Berman, executive producers, *Star Trek: The Next Generation*, Paramount Domestic Television.

Banks, I. M. ([1988] 2012), *The Player of Games*, New York: Orbit.

Bigelow, K. (1995), [Film] *Strange Days*, 20th Century Fox.

Brown, D. (2015), 'Games and the Magic Circle', in N. Lee (ed.), *Encyclopedia of Computer Graphics and Games*, New York: Springer. Available online: https://link.springer.com/referenceworkentry/10.1007/978-3-319-08234-9_32-1?noAccess=true (accessed 18 May 2022).

Buckland, W. (2009), 'Introduction: Puzzle Plots', in W. Buckland (ed.), *Puzzle Films: Complex Storytelling in Contemporary Cinema*, Chichester: Wiley & Blackwell: 1–13.

Card, O. S. ([1985] 1994), *Ender's Game*, New York: TOR.

Cerny, C., S. Hatters Friedman and D. Smith (2014), 'Television's "Crazy Lady" Trope: Female Psychopathic Traits, Teaching, and Influence of Popular Culture', *Acad Psychiatry*, 38: 233–41.

Chalmers, D. J. (2005), 'The Matrix as Metaphysics', *Philosophers Explore the Matrix*, Oxford: Oxford University Press: 132–76.

Cline, E. (2011), *Ready Player One*, New York: Broadway Books.

Consalvo, M. (2009), 'There is No Magic Circle', *Games and Culture*, 4 (4): 408–17.

Cover, R. (2006), 'Gaming (Ad)diction: Discourse, Identity, Time and Play in the Production of the Gamer Addiction Myth', *Game Studies*, 6 (1).

Cronenberg, D. (1999), [Film] *eXistenZ*, scriptwriter David Cronenberg, Alliance Atlantis.

Csikszentmihalyi, M. (1990), *Flow: The Psychology of Optimal Experience*, New York: Harper & Row.

Descartes, R. ([1641] 2013), *René Descartes: Meditations on First Philosophy – With Selections from the Objections and Replies*, Cambridge, MA: Cambridge University Press.

Dick, P. K. ([1959] 2002), 'War Game', in *The Minority Report and Other Classic Stories*, New York: Kensington Publishing, loc. 3913–4283.

Dick, P. K. ([1969] 2012), *UBIK*, Boston, MA: Mariner Books.

Dow-Schüll, N. (2014), *Addiction by Design: Machine Gambling in Las Vegas*, Cambridge, MA: The MIT Press.

Ecklar, J. (1989), *The Kobayashi Maru*, New York: Pocket Books.

Elgin, C. 2007, 'The Laboratory of the Mind', in W. Huemer, J. Gibson and L. Pocci (eds), *A Sense of the World: Essays on Fiction, Narrative, and Knowledge*, New York: Routledge: 43–54.

Elsaesser, T. (2009), 'The Mind-Game Film', in W. Buckland (ed.), *Puzzle Films: Complex Storytelling in Contemporary Cinema*, Chichester: Wiley & Blackwell: 13–41.

Elsaesser, T. (2021), *The Mind-Game Film: Distributed Agency, Time Travel and Productive Pathology*, New York and London: Routledge.

Fassone, R. (2017), *Every Game is an Island: Endings and Extremities in Video Games*, New York: Bloomsbury.

Fincher, D. (1997), [Film] *The Game*, scriptwriters John Brancato and Michael Ferris, Propaganda Films.

Fine, G. A. (1983), *Shared Fantasy: Role-Playing Games as Social Worlds*, Chicago, IL: University of Chicago Press.

Gadamer H.-G. ([1960] 2013), *Truth and Method*, New York: Bloomsbury.

Galloway, A. R. (2006), *Gaming: Essays on Algorithmic Culture*, Minneapolis, MN: University of Minnesota Press.

Goffman, E. (1956), *The Presentation of Self in Everyday Life*, New York, NY: Doubleday.

Griffiths, M. D., D. J. Kuss and D. L. King (2012), 'Video Game Addiction: Past, Present and Future', *Current Psychiatry Reviews*, 8 (4): 308–18.

Gualeni, S. (2017), 'Virtual *Weltschmerz*: Things to Keep in Mind While Building Experience Machines and Other Tragic Technologies', in M. Silcox (ed.), *Experience Machines: The Philosophy of Virtual Worlds*, London: Rowman and Littlefield International, 113–33.

Gualeni, S. and N. Van de Mosselaer (2021), 'Ludic Unreliability and Deceptive Game Design', *Journal of the Philosophy of Games*, 3 (1).

Gualeni, S. and D. Vella (2020), *Virtual Existentialism: Meaning and Subjectivity in Virtual Worlds*, Basingstoke: Palgrave Pivot.

Gualeni, S., D. Vella and J. Harrington (2017), 'De-Roling from Experiences and Identities in Virtual Worlds', *Journal of Virtual World Research*, 10 (2).

Huizinga, J. ([1938] 1955), *Homo Ludens: A Study of the Play-Element in Culture*, Boston, MA: Beacon Press.

Kiss, M. and S. Willemsen (2017), *Impossible Puzzle Films: A Cognitive Approach to Contemporary Complex Cinema*, Edinburgh: Edinburgh University Press.

MacPherson, F. (2020), 'Is Virtual Reality Experience Veridical, Illusory or Hallucinatory? A Complex Answer Based on a New Theory of Illusion and Hallucination and the Nature of the Technology Used to Create Virtual Reality', Working Paper, University of Glasgow.

Mochocki, M. (2020), 'Rhetorics and Mechanics of Player Safety in the Nordic-American Larp Discourse', *Homo Ludens*, 1 (13): 180–202.

Montola, M., J. Stenros and A. Waern (2009), *Pervasive Games, Theory and Design: Experiences on the Boundary between Life and Play*, Boca Raton, FL: CRC Press.

Neely, E. L. (2021), 'Come for the Game, Stay for the Cash Grab: The Ethics of Loot Boxes, Microtransactions, and Freemium Games', *Games and Culture*, 16 (2): 228–47.

Nolan, C. (2000), [Film] *Memento*, Summit Entertainment, Team Todd.

Nozick, R. (1974), *Anarchy, State, and Utopia*, New York: Basic Books.

Obsidian Entertainment (2010), [Digital game] *Fallout: New Vegas*, directed by J. Sawyer and published by Bethesda Softworks.

Polcino, D. (2015, 2 August), [TV series episode] 'Mortynight Run', season 2, episode 2, in D. Harmon, J. Roiland, J. A. Fino and J. Russo, executive producers, *Rick and Morty*, Warner Bros. Television Distribution.

Rheingold, H. (1991), *Virtual Reality*, New York: Summit Books.

Roiland, J. and D. Harmon (2013–present), [Animated series] *Rick and Morty*, USA: Warner Bros. Television Distribution.

Salen, K. and E. Zimmerman (2003), *Rules of Play: Game Design Fundamentals*, Cambridge, MA: The MIT Press.

Schrank, B. (2014), *Avant-Garde Videogames: Playing with Technoculture*, Cambridge, MA: The MIT Press.

Soderman, B. (2021), *Against Flow: Video Games and the Flowing Subject*, Cambridge, MA: The MIT Press.

Stenros, J. and T. Sihvonen (2019), 'Queer while Larping: Community, Identity and Affective Labor in Nordic Live-Action Role-Playing', *Analog Game Studies*, 8 (2).

Stenros, J. and M. Montola (eds) (2010), *Nordic Larp*, Stockholm: Fea Livia.

Stephenson, N. (1992), *Snow Crash*, New York: Penguin Books.

Strick, P. (1997), 'The Game', *Sight and Sound*, 7 (11): 41.

Trachtenberg, D. (2016, 21 October), [TV series episode] 'Playtest', season 3, episode 2, in A. Jones and C. Brooker, executive producers, *Black Mirror*, Zappotron, House of Tormorrow.

Vaughn, C. (2021), *Questland*, Boston, MA: Mariner Books.

Vella, D. (2015), 'The Ludic Subject and the Ludic Self: Investigating the 'I-in-the Gameworld', PhD diss., IT University of Copenhagen.

Wachowski, L. and L. Wachowski (1999), [Film] *The Matrix*, Warner Bros.

Zimmerman, E. (2012), [Blogpost] 'Jerked Around by the Magic Circle – Clearing the Air Ten Years Later', *Game Developer*, published 7 February. Available online: https://www.gamedeveloper.com/design/jerked-around-by-the-magic-circle---clearing-the-air-ten-years-later (accessed 18 May 2022).

5

Fictional Games and Transcendence

The previous chapter focused on the ambiguity and permeability that often characterize the boundaries separating gameworlds from the seriousness and irrevocability of the actual world. The present chapter pursues a somewhat similar theme, concentrating on a particular relationship between the activity of play and everyday existence. Specifically, the chapter analyses fictional games that function explicitly as transformative tools for their (fictional) players. In discussing games in terms of their capability to promote and guide changes in individual players that go beyond the players' in-game roles and aspirations, this final thematic chapter connects the use of fictional games in works of fiction with the themes of human transcendence, post-biological evolution and the future of play in light of the technological augmentation of human beings.

Our exploration of the use of fictional games as transformative tools begins with one of the most famous and interesting fictional games in Western literature: the Glass Bead Game in Hermann Hesse's novel of the same title, originally published in 1943. As is typical of fictional games in general, and despite the central role of the Glass Bead Game in the novel, the features and rules of Hesse's fictional game are vaguely and incompletely described. The game consists of players taking turns placing coloured beads with specific symbols on them[1] on the board in certain arrangements that are considered valid and meaningful, but it is unclear how many beads can be placed on the board by each player in each turn. The game is presented as very simple in its set-up, merely requiring a game board, the prescribed number and types of beads and a starting theme (the preliminary arrangement of a few beads meant to convey the initial idea around which the game will play out). In the novel, playing the Glass Bead Game is often discussed as a close analogue to composing poetry, improvising on a musical theme or working towards the proof of a mathematical theorem. Depending on the circumstances in which it is played (e.g. in training sessions, duels or ritual ceremonies), the Glass Bead Game can be played by one player, in pairs or in a variety of other player configurations (Hesse [1943] 2000: 30).

In Hesse's book, we learn that the process to become an elite Glass Bead Game player requires state-sanctioned training courses and many years of practice. Emphasizing both its complexity and its transdisciplinarity, the narrator of the novel initially describes the game as a 'kind of highly developed secret language drawing upon several sciences and the arts, but especially mathematics and music (and/or musicology), and capable of expressing and establishing interrelationships between the content and conclusions of nearly all scholarly disciplines. The Glass Bead Game is thus a mode of playing with the total contents and values of our culture [...]' (ibid.: 6).

The narrator further specifies that the bead configurations that are possible in the game could reproduce the entire intellectual content of the universe (ibid.: 7). The game, however, should not be understood as being capable merely of replicating various expressive and epistemic forms, but also as a generative device. In various passages in the novel, the Glass Bead Game is described as an instrument that grants access to a universe of possibilities and combinations to be explored and experimented with (ibid.) Reinforcing this idea, in the book, players of the game are often explicitly compared with organ players in that their possibilities are constrained by a complicated mechanism with a fixed structure. Additionally, like organ players, they are free to express themselves and improvise within the specifically constrained kind of freedom (i.e. the 'play') afforded by the game.

The novel *The Glass Bead Game* takes place in a fictional version of our world and is set an unspecified number of centuries in the future. Hesse presents the Glass

---

[1] *The Glass Bead Game* does not specify the quantity or types of beads required to play, but on several occasions the book hints that it is an innumerably vast quantity. For example, in one early passage, Hesse clarifies that the number of all accepted symbols (words, numbers, musical notes, chemical notations and mathematical symbols) on the beads of the game 'long ago by far exceeded the number of the ancient Chinese ideographs' (Hesse [1943] 2000: 33). The book is also not forthcoming about whether the colours of the glass beads are relevant in terms of their in-game meaning.

Bead Game as having undergone transformations and refinements over several centuries. In the book, the narrator dates the origins of the game back to the beginning of the current era (the 'Age of the Feuilleton'), when the game is said to have arisen simultaneously in Germany and England. As in Banks' ([1988] 2012) novel *The Player of Games* (see section 3.1), the reader encounters the Glass Bead Game at an advanced stage of its development, when its ludic form has reached maturity; both books present their fictional games as established social practices that can be considered to have reached an evolutionary plateau. The stability of the developmental phase of the Glass Bead Game is further emphasized when Hesse explains, again leveraging the organ analogy, that the 'manuals, pedals, and stops are now fixed' and that '[c]hanges in their number, and order, and attempts at perfecting them, are actually no longer feasible, except in theory' (Hesse [1943] 2000: 7).

The immensely complicated Glass Bead Game also incorporates notions and ideas from mythology and religion, as well as elements of mysticism. The game itself is preserved and taught by an institutional body that, in many aspects, resembles a monastic order. There are also several obvious overlaps between the process of training to become an elite player of the Glass Bead Game and the phases through which monks or seminarians approach and finally obtain ordination. The analogies between playing the game and practices of self-transcendence, such as prayer, meditation and drug-induced ecstasy, are also evident and are particularly conspicuous on the occasions in the novel when the game is played ceremonially at public events. In such contexts, the novel asserts, it is not unusual for players, for the duration of the multiple-day game period, to 'live an ascetic and selfless life of absolute absorption, comparable to the strictly regulated penitence required of the participants in one of St. Ignatius Loyola's Exercises' (ibid.: 30).

The Glass Bead Game is clearly extremely relevant in multiple ways to our work on fictional games – we could even have dedicated an entire chapter to the game's uses as a literary device or to some of its particularly extravagant formal or material properties. However, we have already provided similar kinds of analyses of other fictional games in previous chapters. In this chapter, focusing specifically on the relationships between fictional games and the idea of transcendence, we concentrate on aspects and uses of the Glass Bead Game that are specific to its use as a practice for self-perfecting and its narrative role as a factor in human beings' development and evolution. Here, our approach to the idea of transcendence is not specific to a certain philosophical current or ascribable to a particular scholar. Rather, we adopt a broad and common understanding of the notion, which also aligns with its etymology. The word 'transcendence' is derived from Latin, in which the prefix *trans-* denotes the idea of going beyond and the verb *scandare* indicates the action of climbing. Accordingly, in this chapter, we apply the term 'transcendence' to refer to the act of deliberately overcoming the obstacles and limitations that bound and define one's condition. This understanding is clearly expansive and non-technical, which inevitably introduces conceptual ambiguities and shortcomings. One such shortcoming emerges because of the wide and unspecific array of ways in which one's situation can be constrained: one can encounter boundaries and interdictions in several modes, ranging from legal and moral constraints to the presence of physical impediments or one's individual capability of perceiving and conceptualizing phenomena. Some of these limitations apply solely to the individual human being, whereas others are shared among members of a community (e.g. in the case of professional deontology or the precepts followed by a specific religious group). The question of intensity is another issue in the broad and unspecific definition we propose: when does a social shift or a moment of personal epiphany qualify as an act of transcendence? Can an action or a phenomenon be considered 'transcendental' if it does not overcome its original frame of reference in some way, or would that qualify, more modestly, as a transformative experience? To push this point even further, if by 'transcendence' we simply mean all possible forms of overcoming one's physical, perceptual and/or cognitive limitations, then almost every artefact and technological advance (and not only those disclosing fictional worlds) could be understood as a tool for human transcendence. The vast majority of the artefacts we use were indeed designed with the explicit objective of enhancing and extending our capabilities for perceiving and acting in the world, understanding ourselves and relating to others. If any activity pursued with the aid of tools can be understood as an act of transcendence of some kind, is this notion of transcendence actually of any analytical use?

To clarify our position on these questions, we refer again to the Glass Bead Game. In analysing the role of this fictional game in Hesse's novel, we want to stress two salient ways in which the Glass Bead Game functions as a tool that guides and stimulates the novel's characters to overcome their 'thrownness'.[2]

---

[2] 'Thrownness' is used here in reference to the writings of twentieth-century German philosopher Martin Heidegger. In Heidegger's work, the idea of 'thrownness' (*Geworfenheit* in the original German text) indicates the fact that one is thrown into existence in a certain way and in a certain world. In the actual world, one finds oneself confronted with qualities, capabilities and conditions over which one initially has no control (Heidegger 2008: 174). Practical examples of such thrownness are one's place and date of birth, one's biological sex, one's congenital defects and the socio-technical contexts in which one finds oneself. In other words, being 'thrown into the world' in a certain way means being characterized and bounded by a contingent set of facts – a facticity – on the basis of which (and against which) one understands and conducts one's existence.

Specifically, the forms of transcendence that we want to focus on in relation to Hesse's fictional game emerge from how the game

1. is purposely played as a practice for self-transcendence; and
2. is designed as a transdisciplinary (or even as a post-disciplinary) activity.

In Hesse's novel, the Glass Bead Game is frequently presented as a practice of self-transcendence – a 'symbolic form of seeking perfection, a sublime alchemy, an approach to that Mind which beyond all images and multiplicities is one within himself – in other words, to god' (Hesse [1943] 2000: 31). The fact that the game is understood and experienced in the fictional society of *The Glass Bead Game* as an activity conducive to self-transformation and self-transcendence is further emphasized in the cloistral and cult-like ways in which the institutionalized schools for elite players are structured and operated.

A second perspective through which we can understand the Glass Bead Game as a playful tool for transcendence involves its being designed as a universal system for thinking and communicating – a 'world language for thoughtful men' (ibid.: 33). Leveraging every facet of human knowledge and human expression, every game of the Glass Bead Game effectively contributes to the expansion of our species' horizons. In this pursuit, the Glass Bead Game encourages and guides player behaviours in ways that are not circumscribed within expressive or disciplinary boundaries. In this sense, the game can be understood as encouraging the transcendence of the discipline-bound knowledge constituted by fragmented institutional domains.

In considering the Glass Bead Game as eliciting and guiding various forms of transcendence, it is also significant that the game does not feature elements of fictionality. The game does not encourage players to act *as if* they were someone else or something else or to feel that they are part of a fictional world (or, to be more precise, a fictional world within the general fictional world of the novel). Fiction, by definition, pursues its experiential objectives by disclosing possibilities for appreciators to imaginatively engage with non-actual states of affairs. This central function of the experience of fiction is discussed in depth in fields such as aesthetics and the philosophy of fiction (see, e.g., Novitz 1980; Nussbaum [1986] 2001; Van de Mosselaer 2020). Fictional elements are very common components of the experience of actually playable games and video games, which typically require players to engage with the world of fiction set up by the games *as if* they were subjects other than their everyday selves and to pursue objectives that are meaningful for those subjects (see Vella 2016; Gualeni and Vella 2020).

Given the important role of fiction in games, one might wonder whether the lack of a clear mandate to entertain self-involving imaginings is a rare or troublesome occurrence in the context of play. The answer is a clear 'no'. Puzzle games, for instance, are often so abstract in their functions that a fictional stance towards their gameworld is not a necessary condition for playfully engaging with them. Consider, for instance, games that do not explicitly introduce a fictional layer to their gameworlds – games such as Go, Sudoku, Mastermind or *Tetris* (Pajitnov [1984] 1989; see Chapter 2). Sports, folk games and some children's games (e.g. hide-and-seek, tag and hopscotch) are further examples of playful activities that do not depend on the lens of narrative fiction to present their rules, boundaries or lusory objectives. The fact that the Glass Bead Game, in its dry, logical constitution, does not feature a fictional layer is, thus, not a particularly rare or problematic occurrence. However, the absence of this common avenue for transcendence makes the Glass Bead Game a useful example of how fictional games can stimulate and guide their players to 'go beyond' their ordinary situations without depending on imaginings about oneself.

To avoid trivializing the notion of transcendence (as well as the point we are arguing in this chapter), we decided not to consider all possible forms in which and degrees to which our human thrownness can be overcome (see footnote 2). Thus, we do not focus on forms of transcendence that require players to fantasize about themselves. To be considered a tool for transcendence, we require a fictional game to effectively prompt and/or allow players to overcome their physical, perceptual and/or cognitive limitations, and not simply to cause them to imagine they have done that. In this chapter, we also do not consider forms of overcoming at the political, legal or moral level, as these have already been discussed in relation to fictional games in Chapter 3 on the utopian potential of fictional games.

Instead of discussing forms of transcendence that rely on imagination about oneself or that happen at the social, intersubjective level, the following sections concentrate on fictional games that stimulate and structure forms of transcendence that concern the playing individual. More specifically, we analyse and discuss fictional games that trigger significant transformations in their fictional players. In this context, by 'significant', we mean that the human or humanoid characters in a work of fiction gain – through play or as a consequence of having played – physical, perceptual or cognitive capabilities that are qualitatively and/or quantitatively beyond those of the fiction appreciator. We concentrate on fictional games that, within the work of fiction, produce physical, perceptual or cognitive transformations that allow the playing characters to overcome their facticity.

As we have already discussed, fictional games can function as a synecdoche for the values and beliefs of particular social groups within the fictional worlds of which they are a part (see Chapter 2). In this role, we presented fictional games as literary devices used to characterize the social context in which these games are played and/or to typify qualities and attitudes that define certain fictional characters. In this chapter, we want to highlight fictional games that specifically signalize the following two (often concurrent) characteristics of the fictional worlds in which they are played:

1. the context in which the narrative takes place is remarkably more advanced compared with the actual world of the fiction appreciator; and
2. the characters in the fiction achieve capabilities and possibilities to act, think and play that are clearly beyond those that can currently be realized by human beings.

The use of fictional games to highlight these aspects of fictional worlds is particularly central in works of fiction where human characters require physical or mental augmentation to participate in play. A case in point is the already-mentioned film *eXistenZ* (Cronenberg 1999; see Chapter 4), where advanced biotechnological devices are utilized to interface computers with the human nervous system, granting players totalizing experiential access to a digital gameworld. Another example of a game that requires players to undergo technological body augmentation is Motorball, a blood sport described in the manga *Battle Angel Alita* (Kishiro 1990–5; see Chapter 1).

Other fictional games such as The Mind Game in *Ender's Game* (Card [1985] 1994; see Chapter 4, section 4.2) or the Kobayashi Maru test in *Star Trek II: The Wrath of Khan* (Meyer 1982; see the introduction to Chapter 4) can be cited as examples of fictional games that do not require a direct or substantial overcoming of one's physical or perceptual apparatus to be played but that can invite and catalyse significant transformative effects. In Card's book, group battle simulations and individual Mind Game sessions are presented as having a profound transformative effect on Ender, the novel's protagonist. Playing these games primes and trains him to perform superhuman feats in terms of both strategic and lateral thinking – skills that are crucial in the narrative development of *Ender's Game*. The same is true of the effects the Kobayashi Maru test has on starship captains in *Star Trek II: The Wrath of Khan* (Meyer 1982).

The two fictional games we analyse in detail in the following sections epitomize, each in their unique ways, the transformative and evolutionary role that fictional games can have within a work of fiction. In the two sections that follow, we discuss:

1. Blood Spire (section 5.1), a fatal fictional game that is central to Alastair Reynolds' 2003 science-fiction novella, *Diamond Dogs*; and
2. *eXistenZ* (section 5.2), an immersive virtual reality game that is uploaded directly into the player's spinal cord in David Cronenberg's 1999 film of the same name.

These focal games will be analysed individually and investigated as artefacts that prompt and support a significant overcoming of the protagonist's physical and cognitive limitations through activities that can be described – at least to some degree – as playful. In ways that are ultimately similar, both fictional games reveal a profound fascination with the idea of overriding one's biological and cognitive set-up. In a way that is reminiscent of the Glass Bead Game, both games also emphasize that the desire to transcend one's condition (which is also evident in religious aspirations) characterizes human existence.

Finally, our discussion of fictional games as tools for transcendence necessarily includes speculation about the projected trajectory of the transformative processes presented in the fictional works considered. Questions concerning who (or what) might be provoking and guiding the changes, and for what reasons, are considered in the analysis of the two exemplary games analysed and discussed in detail in this chapter. These questions highlight and contextualize Reynolds' and Cronenberg's perspectives and fears in relation to the roles and influences of technological development on the process of human evolution.

5.1 Transcendence and technological fatalism in *Diamond Dogs*

In the futuristic fictional world of *Diamond Dogs* (part of Reynolds' ongoing series of science-fiction novels commonly referred to as the 'Revelation Space Universe' series, 1999–present), humans have been a spacefaring and space-colonizing species for a few centuries. Interstellar transport, however, is still very dangerous and expensive – both economically and in terms of the health hazards it poses. Spaceship travel entails spending decades traversing the galaxy in 'reefersleep' (a kind of cryogenic sleep), which takes a progressively higher toll on travellers' bodies with each subsequent freezing cycle. Given these premises, it is unsurprising that, in Reynolds' novel, technologies dedicated to the repair and replacement of organs and body parts are extremely advanced compared with the actual world, as is the science behind human augmentics.[3] Most of the characters in *Diamond Dogs* are examples of posthumans in the sense outlined in Chapter 1 (see section 1.2.3); to different degrees, almost all of them have robotic limbs, bioengineered substitutes for internal organs and various kinds of perceptual and cognitive enhancements. Among the posthumans featured in Reynolds' novels, the 'ultranauts' (often shortened as 'ultras') are some of the most obviously augmented characters. Ultras are heavily modified humans who tend to work as crew members on 'lighthuggers', a class of interstellar spacecraft whose maximum speed is just below the speed of light. The ultranauts who survive interstellar journeys usually live extremely long lives because of the time-dilating effects of near-lightspeed travel, their willingness to replace their organs and limbs with bioengineered alternatives and the long periods that they spend in reefersleep during galactic transit.[4]

Notwithstanding the advancements in space travel and human augmentics, in the four centuries between the actual present day and the time when the events narrated in *Diamond Dogs* occur, there have been no more than glimpses of alien sentience – that is, until the fortuitous discovery of an alien construction, an artefact informally called Blood Spire. A space probe owned by a private space exploration enterprise spotted the Spire on a remote and lifeless planet, Golgotha, which is very far from planets inhabited by human colonists and from common space-faring routes (Reynolds [2003] 2006: 29). A team organized and financed by the private company that discovered Blood Spire is sent to Golgotha.

> For most of its height Blood Spire was no thicker than a few dozen metres, and considerably narrower just below the bulb-like upper part. But, like a slender chess piece, its lower parts swelled out considerably to form a wide base. That podium-like mass was perhaps fifty metres in diameter: a fifth of the structure's height. From a distance it appeared to rest solidly on the base: a mighty obelisk requiring the deepest of foundations to anchor it to the ground.

---

[3] The term 'human augmentics' refers to technologies designed and employed to integrate with human bodies and expand their capabilities and possibilities for perceiving and acting. According to Kenyon and Leigh (2011), one can think of human augmentics as the force driving the non-biological evolution of human beings.

[4] Ultras are described in Reynolds' books as skeletal beings who are heavily technologically modified and often wear locks of braided hair. Each lock commemorates a time they managed to cross interstellar space (i.e. surviving the myriad misfortunes that might befall a spacecraft during decades-long transit; Reynolds [2003] 2006: 28, and ibid. 2000: 87). Interestingly, in one passage of Reynolds' novel *Revelation Space* (2000) – which takes place in the same universe and belongs to the same novel series as *Diamond Dogs* – some ultras are described as betting their braided locks as part of a 'heated card game' of some kind. In that game, the ultranauts put their honour and status at stake by wagering one or more of their locks of hair. In case of a loss, a corresponding number of braided locks are cut from their heads (Reynolds 2000: 109).

> But it didn't.
> The Spire base [...] floated above it, spaced by five or six clear metres of air.
>
> Ibid.: 45

Although nothing is known about the Spire's purpose, its history or what the top of its upper portion houses, the alien artefact appears to be designed as a sort of test for space-faring intelligent lifeforms who might come across it. In line with the literary tradition of deadly games or fatal challenges, Blood Spire confronts its 'players' with a series of trials or – in this case – mathematical puzzles. Structurally, the Spire consists of a linear sequence of rooms connected by doors. These rooms are organized in an ascending spiral from the bottom of the alien construction to its summit. Each room contains a puzzle that must be solved to open the door to the next room. The puzzles focus on different area of mathematics, such as prime number theory or topology, and become increasingly difficult to solve as the group's journey progresses through the Spire's rooms. To fully understand the plot of *Diamond Dogs* (as well as our point here), it is relevant to observe that, as they become more demanding, the Spire's puzzles also venture into areas of mathematical knowledge that have not yet been developed or formalized in the socio-technical context of the novel's protagonists. Curiously, the dimensions of the doors connecting the rooms also change subtly with each room, becoming smaller and narrower as the players make their way up the Spire.

Each room of the mysterious alien construction presents several possible answers to its mathematical puzzle. If the players choose an incorrect solution (or take too long to answer in the more advanced rooms, which also have a completion time limit), the alien spire delivers cruel physical punishments. These penalties vary wildly from room to room but always involve one of the party members suffering some form of dismemberment or even death. Although Blood Spire is often referred to as a construction or a machine, the novella often hints at it giving the semblance of consciousness, as if it were – to some degree – alive. Initially cold and silent, the Spire 'wakes up' and starts warming up and vibrating when the team enters its first room. It also seems to be feeding off the mechanical components of the players' body parts when these are severed as part of a punishment.

The Spire allows players to leave the 'game' space only when the riddle in a room has been correctly answered and the door to the next room has not yet been opened by the players. With the objective of providing medical assistance to injured players, replacing body parts or simply resting, the members of the team investigating the alien construction often decide to retreat to their base camp, which is set on the inhospitable and barren planet of Golgotha, not far from the Spire itself. The base camp on Golgotha serves another crucial purpose; as the fatal challenge progresses in the narrative of *Diamond Dogs*, the team members who have survived and intend to continue with the game often return to the camp to undergo additional cybernetic enhancements and cognitive augmentations. Some of these technologically aided forms of transcendence are meant to help the players deal with the progressively more arcane and abstract level of mathematics. Others are bodily reconfigurations meant to guarantee the players' passage through the increasingly narrow doors. This self-transformation process culminates with the two remaining players becoming indistinguishable from one another and no longer resembling human beings – through multiple iterations, the team surgeon has re-arranged and reconstructed them to the point that the players have effectively become cybernetic greyhounds with artificially accelerated minds.

The challenge implicitly issued by the alien Spire in *Diamond Dogs* is never explicitly referred to as a game, as is frequently the case with fatal games. If fatal games are ever called 'games' within works of fiction, it is by their game designers or the game masters rather than by their often-unwilling players. As the creators of Blood Spire are not part of the narrative of Reyolds' novella, we can only speculate as to whether they might regard it as a game. Without certainty in that regard, we nonetheless decided to include Blood Spire for analysis here on the basis of both its evident set-up as a fatal game and descriptions of two of its players (the ones who end up transforming into dog-like cyborgs) in early parts of the narrative as avid, dedicated gamers who spent years challenging one another with puzzles and logical challenges in their youth. *Diamond Dogs* is thus a story of an obsessive game-like pursuit; it is also a story about abandoning one's humanity. In terms of appearance, physical possibilities, computational speed and cognitive capabilities, as mentioned above, the two dog-like bioengineered players are no longer recognizable as human beings. Through their multiple, iterative augmentations, they can be seen as having ventured beyond even the heavy-handed posthumanism of the ultranauts. Blood Spire can thus be understood as a fictional game that – beyond a certain point – is meant to be unplayable for regular human beings.

The characters in *Diamond Dogs* do not know why the Spire is standing on Golgotha, who built it or what they might find in its bulbous top. The protagonist of the novella speculates that one possible function of the alien construction is forcing players to alter themselves to overcome its challenges (Reynolds [2003]

2006: 159–60). This idea might explain why, upon the successful solution of a puzzle, the fatal game allows players to exit the Spire, attend to their wounds, regroup and plan ahead. Continuing his train of thought, the main character speculates that the ever-increasing complexity of the mathematical challenges, the deadly punishments and the steadily decreasing size of the doors is a way of encouraging suitably motivated individuals to transcend themselves through technological means. The challenges posed by the Spire can be understood as incentives to willingly pursue a very specific kind of evolutionary fitness. This character further speculates that the Spire might have some use for individuals who have undergone drastic modifications and that they will be 'harvested' by an advanced alien civilization when they manage to reach the top of the Spire (ibid.).

This character, the main protagonist of the novella, is initially dubious and mildly disturbed by bioengineered replacements and augmentations. He is also distrustful of the ultranauts on the team and disapproves of the famous (and famously controversial) surgeon who follows the team on their journey to Golgotha. The focal character's initial reservations notwithstanding, however, the sociocultural context in *Diamond Dogs* is generally not presented as critical of posthumanism or of human augmentics. In fact, the opposite seems to be the case; it is a civilization that, in response to planetary catastrophes and hazards related to space colonization, decided to take their chances of survival (and their evolutionary destiny) in their own hands.[5]

The optimistic and uncritical disposition towards human augmentics that is generally displayed by the characters in Reynolds' novel is further corroborated by how some of them respond to the fatal demands of Blood Spire.[6] The most obsessive players, and especially the two who finally decide to undergo the most extreme self-transformations, treat the alien artefact with reverence and appear to be unquestioning in accepting the trials that the Spire puts before them. Their quasi-religious faith in the alien artefact and the consequent decision to continue

---

[5] As exemplified in much of Greek mythology, this disposition does not guarantee a positive outcome and poses existential threats of its own. Any attempt at domesticating destiny appears, in fact, to constitute a new source of danger and to invite new aspects of tragedy into the lives of the individuals and societies deciding to walk this path. For more information and perspectives on this tragic approach to the philosophy of technology, see de Mul (2009) and Gualeni and Vella (2020).

[6] To be sure, techno-optimism and a fatalistic (if not enthusiastic) disposition towards human augmentics are not ubiquitous or general traits of human beings and groups in Reynolds' work. In the 'Revelation Space Universe' series of novels, the reader comes across individuals and political factions that are sceptical about the idea of transcending one's biological body by technological means. Fictional characters harbouring such beliefs are typically distrustful of factions like the ultranauts, refuse to use cybernetic implants and might prefer to die over taking medications that involve implanting bio-technological devices or injecting nanomachines into their bodies.

on the evolutionary trajectory it proposes could be attributed to the compulsive personality traits of the characters involved and their passion for games, but doing so would overlook an important component of the narrative. In *Diamond Dogs*, the characters are exposed to several clues indicating that the Spire is likely the product of an ancient and extremely advanced civilization.[7] The detectable properties of the alien artefact (as well as the rumours surrounding it) seem to grant the Spire an implicit authority over its less-developed visitors. Its demonstration of a currently inconceivable level of techno-scientific advancement and its appearing to be designed around reaching a very specific cognitive and physical standard could also be recognized as providing some characters with enough reason to trust in the Spire and continue playing.

Our analysis of Blood Spire as a fictional game (and this chapter in general) expose and emphasize an aspect of the use of fictional games in works of fiction that has thus far remained largely unacknowledged in our discussion. In addition to demonstrating that there are clear instances of fictional games that can be understood as tools for human transcendence, we also show that the various expressive possibilities of fictional games within a work of fiction are not mutually exclusive. As is the case for other types of narrative devices, fictional games do not necessarily need to stimulate the imagination of fiction appreciators in a way that is unidimensional or that focuses solely on one communication strategy. In the narrative of *Diamond Dogs*, as we have discussed, the alien Spire pursues a variety of interrelated functions simultaneously. It is, among other roles within the work of fiction,

1. a tool for stimulating and guiding a specific kind of transcendence among the human players;
2. a narrative device that presents clues about the core values and inclinations of the civilization that built it, emphasizing this civilization's focus logical-

---

[7] The most obvious signs that the alien artefact belongs to an extremely ancient and advanced civilization can be seen in both technological and conceptual features of the Spire:

Technological: The fact that the Spire floats effortlessly, that it is pristine and functioning presumably after millennia of inactivity, that it is impermeable to any attempts at probing it with the team's analytical tools, drones, and scanning devices, and the fact that it operates at supersonic speed and surgical precision when it comes to punishing its players.

Conceptual: The kind of mathematics that the Spire insists upon oddly resonates with the mathematical capabilities of another (but in this case non-sentient) alien species, that of the Pattern Jugglers. The Pattern Jugglers are a sort of a living superorganism that appear to be functioning as a vast biological archiving system: their networked minds can absorb and integrate the minds and bodies of multiple lifeforms and indefinitely store their collective memories.

mathematical intelligence, rigour and adaptability (i.e. openness towards technology-driven body transformations and augmentations); and
3. a constant source of occasions for the indirect characterization of its protagonists.

A number of other narrative and philosophical functions could certainly be added to this list, including approaching the Spire as the manifestation of a largely inscrutable and potentially horrific form of alterity, exhibiting functions and traits that are often associated with the notion of the 'monstrous' across various types of fiction. One could also approach the Spire as serving as an aptitude test in disguise, evaluating performance and proclivity in ways that are similar to fictional games encountered in other works, such as *Ender's Game* (Card [1985] 1994), *Armada* (Cline 2015), and the fourth episode of the ninth season of the animated television series *South Park* ('Best Friends Forever,'[8] Parker 2005).

5.2 Transcendence of the self in *eXistenZ*

As we have shown, fictional games can function explicitly as transformative tools for their (fictional) players. To illustrate and further discuss this idea, in the previous section, we focused on Reynolds' 2003 novella *Diamond Dogs*, where Blood Spire, a game-like alien artefact, pushes the protagonists towards a radical overcoming of their biological make-up. Accepting the challenge presented by Blood Spire means being confronted with radical questions concerning one's sense of identity, the continuity of one's selfhood and how meaning can be attributed to one's existence. *Diamond Dogs* was also discussed as showcasing what could be described as a fatalistic – if not optimistic – stance in relation to the role of technology in human evolution.

As a counterpoint to Reynolds' perspective, the second focal fictional game in this chapter illustrates a sceptical and even openly pessimistic perspective on the integration and augmentation of biology with technology. *eXistenZ*, a 1999 science-fiction/horror film written, directed and produced by Cronenberg, has

---

[8] In this 2005 episode, one of the characters in the animated series (Kenny) is the first person in town to own a Sony PSP video game system. With skill and dedication, Kenny quickly works his way up to the final level of the fictional action-strategy video game Heaven vs Hell, but, soon after, he is run over by an ice-cream truck. Kenny dies, and, after ascending to heaven, he discovers that God had created the game Heaven vs. Hell as a test to find and recruit someone to command his legions against the forces of hell.

often been cited as Cronenberg's first original script in over fifteen years. After his breakthrough as a major contemporary *auteur* with the science-fiction body horror film *Videodrome* (1983), Cronenberg spent the 1980s and 1990s directing adaptations ranging from Stephen King novels (*The Dead Zone*, 1983) to true crime paperbacks (*Dead Ringers*, 1988). *eXistenZ* is often considered a spiritual successor of sorts to *Videodrome*, similarly presenting technology (especially virtual reality technology) as a threat to the possibility for human beings to express their free will and autonomously construct themselves as individuals. Authors such as Hotchkiss (2003) and Bowler (2007) note how both films can be interpreted as techno-pessimistic or techno-sceptical commentaries on the artificial augmentation of the human body, whose inevitability is summed up by *Videodrome*'s protagonist at the end of the movie, when he proclaims 'long live the new flesh!' before committing suicide.

In the narrative of *eXistenZ*, superstar game designer Allegra Geller (Jennifer Jason Leigh) is on the run from a group of radical 'realists', political activists who oppose the production of hyper-immersive games and have proclaimed a *fatwā*[9] against her. She is escorted in her escape by Ted Pikul (Jude Law), a public relations executive for Antenna Research, the studio publishing Geller's games. Geller has managed to salvage a copy of her latest game, *eXistenZ*, stored in her 'game pod', an assemblage of artificial and organic components, loosely resembling a video game controller. To use the game pod, its cord must be plugged into a player's 'bio-port', an organic socket in the lower back that acts as an interface between the game pod and the player's nervous system. After the game pod has been connected to the player's bio-port, the game data are uploaded directly through the player's spinal cord into their brain – a biotechnological process that results in a radically immersive experience that is indistinguishable from actual reality. Other elements of the film also seem to derive from Cronenberg's interest in the fusion of the organic and the artificial. For example, in several scenes in the movie, characters are shown in the act of crafting or utilizing firearms built with animal parts and loading teeth into those firearms to be used as bullets. Further, when Geller's game pod explodes in a trout farm doubling as a production site for biotech game hardware, the pod releases black spores that 'infect' the assembly line and the parts used in the production process, showing that the convergence of organic and artificial

---

[9] The bounty put on Geller's head by the realists is explicitly referred to as a *fatwā* (a religious ruling in Islamic law) by characters in the film. This is likely because Cronenberg was thinking about writing *eXistenZ* when he interviewed writer Salman Rushdie, who was living in hiding because of a *fatwā* ordering his death.

extends to biological processes such as contagion and infection, which, in the world of *eXistenZ*, can afflict both humans and technological objects.

In this light, it is hard to disagree with Hotchkiss' (2003: 20) description of the film as part of a 'persistent fantasy of transcendence of the body, in part through such eagerly predicted technological advances as the digitization of human consciousness and consequent shedding of human materiality'. The film *eXistenZ* belongs to a strand of 1980s and 1990s cinematic production that reworked the anxieties and predictions of cyberpunk literature asround the human body and its augmentations into more-or-less mainstream cyber-thrillers.[10] Nevertheless, analyses of *eXistenZ* that present the film as a meditation on the future of the human body in an increasingly technologically mediated environment neglect an important component of its message. *eXistenZ*, the revolutionary game designed by Geller, differs from the extremely convincing virtual reality environments portrayed in films such as *The Lawnmower Man* (Leonard 1992) and *Strange Days* (Bigelow 1995) because of it being *a game*. The explicit ludic intention behind Geller's creation and the resulting implications in terms of the characters' interactions with it allow *eXistenZ* (the film) to be seen as Cronenberg's attempt to reflect on the possibility of transcending one's self through play and *eXistenZ* (the game) to be interpreted as a commentary on the existential and evolutionary relevance of video games.

In an interview with *Sight and Sound* magazine (Rodley 1999: 10) that was published immediately after the film's premiere, Cronenberg describes himself as 'a card-carrying existentialist' and the film as 'existentialist propaganda'. Although it is generally advisable to take an author's descriptions of their work with a pinch of salt – especially when they are offered in an explicitly promotional context – Cronenberg's reference to existentialism may be used as an interpretive tool in discussing the transcendental features of the fictional game *eXistenZ*. The game, as portrayed in the film, allows players to live an alternative existence in which they are often openly encouraged to engage in dangerous or illegal activities such as shooting someone who is believed to be a spy or infiltrating a terrorist group. In phenomenological terms – that is, considering the player's perceptions and feelings in relation to the fictional world of the game – *eXistenZ* is indistinguishable from experiences in the actual world. The objects, environments and situations presented in the game are perceived with the same granularity and presence as their actual counterparts, except when a

---

[10] Other notable examples of this tendency are films such as *Robocop* (Verhoeven 1987) and *Total Recall* (Verhoeven 1990).

'bleed-through' effect allows players to glimpse the existence of empirical reality through a glitch in the virtual reality of the game. When these glitches happen, some real phenomena seep into the fictional world of the game, leading to further software glitches and experiential inconsistencies.[11] Although being in the game environment of *eXistenZ* is generally phenomenologically indistinguishable from one's everyday dealings with the actual world, in terms of believability and immersion, the players deem interactions with artificial characters encountered in the fictional world of the game to be less satisfactory. Throughout the film, Geller complains about the predictability of certain lines of dialogue spoken by the game's non-player characters and about the stiffness of their reactions to her own and Pikul's prompts. In other words, although the game *eXistenZ* offers a very detailed and convincing environmental simulation of reality, social conventions appear to be clumsily reproduced and in need of further refinement.

According to cognitive psychologist James J. Gibson (1986), an environment is defined by its affordances – the possibilities that it discloses for its inhabitants. Gibson argues that this is true of both natural environments – understood as environments that are not subject to human intervention – and artificial ones. It would not be a stretch, then, to extend Gibson's theory of environmental affordances to video games (see Linderoth 2013; Fassone 2017: 26). Virtual environments, in fact, are designed specifically to support, or afford, certain actions and to impede or discourage others. For example, a game environment might offer platforms to jump onto or corners to hide in, or present certain paths and options as more conspicuous or desirable than others. From this perspective, the fictional video game *eXistenZ* can be understood as a playful virtual environment in which affordances are deliberately designed to guide and constrain players as they navigate and engage with their fictional surroundings. The world's affordances encourage – and, in the case of *eXistenZ*, often compel – players to adopt certain behaviours or pursue specific objectives and courses of action, introducing a significant degree of determinism into how players exist in the gameworld.

This predicament is exemplified in one of the film's most revealing sequences. Geller and Pikul are playing *eXistenZ*. In the game, they are sitting at a table in a

---

[11] The film is built around the existence of multiple layers of reality. What the spectator initially perceives as Geller and Pikul's actual world is later revealed to actually be a larger game called *transCendenZ*, which includes *eXistenZ* as a nested game (see Chapter 1). The film is also punctuated by numerous hints about the dubious status of the characters' perceived reality. This Russian doll structure is described by Pomerance (2003) as typical of 'elevator films' – films that contain characters who move among several hierarchically structured levels of reality, 'ascending' or 'descending' from one to the next.

Chinese restaurant. Pikul discovers that the bones of the mutant fish he is eating can be used to produce a gun (see Figure 5.1). Although he is hesitant to build a firearm, he finds himself compelled by the game to do so and starts assembling the weapon. Pikul then tells Geller, 'I do feel the urge to kill someone here', to which she responds, 'You won't be able to stop yourself. You might as well enjoy it'. Before shooting the waiter for no apparent reason, Pikul offers a reflection that sounds like an existentialist aphorism: 'Free will . . . is obviously not a big factor in this little world of ours'. This scene deserves special attention for at least two reasons. First, the scene clearly frames *eXistenZ* as a game rather than a generic simulation. Geller's game presents its players with well-defined affordances and mandatory lusory goals (such as killing the waiter at the Chinese restaurant to thwart potential sabotage). Second, the scene establishes winning and losing conditions and explicitly (that is, meta-fictionally) informs the players about the tools and strategies necessary to win. Cronenberg seems to suggest that playing a video game implies abandoning our presumptions of freedom to embrace determinism; as players in the world of *eXistenZ*, Pikul and Geller have no option but to conform to their prescribed destiny.

If we understand Cronenberg's work as inherently speculative – that is, as a way of reflecting on philosophical and existential issues through filmmaking – as Wilson (2011) seems to suggest, we can think of *eXistenZ* as participating in

Figure 5.1 At a Chinese restaurant, Ted Pikul (Jude Law) – the protagonist of the 1999 film *eXistenZ* – is compelled by the game to shoot a waiter with a gun made on the spot using the bones of a mutant fish. Directed by Dmavid Cronenberg © Screenventures XXIV Production Ltd 1999. All rights reserved.

the discourse concerning the relations between games and existentialist philosophy. Philosophers such as Eugen Fink ([1960] 2015) have proposed understanding play as an alternative mode of existence; while our actual life is defined by certain non-negotiable aspects and particular possibilities and aspirations, during play, we are free from these fundamental constraints and can fictionally explore alternative possibilities of being. Building on the work of Fink and other existentialist philosophers (including, notably, Jean-Paul Sartre), several scholars have proposed theoretical approaches applying an existentialist understanding of play to video games – and virtual worlds more generally (Leino 2009; de Miranda 2018; Gualeni 2019; Gualeni and Vella 2020). Video games may thus be said to present players with inhabitable worlds that allow them to perform and experiment with different modes of existence; by inhabiting an avatar, players can experiment with alternative 'ludic subjectivities' (Vella 2016; Gualeni and Vella 2020) that emerge as a function of the convergence of the player's subjective experience of the actual world with the features and affordances of their avatar in the environment of the virtual world of a video game.

When Geller and Pikul enter the virtual world of *eXistenZ*, they are confronted with the existential possibilities of their ludic subjectivities, and they discover that their in-game avatars possess the ability to impose their desires, goals and beliefs onto their (assumedly) actual selves. Cronenberg's take on virtual existentialism can thus be recognized as that of a sceptic. The game offers ways of being and behaving that largely override the players' original selves, along with their existential projects, replacing them with virtual selves designed to be in tune with the game's objectives. Pikul, a shy and insecure 'public relations nerd' is coaxed by the game into the role of an action hero who, despite his reluctance, has no option but to execute his pre-programmed actions and speak his scripted dialogues. Similarly, Geller, a reclusive game designer, is forced to follow a script in which she is a mysterious and reckless *femme fatale*.

Is the game of *eXistenZ* merely acting as a hypnotic device whose function is to entrance its players and force them to surrender their subjectivities to the game system? This might well be the case. However, we would like to offer a different interpretation of Cronenberg's work – one that gives some credit to the director's self-appointment as 'a card-carrying existentialist'. With that purpose in mind, we turn to an article by philosopher Mark Fisher. In 'Work and Play in *eXistenZ*', Fisher (2012) proposes a rather unconventional understanding by decentring the prevalent interpretation of the film as a reflection on the possibility of creating different layers of reality and on the instability of our perception of what is real. According to Fisher (ibid.: 71), at the centre of *eXistenZ*'s engagement with philosophy 'is the idea – in some ways stranger and more disturbing than the notion that reality is fake – that subjectivity is a simulation'. From this perspective, Cronenberg's film can be understood as proposing to treat *eXistenZ*, the video game, as a playful stimulus towards the transcendence of our notion of the self as determined by our free will and to help us recognize the self's dependence on contextual, social and relational factors. Cronenberg himself hints at this notion when he claims that 'all reality is virtual. It's all invented. It's collaborative, so you need friends to help create a reality' (Rodley 1999: 10). However, it is not just reality that is invented and collaborative for Cronenberg – one's subjectivity is similarly always virtual. Accessing the virtual world of *eXistenZ* allows Geller and Pikul to playfully overcome their usual selves and, guided by the game, to more or less willingly assume new subjectivities for themselves. Although the game of *eXistenZ* may seem cruel to its players, forcing them to abandon their usual selves, it serves as a means to understand the artificiality of the very notion of a self.

eXistenZ, the film, certainly engages with some of the core ideas and perspectives of existentialism – from the relevance of free will to Fink's notion of play as an existential condition that is experimental and complementary to our everyday dealings with the actual world – but we believe it can hardly be described as 'existentialist propaganda'. On the contrary, *eXistenZ* seems to point to the necessity of transgressing or transcending factual notions of the self (see footnote 2). This understanding of transcendence resonates in at least two ways with Cronenberg's career-long fascination with the philosophical current of existentialism, a fascination that often results in original and critical approaches to its themes. As a first example, as also noted by Fisher (2012), it is relevant to note that the characters in *eXistenZ* act in ways that contradict one of the tenet's of Sartre's thought, that is the separation between the projectuality of the human being (what Sartre ([1943] 2020) qualified as 'for-itself' because of its existential autonomy and its innate aspiration to 'make something of itself') and the inert nature of common objects, which Sartre (ibid.) identifies as 'in-itself'. Fisher asserts that, in Cronenberg's film, human beings seem to be deprived of their goals and aspirations, while the inert and the apparently inorganic – think of Geller's game pod – reveals an inner life of its own. There is also a second reason why Cronenberg may be seen as a kind of saboteur of existentialism, a stance akin to that of the realist faction in the fictional world of *eXistenZ*. According to Sartre, humans are 'condemned to be free' ([1946] 1970: 37) – that is, they can never break free of the consequences of enacting their free will. The game of *eXistenZ* reveals to its players that the freedom of will that they enjoy in their (assumed) actual world is also an illusion and that their goals, aspirations and, eventually, actions, are almost inescapably determined by external factors. The nested narrative of the film – in which multiple planes of reality are enclosed within each other – seems to reinforce the interpretation that, even in the actual world of the fiction appreciators (provided that there is such a thing), free will is merely an illusion.

Although Pikul is certainly responsible for killing the waiter in the Chinese restaurant, he cannot claim to have committed the murder driven solely by his own free will. Cronenberg's perspective on play, here, is resolutely anti-Finkian. For Fink, play may fictionally disclose alternative, exploratory modes of existence; for Cronenberg, in contrast, games represent a way of being deprived of possibilities and a place where one can acknowledge the irrelevance of free will. In the words of Geller, the creator of the game of *eXistenZ*, in response to Pikul's remark that 'Free will . . . is obviously not a big factor in this little world of ours', 'It's like real life. There's just enough to make it interesting'.

5.3 Conclusions

In this chapter, we presented a particularly interesting – if rather unconventional – narrative role for fictional games. We identified and discussed fictional games as technologies and activities that encourage (or even force) players to overcome some of the facts and possibilities that constrain (and define) their existence. In most of the examples we presented in this book at large, this kind of 'ludic transcendence' was directed towards overcoming physical limitations (as in the case of blood sports or fatal challenges involving the augmentation or modification of one's biological body). In this chapter in particular, we selected two paradigmatic cases of a kind of overcoming that is more involved with cognitive, perceptual, and ultimately existential kinds of overcoming.

In the introductory section of this chapter, we discussed the Glass Bead Game, a fictional game in Hesse's ([1943] 2000) novel of the same name, because of both its literary relevance and the kind of transcendence it proposes. The Glass Bead Game requires a particular kind of cognitive development of aspiring players, but it also requires them to go beyond understanding knowledge and culture as being separated into watertight disciplinary domains. In our exploration of fictional games in terms of their specific function as incentives and playful escorts on the path towards certain forms of human transcendence and evolution, we focused on two fictional games: Blood Spire (section 5.1) and *eXistenZ* (section 5.2). The analysis of both fictional games facilitated reflection on various expressive ways in which fictional games serve as thought experiments concerning our posthuman future and the new roles and possibilities for play within it.

In *Diamond Dogs*, human transcendence is effectively imposed on players by the unquestionable – and unquestionably alien – set of lusory constraints and goals of a fatal game. Players drawn to the deadly challenge found in the mysterious construction informally called Blood Spire could decide to accept this challenge, which meant submitting to the game's merciless demands in terms of cognitive and bodily transformation. Two of the protagonists of the novel are described as obsessive players who live for puzzles. Confronted with the mystery of Blood Spire and with the evolutionary trajectory that the game implicitly lays out for them, these two characters decide to put their lives at stake with particularly fatalistic abandonment.

The immersive video game *eXistenZ* similarly acts as a cruel master to its players, whose free will is denied by the necessity of advancing the game's prescribed plot. Pikul and Geller are forced to perform other subjectivities, imposed by the game, but the transcendental effects of playing *eXistenZ* are found precisely in this denial of their own selfhood and freedom. By being stripped of their perceived original selves, the players realize that free will outside of the gameworld is also an illusion, as their objectives and desires are influenced (and for the most part determined) by external factors such as social and economic pressures. From this perspective, *eXistenZ* can be understood as a game that engages its players in a series of existentialist questions and, more generally, acts as a tool for the virtual exploration of existential themes.

Our analysis of the orientations towards technology displayed in *Diamond Dogs* and *eXistenZ* also revealed a crucial difference between the two works of fiction. Whereas Cronenberg's film presents a critical account of the possibility of transcending one's free will through play, the characters in *Diamond Dogs* almost unquestioningly act on the conviction that the technological transcendence of human beings is not only desirable but worth pursuing at all costs.

As a concluding observation, this last thematic chapter showed that the various expressive possibilities and roles of fictional games are not necessarily mutually exclusive. Especially in the example of Blood Spire, we observe how the alien construction hosts a fictional game that simultaneously pursues a variety of interrelated narrative and philosophical uses. Here, we have pointed out that

Blood Spire has functions such as serving as a tool for the self-transcendence of its human players, an ideological proxy for the civilization that built it, a narrative device for the implicit characterization of some of the protagonists and an aptitude test in disguise, as well as many others. A similar analysis of *eXistenZ* would have revealed that the philosophical and narrative functions of this fictional game within the film are also multiplicitous. Particularly worthy of attention is how *eXistenZ* works simultaneously on two semantic levels – both from the perspective of the fictional players in the game and from the perspective of the viewers of the film. On the first level, the game forces players to transcend their original selves and follow alternative, deterministically prescribed existential paths. On the second level, *eXistenZ* functions as a philosophical thought experiment that prompts spectators to reflect on the illusoriness of free will, both within and outside the context of gameplay.

References

Banks, I. M. ([1988] 2012), *The Player of Games*, New York: Orbit.
Bigelow, K. (1995), [Film] *Strange Days*, Lightstorm Entertainment.
Bowler, A. L. (2007), 'eXistenZ and the Spectre of Gender in the Cyber-Generation', *New Cinemas: Journal of Contemporary Film*, 5 (2): 99–114.
Card, O. S. ([1985] 1994), *Ender's Game*, New York: TOR.
Cline, E. (2015), *Armada*, New York: Crown Publishing Books.
Cronenberg, D. (1983a), [Film] *The Dead Zone*, Dino de Laurentiis Company.
Cronenberg, D. (1983b), [Film] *Videodrome*, Canadian Film Development Corporation.
Cronenberg, D. (1988), [Film] *Dead Ringers*, Morgan Creek Productions, Telefilm Canada, Mantle Clinic II.
Cronenberg, D. (1999), [Film] *eXistenZ*, scriptwriter David Cronenberg, Alliance Atlantis.
de Miranda, L. (2018), '*Life is Strange* and "Games are Made": A Philosophical Interpretation of a Multiple-Choice Existential Simulator with Copilot Sartre', *Games and Culture*, 13 (8): 825–42.
de Mul, J. (2009), 'Awesome Technologies', *Art and Social Change: International Yearbook of Aesthetics*, 13: 120–39.
Fassone, R. (2017), *Every Game is an Island: Endings and Extremities in Video Games*, New York: Bloomsbury.
Fink, E. ([1960] 2015), 'Play as Symbol of the World', I. A. Moore and C. Turner (trans.) (2015), *Play as Symbol of the World and Other Writings*, Bloomington and Indianapolis, IN: Indiana University Press, 33–215.
Fisher, M. (2012), 'Work and Play in *eXistenZ*', *Film Quarterly*, 65 (3): 70–3.

Gibson, J. J. (1986), *The Ecological Approach to Visual Perception*, New York: Psychology Press.

Gualeni, S. (2015), *Virtual Worlds as Philosophical Tools: How to Philosophize with a Digital Hammer*, Basingstoke: Palgrave Macmillan.

Gualeni, S. (2019), 'Virtual World-Weariness: On Delaying the Experiential Erosion of Digital Environments', in A. Gerber and U. Goetz (eds), *The Architectonics of Game Spaces: The Spatial Logic of the Virtual and Its Meaning for the Real*, Bielefeld: Transcript, 153–65.

Gualeni, S. and D. Vella (2020), *Virtual Existentialism: Meaning and Subjectivity in Virtual Worlds*, Basingstoke: Palgrave Pivot.

Heidegger, M. (2008), *Basic Writings*, New York: Harper Perennial Modern Thought.

Hesse, H. ([1943] 2000), *The Glass Bead Game*, London: Vintage.

Hotchkiss, L. M. (2003), '"Still in the Gam": Cybertransformations of the "New Flesh" in David Cronenberg's *eXistenZ*', *The Velvet Light Trap*, 52: 15–32.

Kenyon, R. V. and J. Leigh (2011), 'Human Augmentics: Augmenting Human Evolution', *2011 Annual International Conference of the IEEE Engineering in Medicine and Biology Society*, Boston, MA, 30 August–3 September, *Institute of Electronical and Electronics Engineers* (IEEE): 6758–61.

Kishiro, Y. (1990–5), [Manga series] *Battle Angel Alita*, Tokyo: Business Jump.

Leino, O. T. (2009), 'Understanding Games as Played: Sketch for a First-Person Perspective for Computer Game Analysis', *Proceedings of the 2009 Philosophy of Computer Games Conference*, Oslo, 13–15 August.

Leonard, B. (1992), [Film], *The Lawnmower Man*, Allied Vision, Fuji Eight Company Ltd., Lane Pringle Productions, Angel Studios.

Linderoth, J. (2013), 'Beyond the Digital Divide: An Ecological Approach to Game-Play', *Transactions of the Digital Games Research Association*, 1 (1).

Meyer, N. (1982), [Film] *Star Trek II: The Wrath of Khan*, Paramount Pictures.

Novitz, D. (1980), 'Fiction, Imagination and Emotion', *Journal of Aesthetics and Art Criticism*, 38 (3): 279–88.

Nussbaum, M. C. ([1986] 2001), *The Fragility of Goodness: Luck and Ethics in Greek Tragedy and Philosophy*, rev. edn, Cambridge: Cambridge University Press.

Pajitnov, A. ([1984] 1989), [Digital game] *Tetris*, published by Atari Games.

Parker, T. (2005, 30 March), [TV series episode] 'Best Friends Forever', season 9, episode 4, in T. Parker, M. Stone, B. Graden, D. Liebling, F. C. Agnone, B. Howell and A. Garefino, executive producers, *South Park*, ViacomCBS Domestic Media Networks.

Pomerance, M. (2003), 'Neither here nor there: *eXistenZ* as "Elevator Film"', *Quarterly Review of Film and Video*, 20 (1): 1–14.

Reynolds, A. (2000), *Revelation Space*, London: Gollancz.

Reynolds, A. ([2003] 2006), *Diamond Dogs, Turquoise Days*, New York: ACE Books.

Rodley, C. (1999), 'Game Boy', *Sight and Sound*, 4: 8–10.

Sartre, J. P. ([1943] 2020), *Being and Nothingness: An Essay in Phenomenological Ontology*, London: Routledge.

Sartre, J. P. ([1946] 1970), *L'Existentialisme est un humanisme*, Paris: Nagel.
Van de Mosselaer, N. (2020), 'The Paradox of Interactive Fiction', PhD diss., University of Antwerp.
Vella, D. (2016), '"Who am 'I' in the Game": A Typology of Modes of Ludic Subjectivity', *Proceedings of the 2016 DiGRA and FDG*, Dundee, 1–6 August.
Verbeek, P. P. (2005), *What Things Do: Philosophical Reflections on Technology, Agency, and Design*, University Park, PA: Pennsylvania State University Press.
Verhoeven, P. (1987), [Film], *Robocop*, Orion Pictures.
Verhoeven, P. (1990), [Film], *Total Recall*, Carolco Pictures.
Wilson, S. (2011), *Politics of Insects: David Cronenberg's Cinema of Confrontation*, New York: Continuum Books.

6

Concluding Thoughts

This book has analysed fictional games and their expressive possibilities as narrative devices and philosophical tools. To our knowledge, this is the first time these topics have been at the centre of scholarly inquiry. Accordingly, we designed and wrote this book as an initial exploration of the cultural relevance of fictional games. This pursuit required the articulation of a definition of what, specifically, is meant by 'fictional games' and the proposition of some fundamental conceptual tools to frame and discuss their use and significance.

In the first two chapters, we proposed understanding fictional games as playful activities and ludic artefacts that were conceptualized to be part of fictional worlds. Fictional games are, thus, meant to trigger the imagination of the appreciator of a work of fiction and cannot be – or, at least, were not originally meant to be – actually played. In these first two chapters, we also noted that games in fictional worlds are hardly ever presented in ways that are formally complete: their rules, affordances, boundaries, exceptions and criteria for success are typically simply hinted at and defined just clearly enough to achieve their intended narrative functions. In line with this observation, one of the foundational analytical tools we proposed for the analysis of fictional games is a fourfold taxonomy of the various forms of unplayability that can characterize these games.

Some fictional games are unplayable because the author of the work of fiction of which the game is a part simply did not provide enough detail and information for it to be playable without substantial integrations (see section 1.2.1) and/or because some of its components or required behaviours are clearly not (or not yet) possible in the actual world (section 1.2.2). Other forms of unplayability depend on the physical, cognitive and perceptual limitations that (currently) define human players (section 1.2.3) or are because of interdictions that define our current moral communities (section 1.2.4). As we discussed in Chapter 1, the first two types of unplayability result from objective qualities of how a fictional game is represented, whereas the second two depend on subjective and contextual factors.

After introducing the four types of unplayability of fictional games, we moved on to the question of how to analyse and discuss these games' relevance in the works of fiction in which they are played (or even simply mentioned). In that regard, in Chapter 1, we proposed understanding fictional games as belonging to one of two broad categories that depend on their narrative relevance:

1. fictional games that serve as background elements contributing to the fictional worldbuilding (i.e. as part of the 'ground' over which more relevant acts of communication and events that are more significant to the plot take place); and
2. fictional games that have a more focal, central function in the fiction as narrative devices (i.e. games that have a primary importance in the fictional world in question).

Drawing on these distinctions and conceptual tools (as well as several other models and perspectives from disciplines such as the philosophy of fiction, narratology, game studies and science-fiction studies), we then proceeded to present various close readings of exemplary fictional games. In this pursuit, we identified four particularly frequent or especially interesting uses of fictional games and dedicated a thematic chapter to each of these uses. The function-specific chapters focused on the following topics:

1. the ideological use of fictional games (Chapter 2);
2. the possibilities for employing fictional games for subversive and utopian purposes (Chapter 3);
3. the capability of fictional games to infiltrate reality or to disguise reality as play (Chapter 4); and
4. and the potential of fictional games for stimulating and guiding the characters' transcendence (Chapter 5).

Obviously, the four functions we chose to cover in depth in the analytical chapters of this book do not exhaustively map the expressive potential of fictional games. In fact, in this book, we have mentioned several possibilities and uses beyond these four categories, including the potential of fictional games to be employed for comedic estrangement (briefly discussed in section 1.2.1). In this concluding chapter, before suggesting some potentially fruitful avenues for future research, we home in on one additional family of functions that we consider relevant as part of this pioneering exploration of the topic: a communicative function of fictional games that is transversally present in all the philosophical reflections and close readings that we have offered to this point – their capability to function as meta-referential (or meta-reflexive) devices. By approaching fictional games as meta-reflexive devices, we focus on their aptitude for suggesting critical and/or satirical perspectives on how actual games are designed, played, sold, manipulated, experienced, understood and used as part of our culture (see Gualeni 2016).

Because they frequently present unfamiliar experiences, and also as a consequence of their various forms of unplayability, fictional games can serve the often implicit purposes of revealing the biases and limitations that frame our understanding of games, the meaning and values we attribute to play, and the relationships that both games and play have with society and technology. In other words, fictional games show – in ways that are often surprising and unfamiliar – what games could be, what threats they pose (or might pose in the future) and what sociocultural relevance they could aspire to have. For example, by presenting imaginative ways that play can be utilized to normalize and promote values and beliefs within a certain social group, fictional games invite us to reflect on what the games we play *already* reveal about our culture and the ideologies we live by (see Chapter 2). In that regard, one rather common epiphany that can be facilitated by our encounter with fictional games is that the artefacts we call 'games' in Western societies are almost invariably framed as competitions for resources of some kind and generally push players to be efficient in accumulating, producing and upgrading goods (Dyer-Witheford and de Peuter 2009: 123–51; Möring and Leino 2016; Gualeni and Vella 2020: 80–3). On the basis of the isomorphism that we, along with other scholars, have identified between structured play and sociocultural arrangements, it is not surprising to observe how often game and play sneakily permeate – and often overlap with – our jobs, the functioning of our economy and some of our relationships with other people. As discussed in Chapter 4, this blurring of boundaries between the playful and the serious – the overlap and confusion between aspects of play and non-play – are possible precisely because the games we already play build upon and replicate values, metaphors and orientations that direct our social behaviour and orient our moral compass (see Flanagan and Nissenbaum 2014). For these reasons, the progressive 'ludification' of our society is perceived as a mounting danger to our culture, in terms of, for example, access to information, surveillance of the individual and trust in democracy and political institutions (see Raessens 2006; Dippel and Fizek 2017).

6.1 Meta-referential fictional games and satire

In Chapter 3, which focused on fictional games that are designed, played or repurposed in a work of fiction as a crucial component of a utopian project, we outlined the kinds of critical communicative acts performed by fictional games when they are explicitly presented as political tools. In this function, we recognized fictional games as pushing the boundaries of our political imagination and potentially shedding light on how games are currently employed and designed in the context of actual countercultural propaganda. Obviously, fictional games can also implicitly suggest new avenues for actual games to become more effective and relevant agents of sociocultural change.

Similar observations also apply to fictional games used to incentivize and guide a path of individual growth and self-perfection. Playing fictional games as a practice of self-transformation also inherently invites reflection on the current use of games as tools for professional training and physical exercise, as well as for psychological therapy, mindfulness and relaxation. Fictional games as media for self-transcendence can anticipate new ways in which interactions with fictional worlds and aspects of structured play may contribute to the self-betterment and evolution of human beings (see Chapter 5).

Another expressive function of fictional games that relies on meta-referentiality is evident in their capability to project visions of future social uses of games and technologies and to anticipate upcoming trends in the design of games. Examples of this future-oriented use abound, from the *OASIS* in *Ready Player One* (Cline 2011), a fictional video game platform that imaginatively anticipates the future of shared virtual reality multiplayer environments (see section 4.2), to *My Dinner with Andre*, a fictional arcade game played in a 1990 episode of the animated television series *The Simpsons* (Archer 1990; see Figure 6.1). In an age when the

Figure 6.1 In the fictional video game *My Dinner with Andre*, the player appears to be guiding the conversation among the characters. This scene both reflects sarcastically on the tone of the film that inspired the fictional game and serves as a moment of indirect characterization for Martin Prince Jr. *The Simpsons* © 20th Century Studios 1989. All rights reserved.

market was dominated by the production and commercialization of action-oriented, violent and narratively unsubtle video game titles, the fictional video game *My Dinner with Andre* wittily predicted the advent and commercial success of works that focused on providing simulations of intimate and often mundane conversations.[1]

---

[1] *My Dinner with Andre* is itself based on the 1981 American comedy-drama film of the same title directed by Louis Malle. The estranging comedic effect of the game ensues from the fact that *My Dinner with Andre* is presented as a cabinet video game – a mode of ludic consumption that is conventionally associated with frenetic gameplay and a crude and shallow fictional component. The first video game that can be compared with the fictional game sarcastically presented in *The Simpsons* was released only two years after the airing of the episode containing *My Dinner with Andre* (Archer 1990). *Dōkyūsei* (ELF Corporation 1992) was the first dialogue-based dating simulation video game to be released commercially. A variety (both in number and in style) of conversation-simulating video games continue to be released today, especially by independent developers. Particularly notable among them is the critically acclaimed artificial intelligence-based conversation video game *Façade* (Mateas and Stern 2005). Another recent, successful example of this kind of intimate, dialogue-based interactive experience is the moving text-messenger conversation video game *Bury Me, My Love* (The Pixel Hunt 2017).

A similar and particularly obvious form of meta-referentiality in fictional games can be recognized in their satirical use[2] – that is, when fictional games present a humorous critique of how actual games are made, played, used and shared socially. Unlike the previous examples of meta-referentiality in fictional games, the satirical function tends to be expressed in ways that are explicit, if not deliberately on-the-nose. The analysis of a few examples of fictional games that have a clear satirical role within a work of fiction should help to clarify what we mean and to show how their parodic intent tends to manifest itself.

Bonestorm, a fictional video game franchise that recurs in the fictional world of *The Simpsons*, first appeared in the eleventh episode of season seven ('Marge Be Not Proud', Scully 1995), which initially aired on 17 December 1995. The original *Bonestorm* is an obvious caricature of *Mortal Kombat II*, which was released two years earlier (Midway Games 1993). In that episode of *The Simpsons*, the various characters fighting one another in the fictional television advertisement for *Bonestorm* bear an unmistakable resemblance to the *Mortal Kombat II* characters Liu Kang, Goro and Kintaro. Presenting a caricature of Midway Games' popular video game franchise, *Bonestorm* satirizes the grotesque character design, brutal representation of violence, unimaginative plot and mindless serialization that characterized 1990s fighting games. The titles of *Bonestorm*'s video game competitors mentioned in the same episode (i.e. *Bloodstorm*, *Bonesquad* and *Bloodstorm 2*) also contribute to this parodic effect.

A comparable example of meta-referential satire can be recognized in the fictional game *Lee Carvallo's Putting Challenge*, a golf-simulation video game that is played in the same episode of *The Simpsons* where *Bonestorm* is introduced. *Lee Carvallo's Putting Challenge* was turned into a fan-made playable game by Aaron Demeter in 2020. In the episode, as a counterpoint to *Bonestorm*, *Lee Carvallo's Putting Challenge* mocks how simulation games were understood and developed at the time, exaggerating features such as their fastidious and overly technical gameplay, their aesthetical blandness and the patronizing way in which they established relationships with the players.

The fictional, radio-operated, multiplayer role-playing adventure game, Wirrâl Untethered, in the digital gameworld of *Disco Elysium* (ZA/UM 2019) offers

---

[2] In this context, satire is understood as a form (or genre) of fiction in which human or individual vices, follies, abuses and shortcomings are held up to censure by means of ridicule, derision, irony, parody, caricature or other methods (Caselli et al. 2020: 2). Accordingly, we conceive of satire as an expressive form that has aspirations of both entertainment and criticism. Ways of detecting, understanding and crafting satire in relation to games and game design have been presented and discussed in the field of game studies (but exclusively in relation to actually playable games) by Caselli et al. (ibid.) and by Schellekens et al. (2020).

another extremely interesting example of humorous meta-criticism. Developed by the (fictional) independent game company Fortress Accident, Wirrâl Untethered remained unfinished and unplayable. As players, we learn about the fictional game by visiting Fortress Accident's abandoned development studios in Martinaise, where some of the production documents can be examined and interacted with, and by speaking with non-player characters that were formerly part of the development team. Overly ambitious in its mechanical complexity and narrative intricacy, Wirrâl Untethered put the mental health of the game developers to the test for years and eventually forced the game company to discontinue its development and declare bankruptcy. It does not take much imagination to recognize a definite meta-referential intent in ZA/UM's (the developers of *Disco Elysium*) decision to present the story of a small development team biting off more than they could chew in working to produce an original, large-scale title. Wirrâl Untethered thus functions as a satirical *mise en abyme*, a self-mocking *parallel* (see the Foreword and Chapter 1) between the studio that created *Disco Elysium* and the developers of the fictional game within the game. Wirrâl Untethered also proposes a subtle critical reflection on independent game development and the practices within it, in a more general sense; the title of the fictional game references *Camelot Unchained*, a fantasy massively multiplayer online role-playing video game that was partially funded through a crowd-funding campaign and that has been in a beta stage of development since 2018 (with no release date announced at the time of the publication of this book).

A final example of the use a fictional game as a self-referential device can be found in the American streaming comedy series *Mythic Quest* (2020–1). *Mythic Quest* is also the name of the fictional fantasy massive multiplayer online role-playing video game that is being developed by the fictional game studio where the series is set. *Mythic Quest* tells the interlinked stories of different game developers working on various expansions of the game. In terms of its evident caricatural and parodic intentions, the series targets current cultural issues concerning game development, such as overwork, mismanagement, sexism in games and in game studios, and questionable practices of game monetization. The fictional game *Mythic Quest* is a rather generic open-world fantasy role-playing game that serves as a background element in the narrative development of the comedy series. Its thematic function, however, is a particularly present one, as the game's visual appearance and various elements are constant features of both the aesthetics and the plot of the larger work of fiction.

In this section, we have proposed understanding fictional games as expressive devices that are almost inevitably meta-referential. Even when a fictional game does not explicitly reference an existing game, its very existence within a fictional world invites appreciators to reflect upon the games they play in their everyday lives and on the various roles and forms that play adopts in the actual world. In other words, just as we cannot avoid comparing our experiences as beings in the actual world with those of the characters inhabiting a fictional world, we understand ludic experiences and artefacts found in fiction through our own interpretation of what games are, can be and can do. In this sense, our foray into fictional games in the current book – and the resulting recognition of their cultural relevance – demonstrates that the fields of interest and applicability of game studies are wider than is commonly construed.

6.2 Directions for future research

We hope that our present work will inspire future analyses in game studies along several lines that we see as potentially fruitful avenues for future investigation. Through our analyses and close readings of fictional games in this book, we have shown that the knowledge produced in game studies is not limited in its application to analyses and claims concerning games that exist (or that have existed) or of actual experiences of play. Rather, the discipline of game studies has already developed tools and methods that, although they have thus far been exclusively directed to actually playable games, can be fruitfully employed in the study of incomplete and unplayable fictional games.

We see fictional games as condensing and reconfiguring some fundamental characteristics and elements of games and play, and we thus believe that fictional games could be used as important case studies in new scholarly efforts in game ontology. We hope that this book will encourage such projects in the game studies community. Fictional games can be understood as invariably meta-referential because their existence invites new perspectives and interrogatives concerning the artefacts we commonly refer to as 'games' and the activities we categorize as 'playful'. Why do we embrace these abstractions, these paradoxical unplayable activities, as games to begin with? What characteristics and formal elements need to be present in fictional games for us to recognize them as games? In this book, our admittedly unsophisticated (but very practical) response to these questions was to take a nominal approach to defining what a fictional game is. According to this approach, whenever something within a work of fiction was described as a game, we decided to simply treat it as one. Such an operational and clear-cut distinction allowed us to keep the howling void of definitory matters at bay and to focus on offering analytical tools and observations related to the narrative roles of fictional games, as well as philosophical reflections about them. However, in our analysis, we often brought in fictional games that were understood as games before they were explicitly described as such in the works of fiction of which they are part. In some rare cases, we even discussed particular activities or artefacts as 'games' without their being recognized as such anywhere in the work of which they are a part. However incomplete and experientially inaccessible for play, we found that these entities possessed some formal features and/or certain ways of signalizing or inviting playfulness that motivated us to include them in our discussion. As also emphasized by Daniel Vella in his Foreword, further explorations of fictional games dedicated to identifying these characteristics are one strand of research we hope to inspire with this book.

Although game scholars may be the implicit audience for this book, we believe that some of the questions left unanswered in our work may be addressed by scholars in the field of literary studies, especially those exploring science-fiction. A question that has been hinted at throughout the book but left unanswered involves the relationship between the representation of fictional games and the genre of fiction to which they belong. This question was prompted by discussions with Cristina Di Maio, whose work on games and play in literature (Di Maio 2017) led her to recognize this gap in our work. In reflecting on this gap, we came to realize that most of the fictional games analysed in this book are found in works that can be more or less comfortably categorized in the science-fiction genre. From a literary studies perspective, then, one could raise the question of why fictional games tend to appear in certain genres more than others. One provisional answer is that genres such as science-fiction historically employ narrative tools such as technological or social speculation to suggest possible future scenarios and promote embracing a variety of new perspectives that often constitute alternatives to established world views and moral orientations. From this perspective, fictional games could even be considered among the defining tropes of science-fiction, along with, for example, space colonization, sentient artificial intelligences and dystopian technological systems of social control. Nevertheless, this remains a fairly commonsensical conjecture that we hope may encourage more serious scrutiny. This, we feel, is needed not only to produce a taxonomy of the genres, literary or otherwise, in which fictional games are particularly present, but also as a resource for authors who may want to include fictional games in their work.

Another unanswered question in this pioneering foray into fictional games involves medium specificity. Throughout the book, we have taken an agnostic stance on media: we were interested in fictional games found in different types of narrative media (e.g. novels, films, television shows and video games), but we have spent relatively little time discussing the technical limitations and expressive possibilities that define each medium. Our avoidance of this aspect of our subject matter, to some degree, followed inherently from our research agenda, as we adopted a broad understanding of fiction to be able to discuss fictional games generally as transmedia narrative objects. Although we decided not to take on this question in the present book, we consider it an important issue for future investigations on the topic. How do fictional games exist in a way that is specific to a novel, a film or a video game? Is the iconographic explicitness of audiovisual media a tool contributing to the invention of fictional games that appear more believable, or is it a hindrance to their speculative nature? How does describing fictional games in words compare with showing them on screen? What are the defining characteristics of non-playable fictional games found in otherwise playable worlds such as those in video games? These questions remain open, and we believe that addressing them is a needed complement to the work we have done in this book.

This book was conceived as an initial exploration of what is, to our knowledge, a previously uncharted scholarly theme. By looking at what is found at the intersection of narrative imagination, game design and ludic culture, we felt that we could offer useful and stimulating insight into both games and fiction. More specifically, this book has demonstrated that games are a constitutive part of the fictional worlds we encounter as readers, viewers and players. The presence of games and playful activities within fictional worlds contribute to the experience of these worlds as vibrant, with their own culture and history, and experientially rich. Further, this book has presented a case for rethinking the idea of games as artefacts that are not necessarily meant to be played but that can be described or imagined – creations, in other words, that can exist within one's imagination without ever being fully realized or formalized. As a subset of contemporary ludic imagination, fictional games are hybrid objects that variously combine elements of game design, worldbuilding and storytelling. In light of this interdisciplinary hybridity, we hope the ideas and tools offered in this book will be relevant to a variety of scholars and practitioners interested in investigating how game design contributes to imagining fictional worlds or in exploring the importance of narrative imagination in game design.

References

Archer, W. (1990, 11 February), [TV series episode] 'Moaning Liza', season 1, episode 6, in M. Groening, J. L. Brooks and S. Simon, executive producers, *The Simpsons*, Fox.

Caselli, S., K. Rutter Bonello Giappone, J. Schellekens and S. Gualeni (2020), 'Satire at Play: A Game Studies Approach to Satire', Proceedings of the 2020 FDG International Conference, Bugibba, 15–18 September, 2020.

Cline, E. (2011), *Ready Player One*, New York: Broadway Books.

Demeter, A. (2020), [Digital game] *Lee Carvallo's Putting Challenge*, developed by Aaron Demeter. Available online https://aaron-demeter.itch.io/lee-carvallos-putting-challenge (accessed 18 May 2022).

Di Maio, C. (2017), 'All is Fair in Play and War: A Ludic Reading of Conflictual Dynamics in Three Short Stories by Grace Paley', *RSA Journal*, 28: 165–89.

Dippel, A. and S. Fizek (2017), 'Ludification of Culture: The Significance of Play and Games in Everyday Practices of the Digital Era', *Digitisation: Theories and Concepts for the Empirical Cultural Analysis*, New York: Routledge: 276–92.

Dyer-Witheford, N. and G. de Peuter (2009), *Games of Empire: Global Capitalism and Video Games*, Minneapolis, MN: University of Minnesota Press.

ELF Corporation (1992), [Digital game] *Dōkyūsei*, directed by Kinji Yoshimoto and published by ELF Corporation.

Flanagan, M. and H. Nissenbaum (2014), *Values at Play in Digital Games*, Cambridge, MA: The MIT Press.

Gualeni, S. (2016), 'Self-Reflexive Videogames: Observations and Corollaries on Virtual Worlds as Philosophical Artifacts', *G A M E – The Italian Journal of Game Studies*, 5 (1): 11–20.

Gualeni, S. and D. Vella (2020), *Virtual Existentialism: Meaning and Subjectivity in Virtual Worlds*, Basingstoke: Palgrave Pivot.

Malle, L. (1981), [Film] *My Dinner with Andre*, New Yorker Films.

Mateas, M. and A. Stern (2005), [Digital game] *Façade*, developed by Procedural Arts and published by Procedural Arts.

Midway Games (1993), [Digital game] *Mortal Kombat II*, directed by E. Boon and J. Tobias, and published by Midway and Acclaim Entertainment.

Möring, S. and O. T. Leino (2016), 'Beyond Games as Political Education: Neoliberalism in the Contemporary Computer Game Form', *Journal of Gaming and Virtual Worlds*, 8 (2): 145–61.

Raessens, J. (2006), 'Playful Identities, or the Ludification of Culture', *Games and Culture*, 1 (1): 52–7.

Schellekens, J., S. Caselli, S. Gualeni and K. Rutter Bonello Giappone (2020), 'Satirical Game Design: The Case of the Boardgame Construction BOOM!', Proceedings of the 2020 FDG International Conference, Bugibba, 15–18 September.

Scully, M. (1995, 17 December), 'Marge Be Not Proud', season 7, episode 11, in B. Oakley and J. Weinstein, executive producers, *The Simpsons*, Fox.

The Pixel Hunt (2017), [Digital game] *Bury Me, My Love*, developed by The Pixel Hunt and published by Dear Villager and Plug In Digital.

ZA/UM (2019), [Digital game] *Disco Elysium*, directed by Robert Kurvitz and published by ZA/UM.

Appendix

A compendium of fictional games cited in the book

The following appendix lists all the fictional games that were mentioned in this book. They are listed alphabetically and described in a concise manner. Should the reader be interested in locating where a particular fictional game is discussed in the book, we invite them to search the name of the fictional game in question in the Index.

1. **American Cowboy Suit:** A fictional, playful virtual reality toy described by Philip K. Dick in his 1959 short story, 'War Game'. By wearing the suit, a child experiences an immersive and interactive recreation of the American Wild West.

2. **Archipelagos of Insulinde:** This is the title of a fictional board game that is played (and sold) in the fictional world of ZA/UM's 2019 adventure video game *Disco Elysium*.

3. *Armada*: An online flight combat simulation in Ernest Cline's 2015 science-fiction novel with the same name. Originally presented as a fictional video game, later in the novel *Armada* is revealed to be a device for training (and screening) prospective drone pilots.

4. *Azad*: A staggeringly complex and nuanced turn-based military strategy fictional board game that involves multiple boards and various kinds of

pawns, resources and autonomous agents. It is central to Iain M. Banks' 1988 science-fiction novel *The Player of Games*.

5. **Bamboozled:** A labyrinthine, fictional quiz show that is played in the twentieth episode of the eighth season of the TV series *Friends*, titled 'The One with the Baby Shower'.

6. ***The Big Hunt(cerca ovunque):*** A state-sanctioned, televised fictional game found in Elio Petri's film *The 10th Victim* (1965). In it, players are divided into 'hunters' and 'victims' and must kill one another in order to win.

7. **The Bird Game:** An informal way to reference the unnamed, fictional VR action shooting video game that is played (and hallucinated about) in an episode of the TV series *House M.D.* (2009).

8. **Blaggard's Boast:** This is a fictional board game that is mentioned in Banks' 1998 science-fiction novel *Inversions*. As discussed in Chapter 2, its title is already indicative of the interests and orientations that are prevalent among the social groups that play it.

9. **Blood Spire:** This is an alien construction of unknown origin featured in Alastair Reynold's 2003 science-fiction novella *Diamond Dogs*. In line with the literary tradition of deadly games, the spire confronts its players with a series of trials, one per room.

10. **Bonestorm:** A gory, fictional fighting video game franchise that often appears in the fictional world of *The Simpsons*. The game is a blatant caricature of the actual video game *Mortal Kombat 2* (Midway Games 1993).

11. **Boxing in 'Steel':** Richard Matherson's 1956 science-fiction short story 'Steel' takes place in a near future in which human boxing has been banned. Human boxers are, thus, substituted by massive humanoid fighting robots, inaugurating a new fictional sport.

12. **Calvinball:** A spontaneous and open-ended fictional sport that is played in the comic strip *Calvin and Hobbes* by the titular characters. It only features a couple of fixed rules, one of which is that players cannot play Calvinball the same way twice.

13. **Card Wars:** A fantasy deck-building card game played in the animated series *Adventure Time* (2010–18). The game obviously references the actual game Magic: The Gathering, and the protagonists describe it as 'super-complicated'.

14. **Cones of Dunshire:** An extremely convoluted fictional board game that is played in the TV series *Parks and Recreation* (2009–15). It first appeared in the eighth episode of the sixth season titled 'The Cones of Dunshire'.

15. **The Contenders:** A deadly, fictional game played in the 2001 film *Series 7: The Contenders* by Daniel Minahan. In it, six competitors randomly selected among the general population are given a gun and instructed to hunt each other down.

16. **Cripple Mr. Onion:** A fictional card game that is played in the *Discworld* fantasy novel series by Terry Pratchett. It is characterized by elements of both blackjack and poker, and it requires an eight-suited card deck.

17. **The Cube:** A fictional, mechanical device central to the 1997 movie by the same name where players must find a way out of a gigantic cube made of smaller, empty cubic rooms that can autonomously move, shift, rearrange and kill their occupants.

18. **Cups:** Cups is an intricate, fictional card game invented and played in the sixth episode of the sixth season of the TV series *Friends*, titled 'The One on the Last Night'.

19. **Cyvasse:** A turn-based chess-like fictional game played by two competing players in the fictional world of *A Song of Ice and Fire*, a series of epic fantasy novels written by George R. R. Martin (1996–present).

20. **Damage:** A fatal, fictional card game similar to Poker that is played in Banks' 1987 science-fiction novel *Consider Phlebas*. In it, players bet credits as well as the lives of the individuals in their retinue (including the players' own life) on card hands.

21. **Dejarik:** Also known as Holochess, Dejarik is a two-player chess-inspired fictional board game that originally appeared in George Lucas' 1977 film *Star Wars: Episode IV – A New Hope*. It is played on a round board using various holographic, animated pieces.

22. ***Domination*:** A fictional video game about territorial control played in the 1983 film *Never Say Never Again*. In it, the losing player receives a series of electric shocks of increasing intensity that depend on the amount of money wagered on the game.

23. **Duel Monsters:** A fictional spirit-casting deck-building card game that is central to the media franchise *Yu-Gi-Oh!* (1996–2004). It is played competitively by two opposing players or by two rival pairs of players.

24. **eXistenZ:** An immersive virtual reality game that is uploaded directly into the players' spinal cords in the eponymous 1999 film by David Cronenberg.

25. **Fizzbin:** A poker-inspired bluff-based fictional card-game that is played in the original TV series *Star Trek* (1966–9).

26. **'The Game':** In A. S. Byatt's 1967 novel *The Game*, two sisters develop a complex game over their childhood years, involving elements of wargaming and role-playing to simulate a fantastical domain of chivalric adventure.

27. **'The Game':** In David Fincher's 1997 thriller film *The Game*, a wealthy investment banker is given a mysterious gift by his brother: the participation in a game that integrates with his actual life and work in unexpected and troublesome ways.

28. **'The Game' in *Chasm City*:** 'The Game' refers to a fatal, technologically enhanced sport where a human – typically belonging to the lowest classes – is fed, tracked with brain implants, and released in an abandoned part of Chasm City to be hunted and killed.

29. **'The Game' in *Star Trek: The Next Generation*:** 'The Game' is a highly addictive, single-player augmented reality game in the Star Trek Universe. It is played via an advanced technological interface that directly connects to the player's synapses.

30. **The Games in *Alice in Borderland*:** During a firework celebration in Tokyo, three Japanese high school students are inexplicably transported into a different version of the same city where they are forced to take part in a series of fictional fatal challenges.

31. **The Games in *Saw*:** All films in the ongoing *Saw* franchise are based on players having to face deadly riddles and puzzles devised by an evil mastermind. The protagonists must overcome the fatal challenges in question in the attempt to (possibly) save their lives.

32. **The Games in *Squid Game*:** Competing in a series of traditional children's games (but with deadly twists), 456 people put their lives at risk and compete in a survival game show. The prize is a fabulous amount of money, and there can only be one winner.

33. **GANTZ:** A fictional game in which the recently dead protagonist of the series and several other deceased people are mysteriously brought back to life and forced to hunt down and kill aliens armed with futuristic equipment and weaponry. For every hunt, each character receives a score based on their performance.

34. **The Gentleman Misinformant:** A fictional board game that is mentioned in Banks' 1998 science-fiction novel *Inversions*.

35. **The Glass Bead Game:** A two-player fictional game in the eponymous 1943 book by Hermann Hesse. It consists in taking turns in placing special beads on the board following certain arrangements considered valid and meaningful.

36. *Global Thermonuclear War*: A single-player computer game in John Badham's 1983 film *WarGames*. It is a tactical simulation game set in the Cold War era where one can opt to play either as the Soviet Union or as the United States.

37. *Grand Theft Auto VI: Zootopia*: A fictional fourth instalment of the actual role-playing action-adventure video game series *Grand Theft Auto*. It is played in the fictional world of the 2010 novel *Zoo City* by Lauren Beukes.

38. **Gwent:** Originally, Gwent was a competitive two-player turn-based strategic fictional card game played in the fantasy world of the novel series *The Witcher* (1986–2013) by Andrzej Sapkowski. It was adapted in video game form (also single-player) in 2018.

39. *Heaven vs Hell*: A fictional action-strategy video game that is played in the fourth episode of the ninth season of the animated TV series *South Park*. The game was created by God to find a person to lead his legions against the forces of Hell.

40. **The Hunger Games:** A game of survival in Suzanne Collins' series of novels with the same name (2008–20), The Hunger Games take place in a dystopian future in which boys and girls are pitted against each other in a deadly competition by a cruel ruling elite.

41. **Ignis Fatuus:** Ignis Fatuus is a fictional single-player board game in Olga Tokarczuk's 1996 novel *Primeval and Other Times*. Brass pieces are moved through a labyrinth consisting of eight concentric circles. The game requires

certain real-world conditions to be met before certain moves can be made, and, as such, takes years to be played to completion.

42. **Infinite Fun Space:** This is the ironic and understated way in which some artificial intelligences (the Minds) refer to their playful simulation of possible universes within Banks' Culture science-fiction novel series (1987–2012).

43. **Jumanji:** Jumanji is a deadly, fictional board game that is played in Joe Johnson's 1995 movie by the same name. By virtue of supernatural qualities, Jumanji unleashes jungle-related hazards on its players, who need to beat the game to be free of its curse.

44. **Kepesh-Yakshi:** A two-player chess-inspired fictional game in the fictional world of the 2012 video game *Mass Effect 3*. Simulating a space battle, fictional players take turns in moving holographic pieces over the hexagonal sectors on a flat map.

45. **Kobayashi Maru Test:** Never explicitly referred to as a game, the Kobayashi Maru Test is a training exercise designed to evaluate the character and the strategic reasoning of Starfleet Academy cadets in the science-fiction universe of *Star Trek*.

46. **Lee Carvallo's Putting Challenge:** A tedious and patronizing golf-simulation video game that is played in the eleventh episode of season seven of the animated TV series *The Simpsons* 'Marge Be Not Proud' (1990).

47. **Liar's Dice:** A fictional board game that is mentioned in Banks' 1998 science-fiction novel *Inversions*. As discussed in Chapter 2, its title is already indicative of the interests and orientations that are prevalent among the social groups that play it.

48. **Lightcycle Competitions:** Are fictional, futuristic two-wheeled vehicles that can generate a solid wall made of light behind them. They are used in deadly competitions against artificial humanoid players within the fictional world of *Tron* (1982–2013).

49. **The Lottery in Babylon:** First appeared in 1941, 'The Lottery in Babylon' is a short story by Jorge Luis Borges that is set in a mythical Babylon. In the city, all social and political activities are chance-based events dictated by an all-encompassing lottery.

50. **The Maze:** In this fatal game, its amnesiac players need to navigate a gigantic maze in order to leave the restricted area where they are trapped. It is

featured in a 2009 novel by James Dashner titled *The Maze Runner*, and was made into a movie in 2014.

51. **The Mind Game:** An immersive, single-player game that involves a highly advanced artificial intelligence. It is played in Orson Scott Card's 1985 science-fiction novel *Ender's Game* to analyse the personality and psychological traits of the Battle School students.

52. **Monarch's Dispute:** A strategic, turn-based, two-player fictional board game that is played in Banks' 1998 science-fiction novel *Inversions*. Based on chess, the way it is played parallels the conversations between two of the novel's protagonists.

53. **Mornington Crescent:** A conversation-based fictional game featured in the comedy show *I'm Sorry I Haven't a Clue*. The intricate rules are entirely obscure to the audience, and one of the most hilarious topics of contention in the show.

54. **Motorball:** The fictional spectator sport Motorball has a focal role in the manga series *Battle Angel Alita* (1990–5), where it is described as a blood sport on skates with elements borrowed from baseball, gladiator combat and car racing.

55. *My Dinner with Andre*: Based on the 1981 American comedy-drama film directed by Louis Malle with the same title, *My Dinner with Andre* is a fictional arcade game played in the sixth episode of the first series of the animated TV series *The Simpsons* (1990).

56. *Mythic Quest*: A fantasy massive multiplayer online role-playing video game that is being developed by a fictional game studio. The streaming comedy series by the same name (2020–21) builds around problems and events concerning its development.

57. **The *OASIS*:** Acronym for: Ontologically Anthropocentric Sensory Immersive Simulation, is a massively multiplayer online simulation infrastructure that is part of the fictional world of Ernest Cline's 2011 science-fiction novel *Ready Player One*.

58. **Oråki:** A strategic two-player turn-based fictional board game described in Nike A. Sulway's 2013 novel *Rupetta*. Players control pawns with different sizes and possibilities, which also correspond to different amounts of phalanges that players need to cut from their own hands when these pawns are eliminated.

59. **Pai Sho:** A Go-inspired two-player competitive fictional board game that is popular throughout the fantasy world of the animated TV series *Avatar: The Last Airbender* (2005–8).

60. **The Peg Game:** A two-player competitive fictional board game that bears, in its minimal description, some resemblance to draughts. It is played in the fictional world of Reynolds' 2021 science-fiction novel *Inhibitor Space*.

61. **Questland:** With the aid of neurotransmitting devices and other advanced technologies, fantasy fiction becomes playful reality on an island off the north-west coast of the United States. *Questland* is the name of the augmented reality fantasy gameworld at the core of Carrie Vaughn's eponymous 2021 novel.

62. **Quidditch:** One of the favourite pastimes of the students of the magic school of Hogwarts in the fictional world of *Harry Potter* (1997–2007). It can be described as a magical version of hockey that is played on flying brooms.

63. **Quintet:** A backgammon-inspired fictional board game for six players that is widely played in the fictional world of the eponymous 1979 post-apocalyptic science-fiction film directed by Robert Altman.

64. **Raubritter:** This is the title of a fictional board game that is played (and sold) in the fictional world of ZA/UM's 2019 adventure video game *Disco Elysium*.

65. **Rollerball:** The most popular blood sport in the eponymous 1975 film by Norman Jewison. It plays on a skating rink, and is a brutal combination of roller-skating, American football and motorcycle racing.

66. **Roy: A Life Well Lived:** A virtual-life simulation video game that is played in the second episode of the second series of the animated TV series *Rick and Morty* titled 'Mortynight Run' (2015).

67. **The Running Man:** A deadly fictional TV game show that is played in the eponymous 1982 dystopian science-fiction novel by Stephen King (as Richard Bachman) and in the corresponding 1987 film adaptation by Paul Michael Glaser.

68. **Secret Keep:** A fictional board game that is mentioned in Banks' 1998 science-fiction novel *Inversions*. As discussed in Chapter 2, its title is already

indicative of the interests and orientations that are prevalent among the social groups that play it.

69. **Shadowplay:** An often fatal, technologically enhanced sport played in Chasm City in Reynolds' science-fiction novel with the same title. In it, a professional hunter and a voluntary prey are bound by a contract detailing the rules of engagement and the duration of the hunt.

70. **Slayers:** A first-person shooting game where players – through nanotechnological brain implants – control the actions of actual death-row inmates who fight for survival in specially created arenas in the 2009 movie *Gamer*.

71. **Solar Lottery:** A fictional lottery described and played by Philip K. Dick in his 1955 science-fiction novel with the same title. The lottery's chance-based assignment of political roles is, in the novel, a social tool that justifies and upholds hegemonic power.

72. **Stars and Comets:** A fictional space-themed board game that makes its appearance in several science-fiction works by Andre Norton.

73. *Strategema*: A fictional video action-strategy video game that is played in an episode of the science-fiction TV series *Star Trek: The Next Generation* by Lieutenant Commander Data and a renowned alien strategist named Sirna Kolrami.

74. **Subterfuge:** A fictional board game that is mentioned in Banks' 1998 science-fiction novel *Inversions*. As discussed in Chapter 2, its title is already indicative of the interests and orientations that are prevalent among the social groups that play it.

75. **Suzerainty:** A competitive civilization-building fictional board game where a player chooses a nation and sets off to colonize and exploit other cultures. It is the only fictionally playable fictional board game in ZA/UM's 2019 video game *Disco Elysium*.

76. **Swords and Strongholds:** A chess-inspired fictional board game invented by David Petersen as part of his graphic novel series *Mouse Guard* (2006–present).

77. **Syndrome:** Designed by the oppressed Ganymedeans to be played by the Terrans, Syndrome is a Monopoly-inspired fictional board game described

by Philip K. Dick in his 1959 short story 'War Game', in which it serves a utopian, subversive function.

78. **Three-Cornered Pitney:** Exhilaratingly intricate, Three-Cornered Pitney is a fictional game invented by Jack Davis and appeared as a five-page story on issue 241 of *Mad Magazine* (1983).

79. **Thud:** A competitive two-player fictional board game played in the *Discworld* fantasy novel series by Terry Pratchett. Inspired by the Scandinavian 'tafl' strategy board games, Thud's narrative refers to a famous historical battle between dwarfs and trolls.

80. **Travesty:** A fictional board game that is mentioned in Banks' 1998 science-fiction novel *Inversions*. As discussed in Chapter 2, its title is already indicative of the interests and orientations that are prevalent among the social groups that play it.

81. *Treadmill to Bucks:* A cruel fictional game show that appears in the 1982 novel *The Running Man*. In it, contestants with various health conditions are forced to run on a treadmill while answering quiz-style questions in exchange for money.

82. **Triad:** A poker-inspired bluff-based fictional card game that is played in the *Battlestar Galactica* science-fiction television series (2004–9).

83. **True American:** A fictional drinking game played in the TV series *New Girl* (2011–18). Its severe underspecification often gives rise to a variety of exhilarating, paradoxical situations in the fiction.

84. *US:* A multiplayer, immersive virtual reality video game in Michele Cocchi's 2020 Italian novel with the same title. Game missions (or quests) in *US* take place in the contexts of some of the greatest humanitarian tragedies of the twentieth century.

85. **The Viticulturist:** This is the title of a fictional board game that is played (and sold) in the fictional world of ZA/UM's 2019 adventure video game *Disco Elysium*.

86. **Whack-Bat:** A fictional team sport reminiscent of cricket that appears in Wes Anderson's 2009 stop motion animated comedy film *Fantastic Mr. Fox*.

87. **Whiff of Truth:** A fictional board game that is mentioned in Banks' 1998 science-fiction novel *Inversions*. Its title is already indicative of

the interests and orientations that are prevalent among the social groups that play it.

88. **Wicked Grace:** A poker-like fictional game played by the characters of the 2014 adventure role-playing video game *Dragon Age: Inquisition* developed by BioWare.

89. **Wirrâl:** The fictional game of Wirrâl is briefly mentioned in ZA/UM's 2019 digital game *Disco Elysium*, but an expansion for it is a buyable object in the game. Nothing is known about its gameplay, apart from its bucolic illustrations and its human-like pawns.

90. **Wirrâl Untethered:** A fictional, radio-operated, multiplayer role-playing adventure game in the digital gameworld of *Disco Elysium* (ZA/UM 2019). The game is unfinished and unplayable as the fictional game developers went bankrupt.

91. **Wizard's Duel:** A wizard's duel is a formal way for magic users to engage in combat under the condition that only magical means could be used. In the fictional world of the *Harry Potter* media franchise, magic duelling is a safe, competitive sport for wizards.

92. **Zen Sumo:** A form of sumo played with telekinesis and mind-reading that is part of Howard Waldrop's 1983 short story 'Man-Mountain Gentian'.

Index

10th Victim, The 104–5, 110

actuality 13, 125
addiction 120 n.3, *121*, 122
Adventure Time 52
affordance 2, 5, 15, 25, 27 n.2, 28, 32, 60, 99, 161–3, 171
agency 2, 13–15, 32, 40 n.7, 42, 135, 137
American Cowboy Suit 128–30
Alice in Borderland 22, 186
Altman, Robert 11, 67, 75–80
Althusser, Louis 62–4
ambiguity 4, 11–12, 22, 35, 37, 99, 117–41, 145
Anderson, Wes 37, *38*, 192
Archipelagos of Insulinde 26, 183
apparatus 41, 48, 60 n.2, 63–4, 105, 109, 125, 132, 151
Armada 158, 183
avant-garde 100
Avatar: The Last Airbender 30, 190
Azad 11, 23, 94–9, 101–2, 110–11, 183

Badham, John 3, 187
Bamboozled 36, 184
Banks, Iain M. 11, 23, 34, 42, 47, 72, 94–102, 123, 147, 184–5, 187–92
Bateman, Chris 23–4
Battle Angel Alita 39, 151, 189
Battlestar Galactica 29, 192
Beukes, Lauren 66–7, 187
Big Hunt, The 104, 184
BioWare 26, 71, 73, 193
Bird Game, The 52, 184
Björk, Staffan 7 n.4, 23–4
Black Mirror 124–5, 141
Blaggard's Boast 72, 184
Blood Spire 42, 152–8, 166–7, 184
blood sport 39, 44, 102, 151, 165, 189–90
Bogost, Ian 7, 28, 41 n.8, 48, 61 n.4
Bonestorm 176, 184
Borges, Jorge Luis 97–8, 188

boxing 39, 44, 184
Brecht, Bertolt 48, 60 n.2, 88 n.1
Buckland, Warren 134–5
Bust A Cup 43

Caillois, Roger 2, 74, 103
Calvinball 36, *37*, 184
Calvin and Hobbes 36, *37*, 184
Card, Orson Scott 128, 131, 151, 158, 189
Card Wars 52, 184
CD Projekt RED 29
chance 47 n.9, 69, 73, 77, 80–1, 96–100, 110, 156, 188, 191
Chasm City 94, 104, 186, 191
Clarke, Arthur C. 39
Cline, Ernest 129, 131, 158, 174, 183, 189
Cocchi, Michele 192
Collins, Suzanne x, 50, 104, 187
Cones of Dunshire 36, 185
Contenders, The 104–5, 185
Consider Phlebas 47, 101, 185
comedy 21, 36–7, 175 n.1, 177, 189, 192
counterplay 64, 103, 110, 112
Cripple Mr. Onion 30, 185
Cronenberg, David 12, 42, 128, 151–2, 158–60, 162–6, 186
Csikszentmihalyi, Mihaly 120
Cube, The 22, 185
Cups 36, 185
Cyvasse 30, *31*, 185

Damage 47, 52, 185
Dashner, James 50, 189
de Peuter, Greig 60, 63–4, 67, 103, 173
de-roling 140
deception x, 6, 11–12, 71, 117–42
Dejarik 47, 185
detective fiction 20–1, 135
Diamond Dogs 12, 42, 152–8, 166, 184
Dick, Philip K. 49–50, 94, 97–8, 127–8, 183, 191–2
Disco Elysium 26, 72, 176–7, 183, 190–3

Discworld 30, 185, 192
Domination 51, 63, 185
Dragon Age: Inquisition 26, 71, 73, 80, 193
Duel Monsters 39, 186
Dyer-Witheford, Nick 60, 63–4, 67, 103, 173
dystopia 2, 11, 45, 49–50, 66, 72, 78, 87, 91–3, 98–9, 104–5, 110, 120, 127, 179, 187, 190

Elsaesser, Thomas 135–6
Ender's Game 128, 151, 158, 189
eXistenZ 12, 42, 128, 151–2, 158–67, 186
existentialism 160, 163–4
Experience Machine, The 16, 126–9, 131–2, 141

Fassone, Riccardo x–xi, xiii, 7, 10 n.5, 13, 20, 74, 161
fatal challenge 14, 42, 154–5, 165, 186
fictional incompleteness 28, 32, 34–5, 87
Fincher, David x, 5 n.2, 11, 123, 134, 136–8, 141, 186
Fine, Gary Alan 137–8
Fink, Eugen 163–5
Fisher, Mark 63, 163–4
Fizzbin 29, 47, 186
Flanagan, Mary 7, 61, 64, 73, 98–100, 174
flow 33, 69, 106, 120
Foddy, Bennett 61–2
Freyermuth, Gundolf S. 89–90
Friends 36, 184–5

Gabor Jr., Brian 43
Gadamer, Hans-Georg xi, 119–22, 125, 127, 137, 141
game
　design 7, 43, 45, 63, 80, 92, 94, 118, 119 n.2, 155, 176 n.2, 180
　fatal 5 n.2, 14, 42, 47, 52, 152, 154–6, 165–6, 185–6, 188, 191
　folk 68, 80–1, 150
　imaginary 23–4
　nested xi, 10, 21, 26–9, 124, 161 n.11, 165
　pervasive 49–50, 73, 78, 134, 138–9, 141–2
　show x, 49, 94, 102, 105–6, 108, 140, 186, 190, 192
　studies x–xi, 2, 4, 7, 9, 11–13, 23, 43, 59, 60 n.1, 75, 99 n.6, 103, 118, 172, 176 n.2, 178
Gamer 39, 191
gameworld 15, 25–9, 33, 91 n.5, 92–3, 117, 123–4, 134, 145, 150–1, 161, 166, 176, 190, 193
GANTZ 22, 187
Gentleman Misinformant, The 72, 187
Getting over It with Bennett Foddy 61–2
Gibson, James J. 161
Glaser, Paul Michael 11, 50, 105, 107–8, 190
Glass Bead Game, The x, 12, 42, 145–50, 152, 165, 187
Global Thermonuclear War 3, 187
Grand Theft Auto 67, 187
Gualeni, Stefano x–xi, xiii, 2, 6, 7, 10 n.5, 13–14, 19, 23, 33, 41 n.8, 64, 73, 75, 95, 98, 102, 119 n.2, 129 n.8, 132, 138, 140, 149, 156 n.5, 163, 173
Gwent 29, 187

Harry Potter 29–30, 38, 190, 193
hallucination x, 11–12, 117–42
Heaven vs. Hell 158 n.8
hegemony 94
Heidegger, Martin 148 n.2
Hesse, Herman x, 12, 145–9, 165, 187
Holquist, Michael 49, 111–12
Hotchkiss, Lia M. 159–60
House M. D. 52, 184
Huizinga, Johan 2, 33 n.5, 74, 118
Hunger Games, The x, 50, 104–5, 110, 187
Hutchinson, Peter 20–2, 34

ideological State apparatus 63–4
ideology 10, 15, 48, 59–81
Ignis Fatuus ix, 187
imagination xiii, 2, 6, 8, 16, 23–4, 33, 38, 42, 60 n.3, 88, 90, 99–100, 150, 157, 171, 174, 177, 180
incompleteness xi, 2, 10, 28, 32–6, 73, 87
indeterminacy 93–102, 110
indirect characterization 50–1, 133, 158, 175
Infinite Fun Space 42, 188
Inhibitor Space 52, 190
Inversions 34, 72, 184, 187–92

Jameson, Frederic 49, 90, 109
Jewison, Norman 65, 77, 190
Johnson, Joe 188
Jumanji 22, 188
Juul, Jesper 7 n.4, 23–4

Kepesh-Yakshi 25, *26*, 188
Kershner, Irvin 51
King, Stephen 11, 105–10, 159, 190
Kobayashi Maru Test 123, 151, 188

LARP 138–40, 142
Lee Carvallo's Putting Challenge 176, 188
Liar's Dice 72, 188
Lightcycle 188
literary device 4, 21, 147, 151
Lottery in Babylon, The 97–8, 188

McLuhan, Marshall 46, 75
Mad Magazine 37, 192
magic 6, 29, 32, 37–40, 66, 190, 193
magic circle 118–19, 134, 137, 141
Magic the Gathering 184
Man-Mountain Gentian 38, 193
Martin, George R. R. 30, 185
Mass Effect 3 25, *26*, 188
Matherson, Richard 184
Maze, The 188
Maze Runner, The 50, 189
meta-referentiality 12, 174, 176
meta-reflexivity 6
metaverse 129 n.7
Mind Game, The 128–9, 131, 151, 189
Minahan, Daniel 104, 185
minigame 10, 26–8, 96, 128–9
modernism 100
Monarch's Dispute 34–5, 72, 189
Mornington Crescent 36, 189
Motorball 39, 151, 189
morality 43, 93
moral dilemma 14, 43–5
More, Thomas 11, 72–3, 80–1, 89
Mouse Guard 30, 191
Murray, Janet 13, 59–60
My Dinner with Andre 174–5, 189
Mythic Quest 177, 189

Natali, Vincenzo 22
Never Say Never Again 51, 185

New Girl 8, 192
Nissenbaum, Helen 7, 61, 73, 174
Norton, Andre 47, 191
Nozick, Robert 16, 126–7, 129, 131–2

OASIS, The 129, 131, 174, 189
Oråki 35, 189

Pai Sho 30, 190
Parks and Recreation 36, 185
Peg Game, The 52, 190
Petersen, David 30, 191
Petri, Elio 104, 184
Player of Games, The 11, 94–102, 123, 147, 184
play
    bad 103 n.7
    critical 6, 64, 73, 98, 131, 173–4
    romantic 74, 140
    transgressive 44
playtest 124–5, 141
posthumanism 40, 155–6
Pratchett, Terry 30, 185, 192
Primeval and Other Times ix–x, xii–xiii, 187
puzzle film 134–6

Questland 122, 190
Quidditch 29, *30*, 38, 190
Quintet 67–8, 73–81, 190

randomness 98–9
Raubritter 26, 190
Ready Player One 129, 141, 174, 189
Reynolds, Alastair 12, 42–3, 52, 94–5, 104, 152–3, 155–6, 158, 190–1
Rick and Morty 12, 125, 128, 130–3, 141, 190
Rollerball 45, 65–6, 77, 190
Rowling, Joanne K. 29, 38
Roy: A Life Well Lived 12, 125–33, 141, 190
rules xi, 2, 15, 28–9, 32–8, 44, 48, 52, 59–60, 66, 68, 75–6, 78, 80, 95–7, 99–100, 102–6, 108–11, 133, 137 n.9, 138, 145, 150, 171
Running Man, The 11, 49, 94, 102–10, 190, 192
Rupetta 35, 189

Salen, Katie 118
Sartre, Jean-Paul 163–4
satire 9, 174–8
Saw 5 n.2, 45, 186
Schrank, Brian 43, 99 n.6, 118
Schwarzenegger, Arnold 105–9
science-fiction 4, 11–12, 29, 34, 37, 42–3, 49, 72, 77, 87–8, 90, 94–5, 101, 103–4, 127–9, 152, 158–9, 172, 179, 184–5, 187–92
Secret Keep 72, 190
selfhood 158, 166
Series 7: The Contenders 104–5, 185
Shadowplay 95, 191
Sharp, John 73–5
Sigler, Scott 44
Simpsons, The 174–6, 184, 188–9
Slayers 39, 191
Snakes and Ladders 68–70
Solar Lottery 49, 97–8, 191
Song of Ice and Fire, A 30–1, 185
South Park 158, 187
Squid Game 104, 186
Stars and Comets 47, 191
Star Trek 29, 47, 52, 120–3, 141, 151, 186, 188, 191
Star Wars 47, 185
Steel 39, 184
Strategema 52, 191
Subterfuge 72, 191
subversion 8, 22, 50, 61, 87, 98–9, 103, 109, 134, 172, 192
Suits, Bernard 20–1, 74
Sulway, Nike A. 35, 189
Suvin, Darko 49, 88
Suzerainty 26, 72, 191
Swords and Strongholds 30, 191
Syndrome 94, 191
synecdoche 1, 10, 44, 48, 50 n.11, 81, 94, 111, 151

techno-pessimism 159
Tetris 25, 59–60, 150
Thomas, David 73–5

thought experiment 5–6, 12, 16, 19, 24, 45, 90, 95, 126–7, 129, 132, 135, 166–7
Three-Cornered Pitney 37, 192
thrownness 148, 150
Thud 30, 192
Tokarczuk, Olga ix, xii, 187
transcendence 6, 8, 12, 42, 145–67, 172, 174
transgression x, 44, 94, 97
Travesty 72, 192
Treadmill to Bucks 106, 192
Triad 29, 192
Tron 39, 188
True American 8, 192

uncertainty 5, 11, 22, 88 n.1, 95, 98–101
unplayability xi, 2, 24, 28, 31–46, 93, 171–3
unplaying 64, 99
US 192
Utopia 11, 72–3, 80–1, 89

Vella, Daniel 7, 33, 75, 129 n.8, 138, 140, 149, 156 n.5, 163, 173, 179
virtual reality 122, 124–5, 128–9, 134, 141, 152, 159–61, 174, 183, 186, 192
virtual world 163–4
Viticulturist, The 26, 192

Waldrop, Howard 38, 193
WarGames 3, 187
War Game 50, 94, 128, 183, 192
Whack-Bat 37–8, 192
Whiff of Truth 72, 192
Wicked Grace 26, 71, 73, 80–1, 193
Wirrâl 26, 193
Wirrâl Untethered 176–7, 193
Witcher, The 29, 187
wizard's duel 38, 193

Yu-Gi-Oh! 39, 186

ZA/UM 26, 72, 176, 193
Zen Sumo 38, 193
Zimmerman, Eric 118
Zoo City 66–7, 187

www.ingramcontent.com/pod-product-compliance
Lightning Source LLC
Chambersburg PA
CBHW061827300426
44115CB00013B/2274